Why War?

THE BUCKNELL LECTURES IN LITERARY THEORY
General Editors: Michael Payne and Harold Schweizer

The lectures in this series explore some of the fundamental changes in literary studies that have occurred during the past thirty years in response to new work in feminism, Marxism, psychoanalysis, and deconstruction. They assess the impact of these changes and examine specific texts in the light of this new work. Each volume in the series includes a critical assessment of the lecturer's own publications, an interview, and a comprehensive bibliography.

Forthcoming volumes by Peter Brooks, Barbara Johnson, and Stanley Cavell.

Why War? – Psychoanalysis, Politics, and the Return to Melanie Klein

Jacqueline Rose

BLACKWELL
Oxford UK & Cambridge USA

First published 1993

Blackwell Publishers
108 Cowley Road
Oxford OX4 1JF
UK

238 Main Street
Cambridge, Massachusetts 02142
USA

British Library Cataloguing in Publication Data

A CIP catalogue record for this book is available from the British Library.

Library of Congress Cataloging-in-Publication Data
Rose, Jacqueline.
     Why war? — psychoanalysis, politics, and the return to Melanie Klein / Jacqueline Rose.
         p.   cm. — (The Bucknell lectures in literary theory)
     Includes bibliographical references and index.
     ISBN 0–631–18923–8 (alk. paper). — ISBN 0–631–18924–6 (pbk. alk. paper)
     1. Psychoanalysis and culture. 2. Psychoanalysis and literature.
3. War—Psychological aspects. 4. Political psychology. 5. Death instinct. 6. Klein, Melanie. I. Title. II. Series.
BF175.5.C84R67   1993
150.19′5—dc20   93–13027
                                                                  CIP

Typeset in 11 on 13 pt Plantin
by Pure Tech Corporation, Pondicherry, India
Printed in Great Britain by Biddles Ltd, Guildford
This book is printed on acid-free paper

For Sally Alexander

Contents

Preface

Fundamental and far-reaching changes in literary studies, often compared to paradigmatic shifts in the sciences, have been taking place during the last thirty years. These changes have included enlarging the literary canon not only to include novels, poems, and plays by writers whose race, gender, or nationality had marginalized their work, but also to include texts by philosophers, psychoanalysts, historians, anthropologists, and social and religious thinkers, who previously were studied by critics merely as 'background'. The stance of the critic and student of literature is also now more in question than ever before. In 1951 it was possible for Cleanth Brooks to declare with confidence that the critic's job was to describe and evaluate literary objects, implying the relevance for criticism of the model of scientific objectivity while leaving unasked questions concerning significant issues in scientific theory, such as complementarity, indeterminacy, and the use of metaphor. Now the possibility of value-free scepticism is itself in doubt as many feminist, Marxist, and psychoanalytic theorists have stressed the inescapability of ideology and the consequent obligation of teachers and students of literature to declare their political, axiological, and aesthetic positions in order to make those positions conscious and available for examination. Such expansion and deepening of literary studies has, for many critics, revitalized their field.

Those for whom the theoretical revolution has been regenerative would readily echo, and apply to criticism, Lacan's call to revitalize psychoanalysis: 'I consider it to be an urgent task to disengage from concepts that are being deadened by routine use the meaning that they regain both from a re-examination of their history and from a reflexion on their subjective foundations. That, no doubt, is the teacher's prime function.'

Many practising writers and teachers of literature, however, see recent developments in literary theory as dangerous and anti-humanistic. They would insist that displacement of the centrality of the word, claims for the 'death of the author', emphasis upon gaps and incapacities in language, and indiscriminate opening of the canon threaten to marginalize literature itself. In this view, the advance of theory is possible only because of literature's retreat in the face of aggressive moves by Marxism, feminism, deconstruction, and psychoanalysis. Furthermore, at a time of militant conservatism and the dominance of corporate values in America and Western Europe, literary theory threatens to diminish further the declining audience for literature and criticism. Theoretical books are difficult to read; they usually assume that their readers possess knowledge that few have who have received a traditional literary education; they often require massive reassessments of language, meaning, and the world; they seem to draw their life from suspect branches of other disciplines: professional philosophers usually avoid Derrida; psychoanalysts dismiss Freud as unscientific; Lacan was excommunicated even by the International Psycho-Analytical Association.

The volumes in this series record part of the attempt at Bucknell University to sustain conversation about changes in literary studies, the impact of those changes on literary art, and the significance of literary theory for the humanities and human sciences. A generous grant from the Andrew W. Mellon Foundation has made possible a five-year series of visiting lectureships by internationally known participants in the reshaping of literary studies. Each volume includes a comprehensive introduction to the published work of the lecturer, the Bucknell Lectures, an interview, and a comprehensive bibliography.

Introduction

The writings of Jacqueline Rose situate themselves at the intersection of feminist theory, psychoanalysis, and literary criticism. Her four books – *Feminine Sexuality: Jacques Lacan and the école freudienne* (1982, with Juliet Mitchell); *The Case of Peter Pan or The Impossibility of Children's Fiction* (1984, second edition 1992); *Sexuality in the Field of Vision* (1986); and *The Haunting of Sylvia Plath* (1991) – have established her reputation as one of the most important cultural critics writing in Britain.

Feminine Sexuality is a complex text that includes two introductions – one by Juliet Mitchell, the other by Jacqueline Rose – as well as Rose's translations of papers by Lacan and members of the École Freudienne on the topic of feminine sexuality. Except for 'The Meaning of the Phallus', the papers by Lacan, which are from *Écrits* and the seminars, are not otherwise available in English. These papers are of major importance for an understanding of Lacan's continuing significance for French feminism. Rose argues in her introduction that the history of psychoanalysis can profitably be charted in terms of its engagement with the problems of feminine sexuality. Freud's psychoanalytic work began with an analysis of hysterical patients who were woman, although he claimed that hysterics could be either male or female. His manifest failure to analyse one of these patients,

Dora, resulted in his writing a critique of normative concepts of woman, concepts, he candidly acknowledged,
that he had erroneously employed himself. Freud's
subsequent theories of sexuality – its fragmented and
aberrant nature and attempts to order it – arise out of his
early misperceptions of feminine sexuality, Rose argues.
Freud returned to this topic when he set out to reformulate his theory of human subjectivity in his later work.
When Freud's dynamic processes of theoretical self-
reflection are understood, feminine sexuality can be seen
as a topic that was extraordinarily important in the
development of Freudian theory. Lacan recognized the
interdependence of Freud's theories of subjectivity and
femininity. The principal critics of Freud's theory of femininity, in Lacan's view, have proceeded from an attempt
to oppose 'the truth about women' to Freud's theory;
but in the process of doing this, they have invariably
sacrificed both. Arguments against Freud that de-
problematize femininity invariably miss Freud's 'stress
on the division and precariousness of human subjectivity
itself, which was, for Lacan, central to psychoanalysis'
most radical insights' (*FS*, 29). Rose works to reopen
the debate on feminine sexuality, which she hopes to
foster simultaneously – but by no means separately –
within both psychoanalysis and feminism.

*The Case of Peter Pan or the Impossibility of Children's
Fiction* focuses on the history of J. M. Barrie's famous
story. *Peter Pan* first appeared in a novel for adults, *The
Little White Bird* (1902), which Barrie was writing at the
time that Freud made his important discovery that sexuality works most powerfully on the level of fantasy. In
the novel, the story of Peter Pan is told to a little boy as
part of the narrator's attempt to abduct the child. This
seemingly quintessential narrative about the innocence
and permanence of childhood, when restored to its
context in the novel of 1902, can be seen as a story
about the use of children's literature to steal childhood.

Strangely, the ejection of the story from its 1902 context was an act of censorship by Barrie himself. His play of *Peter Pan* did not get written until twenty-four years after its first production; and when the narrative version was published on its own, it was issued as an expensive art book, deliberately bypassing what was then the new market for children's books. Barrie's first attempt to write a narrative version of the play was a failure, and it was subsequently rewritten in light of new state educational policy on language. Finally, Barrie authorized the story to a number of other writers, which greatly complicates – even as it would seem an attempt to obscure – Barrie as origin, source, or author. By focusing on this story of Barrie's novel/play, Rose is able to examine not only the possibility (or impossibility) of children's fiction, but also assumptions about childhood, subjectivity, and fantasy implied by the notion of books for children; the systematic misreadings of Freud that have sustained many of those assumptions; and the complex political, economic, and psychoanalytic networks in which even so seemingly innocent a story as *Peter Pan* is inescapably caught. In the Preface to the recent reissue of her book, Rose effectively summarizes her argument: '*Peter Pan* is a front – a cover not as concealer but as vehicle – for what is most unsettling and uncertain about the relationship between adult and child. It shows innocence not as a property of childhood but as a portion of adult desire' (*P*, xii).

Sexuality in the Field of Vision widens the theoretical focus of the Rose's first two books by collecting ten of her major papers, which she arranges in two parts: Part I – 'Femininity and Representation' – includes studies of Freud's 'Dora case', a reprint of the introduction to *Feminine Sexuality*, a detailed consideration of some major feminist criticisms of psychoanalysis, and studies of George Eliot, *Hamlet*, and Julia Kristeva; Part II – 'The Field of Vision' – includes an exposition of the concept of the imaginary in psychoanalytic (especially Lacanian) theory, a critique of the cinematic theories of Jean-Louis Comolli and Christian Metz, a critical examination of the concepts of the imaginary and identification as used in film theory, and an assessment of Freud's writings on Leonardo da Vinci. In her introduction to this volume Jacqueline Rose positions the problems considered in these papers within the history of the confrontation of psychoanalysis with feminism. This book keeps in the foreground of its arguments, first, a recognition of the national and social differences that have had an impact on psychoanalytic and feminist theory in England, the United States, and France; and second, the problematic consequences for theoretical work that simultaneously invokes psychoanalysis, feminism, and Marxism.

The paper on 'Feminism and the Psychic', which serves as an introduction to *Sexuality in the field of Vision*, anticipates the psycho-politics of the succeeding chapters. Here Rose begins with a reference to Freud's plea to H.D. that no attempt should be made to defend his work in any time or circumstance, lest such a defence drive hatred, fear, or prejudice concerning his work in more deeply. Rose offers no defence. She does, however, point out that although Freud and Lacan were considered scandalous by many less advanced in their thinking than they, both have partly replicated – in their images as patriarchs – the 'insidious effects' of patriarchy on the psychic life of us all, which they, none the less, attempted 'to undo or defy'. The immediate problem Rose chooses to address (as did her colleague Juliet Mitchell) is again the relation of psychoanalysis to feminism. Rose argues not only for such a relation, but also for the importance of both 'for the larger terms of contemporary political debate' (*SV*, 2). Recent feminist challenges to psychoanalysis replay similar critiques that are part of the history of psychoanalysis itself. Lacan's dissolution of the École Freudienne in 1980 – which can be read either as an act of patriarchal arrogance or a gesture of liberation – provides a historical point of departure for a reconsideration of the political import of psychoanalysis.

That history for Lacan begins with his critique of American ego psychology and its efforts, in the interest of shaping a psychology of social adaptation, to tame and order the concept of the unconscious, thereby eclipsing – or betraying – Freud's theory with a normative concept of identity. Lacan's 'critique of autocracy and the critique of the ego should be taken together', Rose argues (*SV*, 5). For feminism, patriarchy is the supreme autocracy. Lacan's attempt to counter the appropriation of psychoanalysis by ego psychology and his efforts to challenge autocracy within the psychoanalytic institutions with which he was associated – the Société psychoanalytique de Paris in 1953 and the École Freudienne in 1980 – can, however, be read two ways. On the one hand, Lacan's work can be seen as uncovering within the history of psychoanalysis a betrayal of Freud in the handing over to agencies of political oppression theories of the ego in its relation to the unconscious that sustain oppression. Thus, Lacan's entire project of calling for a return to Freud, as well as a return to the unconscious, can be seen as political to its core. On the other hand, the cult of Lacan (Lacanianism) and Lacan's unilateral strategies signal a return to autocracy in the very efforts to undo it. Lacan thus becomes the patriarchal autocrat, 'a father whose status goes without question and beyond which there is no appeal' (*SV*, 5). In the face of this politically crucial Lacanian ambiguity, Rose applauds the decision of such feminists as Michèle Montrelay, who continues to work within psychoanalysis in order to confront the problems, force, and impossibility of identification. 'The question of identity'. Rose emphasizes, 'is . . . the central issue through which psychoanalysis enters the political field' (*SV*, 5).

Rose concludes her paper with an assessment of Derrida's critique of Lacan and Freud. Derrida sees in the discourse of psychoanalysis a reinforcement of the category of the subject, which for him is 'a vestige of the logocentrism of the West' (*SV*, 18). His objection to Lacan's and Freud's phallocentrism, then, is an attack not on patriarchy *per se*, but on the whole metaphysical order that supports it. Against that logocentric (or phallogocentric) order, Derrida affirms the slippages, deferrals, and differences of language – in a word, *différance* – which oppose gender identity as a classic binary opposition that would fix and repress the aberrant ways of sexuality and the unconscious. Consistent with its enshrining of the concept of identity, the psychoanalytic community, in Derrida's view, detaches itself from the political realities at work in the societies of which it is a part, rather than championing 'an endless dispersal of subjectivity' (*SV*, 20). Rose challenges his argument on two points. First she suggests that if, as Derrida argues, *différance* lies behind – or is forgotten by – the Western logocentrism of presence, then a psychic account of how and why that forgetting takes place is necessary. Secondly, his own writing is tropologically infused with sexual difference, which finally outweighs and outwits the deconstruction to which he subjects them. (To Rose's references to his concepts of 'hymen' and 'double chiasmatic invagination of the borders' might be added his recurring image of childbirth to represent the moment of the deconstructive birth of the new.) Rose concludes that psychoanalysis is an institution that 'knows the necessity and impossibility of its own limits', suspended as it is 'between the too little and too much of a subject' (*SV*, 22).

Jacqueline Rose's most recent book, *The Haunting of Sylvia Plath*, is her subtlest introduction of psychoanalytic and feminist theory into literary critical practice. The book begins with what amounts to a hermeneutical declaration of independence:

Interpretation of a literary work is endless. There is no one true place where it can be halted. It cannot be arrested at the point where it comes into conflict with how a writer sees their own depiction of others or of themselves. Once a piece of writing has been put into circulation, it ceases – except in the most material sense – to be the property of its author. Nor can it be controlled and limited by the views of any one individual, no matter how close to the subject they may have been, or still feel themselves to be. (*HSP*, xi)

Nevertheless, as Rose goes on to show, elaborate attempts have been made to restrict the interpretation of the writings of Sylvia Plath, including threats of legal action against those who refuse to submit to such restrictions. In sharp contrast to such interpretive restriction is the extraordinary generosity with which Plath admits her readers into her mind, into her private and intimate plays of fantasy. Rose chronicles the equally extraordinary lengths to which Ted Hughes, Aurelia Plath, and a host of critics and reviewers have gone in an effort to arrest this interpretive freedom and psychic access.

The final chapter of *The Haunting of Sylvia Plath* is a magnificent performance in critical reading that is informed by what is most ideologically compelling and imaginatively energizing in contemporary theory. Here Rose's prose is remarkably modest, much of it in monosyllables, which matches the text of Plath's 'Daddy'. There is very little here of what might be called 'overt' theory. The inheritances of Lacan, Derrida, Kristeva, and others are, with exemplary hermeneutical tact, kept subdued by the language of the poem. The manifest argument is an answer to the charge that Plath's 'metaphor' of the Holocaust is opportunistically appropriated and too easily invoked by the poet. At first this seems an invitation to a digression in the form of a recollection of the Hamburg Congress of the International Association of Psycho-Analysis of 1985, which was the first Congress

of the Association held in Germany since 1932. The
theme of the Congress was Nazism and the Holocaust
only in the sense that difficult circumstances allowed it
to be so, given the decision by the organizers to avoid
direct historical reference. Patients who were survivors,
children of survivors, and children of Nazis provided an
indirect means of address to the theme that could not
be spoken. (Rose points out that even the term 'Holocaust' is a rhetorical figure, in that it is a word projected
back from the nuclear threat of 1949 to the horror of the
camps a decade or so earlier.) Problems of language,
memory, survival, history, and psychoanalysis were all
reflected by the politics of the Congress itself. When
Rose turns to Plath's 'Daddy', only part of her purpose
is to refute the argument that the Holocaust is more than
a poetic truth.

Since it is impossible to summarize Rose's brilliant
reading of this poem, an enumeration of some of its
argumentative moves will have to stand as an inadequate
sort of metonymy. When Anne Sexton and Plath were
students in Robert Lowell's poetry class, Sexton wrote
'My Friend, My Friend', which makes being Jewish a
state that is enviable because it confers a sense of origin
and divine paternity. Whereas in that poem guilt is
located in the mother, Plath in her text shifts it to the
father, and thereby projects the drama 'into the realm of
symbolic as well as personal law' (*HSP*, 219). The poem
opens with an admission that the conditions that make
communication possible have been lost. In their place,
the German voice, which cannot be heard or understood, offers a substitution of empty signs; and in place
of the silenced or unintelligible father, the speaker here
and in 'Little Fugue' offers 'a narrative of silence' (*HSP*,
221). In Freudian terms, Rose observes, this is a murder
that has taken place after the fact, a killing of the father
who has died and already been mourned. Such a reading
makes any easy identification of 'Daddy' with Otto Plath

impossible. In the poem the father is personal, prehistoric, symbolic: Kristeva's *'Père imaginaire'*. The death of the father and the death of language – the death of the language of the father – are yoked together. By way of the German language – 'his' language – the father becomes every German, and 'she' becomes a Jew, whatever he or she was 'in fact'. Rose underlines the point here: 'It is not the character of Otto Plath, but his symbolic position which is at stake' (*HSP*, 230). Thus, his text on bees – his 'violence of writing' (*HSP*, 231) or his violence in writing (he was an entomologist) – is more pertinent than biography (see also Plath's 'The Bee Meeting' and 'The Arrival of the Bee Box'). If the poem dramatizes identification, it at least opens up the question of whether it is about one single identification with another, especially given its destabilizations of language and of the identify of the father. Analogously, then, if 'Every woman adores a fascist' who puts the 'boot in the face', who has the 'Brute heart'? Father, daughter, both? Further, what does the word 'through' signify in 'I'm through'? Finished speaking, finished living, or finished at last in driving the point home, like the stake in the 'fat black heart'? Even the address, 'You bastard', maintains the ambiguity of identity/difference, inheritance/disinheritance.

Rose's project is remarkably comprehensive and theoretically ambitious. She works from a meticulous knowledge of the literature of psychoanalysis, while pushing psychoanalytic theory to confront feminist issues – this, she demonstrates, Freud himself and many of his disciples were ready to do – and she does these things at a time when the increasingly marginalized concerns of European socialism are only too obvious, and any possible American equivalents virtually invisible. Accordingly, Rose's work keeps returning to the points of intersection between fantasy and culture, or, perhaps more specifically, to unsuspected eruptions of fantasy in cultural, political, and aesthetic life. (Here it may be useful to recall that Freud's German word *Phantasie* may be translated into English by the word 'imagination', signifying the contents and creative processes of an imaginary world rather than the faculty of imagining (*Einbildungskraft.*)

In 'Margaret Thatcher and Ruth Ellis' (chapter 2 below), Jacqueline Rose offers her most sustained and intellectually powerful political critique, which brings together the feminist argument that 'the symbolic order is always gendered' with the insight made possible by psychoanalysis that 'right-wing ideologies thrive on and strain against the furthest limits of psychic fantasy'. This chapter is a self-reflective attempt at analysing the confrontation of these two propositions in terms of the complicating factor that Margaret Thatcher, in Rose's view, has come 'to embody them at their most extreme'. While not dismissing the 'rational reasons why people may have voted for Thatcher', the chapter argues against any 'single political determinant or cause', and has a comprehensive agenda that includes examing the symbolic and fantasy components of political life as they manifest themselves in Mrs Thatcher; arguing for the political usefulness of a co-operative relationship between feminist and psychoanalytic theory; considering the challenge to unreflective feminist and psychoanalytic thought posed by the phenomena of Mrs Thatcher and Ruth Ellis ('For a feminism which has argued for the perversity and even deadliness of the social, and then called it male, Thatcher presents a particular difficulty and anxiety which has perhaps been operating in the form of a taboo. . . . The fact that Thatcher is a woman allowed her to get away with murder'); exposing the manipulation of reason – or what goes under the name of reason – in the prosecution of Ellis, in arguments for reinstating capital punishment, and in Thatcher's rhetoric and political practice; and continuing the critique of Julia Kristeva initiated in *Sexuality in the Field of Vision*.

In that earlier book Rose points to the importance of
Kristeva's work, especially for 'the way it is poised on
that interface of politics/psychoanalysis/feminism' (*SFV*,
163), which is where, as I read her, Rose's work is also
poised. Kristeva has refused to absorb sexual politics
into the politics of class, for which some forms of Marxism would argue; she has also refused to absorb the
concept of sexuality into a normative concept of identity,
for which some forms of feminism would argue. For
Rose, Kristeva's work is exemplary with regard to the
difficulties that productively arise when 'politics tries to
open itself up to the ravages of the unconscious mind'
(*SFV*, 164). The challenge of Kristeva's theory – and the
corresponding challenge of the examples of Ruth Ellis
and Margaret Thatcher – is that they call into question
the too easy identification of violence with the male.
Here there would seem to be two readings of Kristeva,
Ellis, and Thatcher that one might consider. According
to reading A, Kristeva might be seen as arguing that we
are now ready to enter the third stage of feminism –
'post-feminism', perhaps – having progressed through
demands for equality and then for separation and difference. According to this reading, sexual difference itself is up for deconstruction as a metaphysical category.
Here the examples of Ellis and Thatcher may be said to
demonstrate that physical violence and political violence
are not uniquely the curse of the male and that a major
portion of the rhetoric of feminism must, therefore, be
questioned. According to reading B, Kristeva may be
seen as arguing that the three stages of feminism she
outlines in 'Women's Time' are cumulative rather than
discrete, that the violence of patriarchy may be adopted
by males or by females, that women are uniquely positioned in the socio-symbolic contract, that such a contract is founded on a moment of violence, that sexual
difference itself is a form of violence, and that 'for Kristeva it is feminism's importance that it confronts the

furthest extremities, or perversion, of what it is that constitutes the social bond' (*SFV*, 4). For Rose, Ruth Ellis and Margaret Thatcher occupy two such positions of extremity or perversion.

In Rose's work, poetry and theory, feminism and psychoanalysis, politics and fantasy meet without either identifying with the other or affirming identity against the other. The assurance of stable identity that forgets the aberrant ways of sexuality, the fantasies of culture, or the autocracy of patriarchy has in her work been subjected to a sustained and eloquent critique.

Michael Payne

REFERENCES

The following works by Jacqueline Rose are cited in the Introduction:

Feminine Sexuality – Jacques Lacan and the École freudienne, with Juliet Mitchell (London: Macmillan, 1982) (*FS*)

The Haunting of Sylvia Plath (London: Virago, 1991, Cambridge, Mass.: Harvard University Press, 1992) (*HSP*)

The Case of Peter Pan or The Impossibility of Children's Fiction (London: Macmillan, 1984); rev. edn, Philadelphia: University of Pennsylvania Press, 1992) (*P*)

Sexuality in the Field of Vision (London: Verso, 1986) (*SV*)

Part I Psycho-Politics

1 'Why War?'

It is funny about wars, they ought to be different but they are not.

Gertrude Stein, *Wars I Have Seen*, 1945

No guess

Anticipative of a wrong unfelt,
No speculation on contingency,
However dim and vague, too vague and dim
To yield a justifying cause.

Coleridge, 'Fears in Solitude', 'written
in 1798, during the alarm of an invasion'

Perhaps the first thing one notices on reading Freud's famous exchange with Einstein on the subject of war is the dissatisfied, impatient, self-deprecating tone with which Freud writes.[1] By all accounts, Freud found the discussion tedious and sterile. He insists at the beginning that Einstein's opening letter has already said all there is to say on the matter; he ends by apologizing in advance for the disappointment he feels sure he will have incurred. Freud's answer to the question 'Why War?' seems to be struck with the mark of futility, as if he had incorporated into his writing the epithet which most commonly attaches to his object (viz. the 'futility of war'). And yet, in this exchange of 1932, Freud writes as much about the necessity as about the futility of war. War does not only threaten civilization, it can also advance it. By tending towards the conglomeration of nations, it operates less like death than like eros which strives to unify. Likewise, civilization has its 'advantages and perils'; we owe to it 'the best of what we have become as well as a good part of what we suffer from' (pp. 214–15). If, therefore, war neither simply threatens nor simply advances the cause of civilization, it is because it mimics or participates in the fundamental ambivalence of civilization itself.

eros ←

I want to try and use this talk to reopen the question which heads that exchange between Einstein and Freud – not in order to attempt an answer, but because I think there is something to be retrieved from Freud's at least partial sense of his own failure to produce one. War, I will be suggesting, operates in Freud's discourse, and not only in that of Freud, as a limit to the possibility of absolute or total knowledge, at the same time as such absolute or total knowledge seems over and again to be offered as one cause – if not *the* cause – of war. If war is a brake on knowledge, then to try and give a complete answer to the question – something that still seems today of devastating urgency – or rather, to try *only* to answer the question, might paradoxically involve an evasion of its force.

For Gertrude Stein, from whom the first epigraph is taken, war – or more specifically the Second World War – is an emblem of modernity. Something like Winnicott's transitional object, it straddles the space between the nineteenth and twentieth centuries, between childhood and adulthood, between the realist and the modernist literary text. Stein uses the war to think these transitions. In the 'dark and dreadful days of adolescence', what predominates is the fear of death or dissolution: 'Naturally war is like that. It is and it is not. One can really say that in war-time there is death death and death but is there dissolution. I wonder. May not that be one of the reasons among so many others why wars go on, and why particularly adolescents need it?'[2] What adolescents seem to need here is not just death (or dissolution) but that suspended state – 'It is and it is not.' The familiar destructiveness of war represents not, as is commonly supposed, finality but uncertainty, a hovering on the edge of what, like death, can never be totally known. Likewise, what characterizes the twentieth century and distinguishes it from the one that came before it is randomness, coincidence, and chance: 'this coincidental war this meaningless war, this war that put an end a real end and entire end to the nineteenth century there were so many coincidences and they were the only reality in this time of unreality' (p. 12). Unreality – hence the end of realism: 'there is no point in being realistic about the here and now, no use at all not any, and so it is not the nineteenth but the twentieth century, there is no realism now, life is not real it is not earnest, it is strange which is an entirely different matter' (p. 28).

For Stein, this new unreality, this strangeness, belongs to a shift in the register of knowledge; it signals the breakdown of the nineteenth-century faith in evolution, progress, and science. If everything was understood, so it was then believed, 'there would be progress and if there was going to be progress there would not be any wars, and if there were not any wars then everything could and would be understood' (p. 40). The end of war as the end of knowledge, or knowledge as the confident *means* to a sure *end* (the circularity of the argument as laid out by Stein merely underlines the one-track purpose). The ending of war becomes the guarantee or stake of this form of knowledge, the only terms on which it can justify or perpetuate itself. In the transition from the nineteenth to the twentieth century – which, of course, many writers in fact situate at the time of the First World War – what has collapsed is the belief that knowledge can bring war to an end: 'Certainly nobody no not anybody thinks that this war is a war to end war . . . they cannot take on the future, no really not, certainly not as warless certainly not as future' (p. 122).[3]

In Freud's exchange with Einstein, war could also be said to precipitate a crisis of knowledge. 'As a result of a little speculation', Freud writes, 'we have come to suppose that this [destructive] instinct is at work in every living creature' (p. 211). If Freud offers here an explanation of war, he does so by means of the death drive. But the death drive, and hence the truth of war, operates, it has often been pointed out, as the speculative vanishing-point of psychoanalytic theory, and even, more boldly, of the whole of scientific thought: 'It may perhaps seem to you as though our theories are a kind of mythology and, in the present case, not even an agreeable one. But does not every science in the end come to a kind of mythology like this? Cannot the same be said to-day of your own Physics?' (p. 211). So while Freud undoubtedly proposes at the end of this exchange a resolution of sorts to the problem of war – a constitutional drive towards pacifism in all human subjects and civilization as the advance guard against war – we could argue that he has himself undermined both these claims in advance: through his earlier stress on the ambivalence of cultural progress on the one hand ('its advantages and its perils'), by his account of the destructive instinct on the other; but more radically than either of these two, although centrally implicated in both, by the instability, the necessary failure, of knowledge as resolution that he places at the foundation, or limit, of all scientific thought.

In much of the psychoanalytic writing that I have read on the subject of war, the problem of war is placed in the context of mourning. For Franco Fornari, war is a 'paranoid elaboration of mourning'.[4] We project on to the alien, or other, the destructiveness we fear in the most intimate relations or parts of ourselves. Instead of trying to repair it at home, we send it abroad. War makes the other accountable for a horror we can then wipe out with impunity, precisely because we have located it so firmly in the other's place. This saves us the effort of ambivalence, the hard work of recognizing that we love where we hate, that, in our hearts and minds at least, we kill those to whom we are most closely and intimately attached. Cleaving, as Geza Roheim puts it in his *War, Crime and the Covenant*, could almost be taken as a synonym for mourning, so graphically does it conjure up the idea of an attachment which suffocates, grasps, and attacks.[5] If we mourn, therefore, it is because we know that we have destroyed as well as lost. Enemies, on the other hand, are like possessions, writes Gertrude Stein, they allow us to forget the fear of death (p. 23).

In 'Thoughts for the Times on War and Death', written shortly after the outbreak of the First World War, Freud places mourning at the origins of speculative thought. Against those philosophers who see the enigma of death as the starting-point of all speculation, Freud argues that 'what released the spirit of enquiry in man was not the intellectual enigma, and not every death, but the conflict of feeling at the death of loved yet alien and hated persons'.[6] Death is a problem, not because we cannot surmount its loss or imagine our own death, but because it forces us to acknowledge that what belongs to us most intimately is also a stranger or enemy, a type of foreign body in the mind: 'those loved ones are on the one hand an inner possession, components of our own ego; but on the other hand they are partly strangers, even enemies' (p. 298). Mourning appears here almost as a metaphor for psychoanalysis itself, or at least for the mental processes it describes: estrangement of conscious from unconscious thinking, the symptom as 'alien', the 'foreign body' of the repressed. More important, the thought provoked by mourning takes the form of a dissociation. It is not thought as assured knowledge, but a form of thinking unable, in any single or singular way, to own or possess itself. This dissociation starts with the division of the individual into body and soul: 'In this way his train of thought ran parallel with the process of disintegration that sets in with death' (p. 294). Thought originates in love and hate of the dead, and mimics the falling apart of the body which it both celebrates and mourns. So if mourning initiates thinking, it also severs us once and for all from any certainty of thought. In Freud's essay 'On Transience', mourning appears as the end-point of speculation, the 'great riddle' which attracts all other forms of uncertainty to itself: 'to psychologists, mourning is a great riddle, one of those phenomena which cannot in themselves be explained but to which other obscurities can be traced back.'[7]

It is in this form of unknowing that Freud none the less grounds the origins of ethical life. The earliest ethical commandment, the first prohibition – 'Thou shalt not kill' – arises out of this fragile moment of self-recognition in contemplation of the dead: 'It was acquired in relation to dead people who were loved, as a reaction against the satisfaction of the hatred hidden behind the grief for them; and it was gradually extended to strangers who were not loved, and finally even to enemies' (p. 295). It is, paradoxically, because we hate our enemies and recognize in that hatred our psychic alienation from those we are presumed to love, that we do not kill them. Another way of putting this would be to say that we do not kill them in so far as we recognize them – their alien-ness – as internal to our own egos, as part of our relationship to ourselves. In a striking reversal, the problem then becomes not that we hate those we love, but that we do not love – we fail to recognize ourselves in – those we hate.

It is for this reason that Freud argues that one of the things that distinguishes modern from 'primitive' man – to his advantage – is that we no longer mourn our enemies. According to Roheim, the blood avenger in the Ngatatara tribe of Central Australia takes his victim in his arms. If he does not, he too might die, 'for he himself is identical with his victim and might die of his own aggression' (p. 18). Among the Papago Indians of North America, when the war hero returns to his tribe, he is placed in isolation as if he was inflicted with a terrible disease. He sits motionless, arms folded, with his head on his breast. The parallelism between the behaviour of the hero or homicide and the mourner, writes Roheim, is 'quite evident': 'They both behave like a case of melancholia, i.e. with aggression turned inward and identification with the dead' (p. 61).

Here again, it seems that, as much as an issue of militarism and its ethics, something about knowledge or the possibility of acquired and definitive certainty is at stake. One of Roheim's main informants in Normanby Island explained to him that they were 'different from the white people because their anger [the Islanders'] was never finished' (p. 98). The idea that one can have done with, or finish with, anger could be seen as a parallel to the idea of a final end to knowledge, the belief that knowledge, like war, can be brought to a definitive end. The idea of an end to war would then appear not as conclusion, but as repetition. As one of the soldiers puts it in Henri Barbusse's *Under Fire*, his account of the front line in Artois and Picardy during the Great War, ' "War must be killed . . . war must be killed in the belly of Germany. War must be killed; war itself." '[8]

In probably the most famous text ever to be written on war, Clausewitz's *On War*, the question of war and the question of knowledge bear the most intimate and troubled relation to each other.[9] Clausewitz is famous for the theory he proposes of total or absolute war – that is, war which aims for the total destruction or subordination of the enemy (a 'massive Clausewitzian deployment of force' is what, we were told, we witnessed in the buildup to the Gulf War).[10] War, Clausewitz states on the first page, is 'an act of violence intended to compel our opponent to fulfil our will' (p. 101). Violence forces the enemy to fulfil our purpose and simultaneously drives war to the realization, or fulfilment, of its own conception of itself: 'The more violent the excitement which precedes the War, by so much the nearer will the War approach its abstract form' (p. 119). Yet, to experience Clausewitz's text is above all to experience an abstract concept constantly failing to achieve its aim. In Clausewitz's discourse on war, theory always falls short. It is incapable of calculating, or mastering, the chaos, inconsistency, and randomness of the object it is meant to predict and represent: 'in this labyrinth [logic] sticks fast . . . This inconsistency . . . becomes the cause of the War being something quite different to what it should be, according to its concept [*Begriff*] – a half-and-half production, a thing without perfect inner cohesion' (pp. 368–9). 'Why', Clausewitz asks, 'is the philosophical conception not satisfied?' (p. 368).

For Clausewitz, theory founders first and above all on the moral factor. Wrongly omitted, from previous discourse on war, he argues, this moral element is war's first 'peculiarity': 'as soon as the moral activities begin their work, as soon as moral pressures and feelings are introduced, the whole set of rules dissolves into vague ideas' (p. 185). The moral element is 'most fluid'; rather like Freud's image of the libido, it distributes itself and spreads 'through all the parts' (p. 134). Not just a complicating factor in the sure calculation of war, the moral becomes the very image of complication, partiality, or dissemination, indicating what cannot – either for the theory or for war itself – be held to its proper place. The particularity of war is a moral factor which slides and deceives. Like the body – an 'indefinite', 'elastic' quantity 'the friction of which is well known to be difficult to calculate'; or the dubious, contradictory, and false nature of all information in war; or the 'living', 'reciprocal' reaction of the forces acted on in war which 'by its nature opposes anything like a regular plan' (pp. 161–2, 189). All these 'impediment effects' (p. 167) are what make for the 'difficulty' or 'impossibility' of theory ('Positive theory is impossible', the title of sect. 25, ch. 2, Bk. 2, pp. 189–90). War thus becomes the failing or imperfection of its own form.

Friction, dissolution, fluidity – it is easy to recognize in these terms, as they surface in defiance of a resistant totalization, the concepts which will appear at the heart of the yet to emerge language of psychoanalysis. For psychoanalysis could be said to display the same isomorphic relation between its meta-discourse (some would say the impossibility of any meta-discourse) and the intangible, theoretically recalcitrant entities and processes which it seeks to describe. In Clausewitz's text, war seems to figure as the the violent repressed of its own rationalization. It becomes, so to speak, the unconscious of itself:

> We must therefore decide to construe War as it is to be, and not from pure conception, but by allowing room for everything of a foreign nature which mixes itself up with it and fastens itself upon it – all the natural inertia and friction of its parts, the whole of the inconsistency, the vagueness and hesitation (or timidity) of the human mind. (p. 369)

I am sure I don't have to underline the nature of the metaphors involved here – war as an intruder or foreign body that fastens and destroys. It is the perfect image of the alien-ness that Freud places at the heart of human subjectivity, the alien-ness whose denial or projection leads us into war. In Clausewitz's text, the theorization of war seems finally to be taken over by its object. The attempt to theorize or master war, to subordinate it to absolute knowledge, becomes a way of perpetuating or repeating war itself. But to suggest that war is in some sense the repressed of its conceptualization – that is, of any attempt to think it – might be one way of explaining why we are never prepared for the full horror of war.

The issue then seems to be not so much what might be the truth about war, but the relationship of war to the category of truth. 'Truth', writes Franco Fornari (and not of course only Fornari), 'becomes the first casualty of war.' In war, he suggests, killing becomes the sole criterion of truth (p. 147). If truth is destroyed by war, truth as abstraction on the other hand is identified by several psychoanalytic writers as one of the determinants of war. According to a note on strategy that Clausewitz wrote in 1809, more than twenty years before *On War*, abstraction kills – it is a 'dry skeleton' or 'dead form' (the destructive element here is not the invasive reality, but the constricting, suffocating theory of war). For Money-Kyrle, our psychic commitment to 'personified abstraction' is a central problem of our political life: 'The ordinary individual who is realistic enough in his domestic world of concrete objects is very apt to think irrationally as soon as he moves into the political world of personified abstractions.'[11] In *The Future of an Illusion*, Freud describes politics as a world of false conviction, as fully delusional as that of sex: 'Must not the assumptions that determine our political regulations be called illusions? . . . and is it not the case that in our civilisation the relations between the sexes are disturbed by an erotic illusion or a number of such illusions?'[12] *As* delusional, or even *more so*. Ernest Jones comments wryly on the fact that, in the field of political controversy (as opposed to that of personal relations), people who have been analysed seem to be no different from people who have not.[13] In an article 'How can Civilisation be Saved?' written in 1943 right in the middle of the war, he relates such delusion to the category of the absolute, the conviction of a total, omnipotent form of truth: 'The French proverb "*Le mieux est l'ennemi du bien*" would make better psychology if it were reversed into: the good, that is the absolutely good, is the enemy of the better.'[14] Likewise, Edward Glover, anticipating the outcry over his refusal to distinguish between the 'evil' of militarism and the 'virtues' of pacifism at the level of the drives, comments: 'The Virtuous like the Beautiful and the True shelters under the wing of the Absolute.'[15]

The conviction of absolute truth, or of truth as an absolute, appears here as the ultimate delusion. Conviction, Money-Kyrle writes, saves us from the work of mourning, since it offers a way of being without flaw. It is only in so far as we believe absolutely in our own virtue, for example, that we are able to go to war (pp. 173–4); which is why Winnicott will argue in his 1940 article 'Discussion of War Aims' that it is crucial that 'we should win a military and not a moral victory': 'If we fight to exist we do not claim to be better than our enemies.'[16] But of course we always do. Only if Hussein was evil personified could Bush – in what appeared so often as a battle of wills between the two men – claim the right to go to war ('Sheriff Bush and the outlaw Saddam approaching high noon'[17]). The absolute veils the more troubling forms of ambivalence and mutual implication: the shadow of self-interest (oil), the fact that the West had at the very least armed, and could in some sense be said to have created, Saddam Hussein.

If, therefore, psychoanalysis has something to say about war, one might also reverse the proposition and suggest that war has something to say about psychoanalysis, or at the very least about its own relationship to knowledge, its own conception of what constitutes the truth. War does not only appear as an object of psychoanalytic investigation, of course. It provides the living context for key moments in the history of psychoanalysis. Psychoanalysis has also found itself at war. In the heat of the controversial discussions, which took place between Melanie Klein, her supporters, and her critics at the British Psycho-Analytical Society in 1943–4 (see chapters 5 and 6 below), Joan Rivière comments: 'The conflict is extraordinarily like that which is taking place in many countries and I feel sure that it is in many ways a tiny reverberation of the massive conflict which pervades the world.'[18] Not just because the manifest conflict between democracy and autocracy inside the analytic community seemed to reproduce, or was experienced as reproducing, the central conflict of the Second World War; nor because the war provided the framework for the questions the Society asked of itself (Who governs in war? Should constitutional changes be permitted in war? How long can change be suspended? What is the duration – the potential interminability – of war?); but because of the way that the dispute took on, assimilated, or incorporated, the language and discourse of war. If war is present here as the most concrete of references (Freud's emigration to England, the absence of Klein from London during the blitz and her subsequent return), it is no less strikingly present as trope, running – spreading – through the language of the British Society, like the moral element that Clausewitz took as the first 'peculiarity' of war. 'Hostile camps', 'front lines', 'closing ranks', 'ramparts', 'weapons', 'sabotage', the controversy itself as an 'evil' that 'kills', the fight between democracy and autocracy as the acknowledged repetition of the external, global war – the 'political militarisation of differences', to use Riccardo Steiner's term.[19] The 'scientific discussions' themselves then appear as an attempt to resolve in the register of knowledge or doctrine the interminable problem of war. Only an 'armistice' – 'A strange peace descended on the committee' (p. 147) – can produce the conditions under which controversy can transmute itself into science: 'Following the military analogy, one can sincerely hope for a fair plebiscite under an armistice till all armies of occupation have withdrawn to the frontiers' (p. 186). The question of training, of governance, of power, gives way, temporarily, to the question of knowledge ('It is the main object of the Society to discover the truth', p. 177). For somebody looking in from the outside, it is hard to avoid the impression that science or truth (science *as* truth) was being asked to settle – suspend, repress? – the problem of war.

This is not just my reading, but that of a number of the key protagonists involved. 'Scientific truth can never be absolute,' Brierly states in 1942 (p. 926). For Strachey, in his key memorandum of 1943, there can be no legislating in the field of scientific difference without imposing an omniscient leader, a legislator precisely, whose function would be to bring all controversy, all knowledge, to a close (p. 604). The issue of knowledge is therefore inseparable from that of power, and the attempt to separate them, to resolve the second by means of the first, therefore futile. A science claiming the status of absolute truth can only be a dictator in its own home. Conflict submits to the higher authority of truth, only to find that all it has reproduced is authority – the sure guarantee that conflict will start all over again. The right to open up the Freudian corpus, to transform it, to recognize its interminability, is the sole condition for the continuation of Freud's own work – even if that means 'continual disruption'; even, therefore, if it means war. Perhaps, then, we remain 'truer' to the spirit of psychoanalysis if we don't try to solve the problem of war.

If, as I have been suggesting, the category of absolute truth is troubled by war, so – I want to suggest now – is that of reality, a category often associated with truth, but to which, in the psychoanalytic literature, it is more often opposed. We have already seem this opposition in Clausewitz – between theory as abstraction and the unmaneageable reality, or friction, of war. Clausewitz's distinction corresponds to the philosophical opposition between the ideal and the empirical (one which a dialectical account of war should manage to resolve). It also reflects the clash between the Enlightenment philosophy of war as reason and an emergent romanticism which stresses the unique and singular instance, the place of the incalcuable and imaginative in the human mind (Clausewitz is read by one of his most recent commentators as above all encapsulating this shift[20]).

But when the same distinction appears within the psychoanalytic accounts of war, it brings with it a new opposition between fantasy and reality, between – in the case of Money-Kyrle, for example – a self-blinding allegiance to personified abstraction and the reality-seeking principle of the rational, normal mind. The aim of psychoanalysis then becomes to correct the distortions of unconscious life. Paranoia – and hence the likelihood of war – will diminish if the ego is allowed to take its measure of the real world. And yet, that seemingly secure distinction between projection and reality is just what is disturbed, according to his own account, by the phenomenon of war. Paranoia crosses over into reality where it comes out as unavoidable truth. If I project aggression on to the other, she or he is likely to become – in reality – the mirror or embodiment of the aggression I am trying to displace on to her or him. In other words, paranoid impulses don't just project on to reality as delusion; they affect reality and become a component of it. At which point, to deny the real danger, even though you may have created it, would be as pathological as to imagine, falsely, that danger is there: 'It is as easy to deny a real danger as to imagine one that doesn't exist' (p. 161).

How can you recognize the real enemy in this scenario? Or rather, how can you distinguish, with any absolute certainty, between your own projections and real external danger? If you produce the enemy, then you must fight him. The category of reality is unable to secure the political distinctions or effects it is being required to perform. One could in fact say that, instead of a just appreciation of reality being the means whereby one cures the individual and the culture of its propensity to war, it is war which, in this argument, has the victory, by undermining the undiluted appeal to reality which is meant to bring it to an end. The distinction between fantasy and reality cannot withstand, or is revealed in its most difficult relation under, the impact of war. We can never finally be sure whether we are projecting or not, if what we legitimately fear may be in part the effect of our own projection. How much of the preamble to the Gulf War turned on the seemingly unanswerable question of to what extent Hussein was really evil (Hitler reborn) and to what extent a projection, the newly desired enemy – post-cold war – of the West? (Both of course can be true.) Certainly, in more than one analysis, the problem for Bush was that, having called up the image of Hussein as utter monstrosity, he *had to* go to war; that is, war became inevitable in so far as he could not leave his own creation, or to the extent that he could not leave his own creation, in place. Money-Kyrle himself asks in a footnote added to his 1934 broadcast 'A Psychological Analysis of the Causes of War' why its tone was so mild, why he did not say that, in his view, by 1934 Hitler was already beyond the point of no recall, and wonders whether one reason was 'the fear of making things worse'.[21]

For Money-Kyrle, the benevolence of the real parents and a benign humanist state are the means – in reality – of countering the delusions of our unconscious life. It is because reality is finally (really) benign that there can be a solution to the problem of internal and external war. But, as if symptomatically, in *Psychoanalysis and Politics*, a very different vision of reality erupts at one extraordinary moment in his text. There is a common myth, he writes, especially prevalent at the end of an unsuccessful war, that one had always wished to live in peace and treat the whole world as a brother: 'In order to support this myth, the very limitations of our world are themselves denied. In reality, there has never been enough for all and we have lived by competition' (p. 167). It is a myth to believe that 'our own desires can be met without depriving others'; but, he adds in a footnote, 'Any reference to the concept of an optimum population is almost taboo in political debate' (pp. 167–8). Each against all, and each for himself. The reality that Money-Kyrle opposes to the delusional precipitates of war is already, and irreducibly, at war. This is a combination of Malthus and Darwin – a violent struggle for survival legitimated by the limited resources of the real world. And as if in reply, Malthusianism erupts inside German war propaganda as proof of the unusual cruelty of the English. Listening to the radio during the occupation, Gertrude Stein hears the Germans offering two examples of enemy excess: birth control ('the killing of unborn children') and, 'almost more frightful', 'Malthus one of their great men who says people should be killed off by plagues, by famine, and by wars' (p. 79). One man's truth is another man's poison, one might say. Or, what is the projection, what the reality in this case?

For Winnicott, of course, not to know whether something is real or not (whether you have made it up), to leave the question in suspense, is a form of creativity. It is the fundamental characteristic of transitional space. Fornari uses this very property – 'beyond reality testing' – to characterize the peculiarity (the pathology) of the group. As in the dream, as in mourning, 'the problem of whether or not mourning as a social phenomenon corresponds to an objective reality does not arise' (p. 142).

This is not of course to argue that there can be no such thing as a justified war. In fact, Money-Kyrle wrote *Psychoanalysis and Politics* in 1951 as an answer to the

ethical relativism whose inadequacy (ethical and political) was for him – and not only for him – established by
the Second World War. But this very fact seems to be
what places his own psychoanalytic argument under the
greatest strain. To take the status of guilt in his account:
war, he argues after Freud, can be seen as the acting out
or projection on to the other of an inner guilt which the
other is then required to carry and which legitimates the
non-guilty aggression of the one who projects. What is
involved, therefore, is a denial of a component of psychic
reality, a denial of guilt in the mind. For psychoanalysis
there is no aggression without guilt. But there are wars
– for example, the Second World War – which we would
be guilty of *not* participating in, where 'an aggressive
country launches an unprovoked and brutal war against
its inoffensive neighbours' (p. 101). (This of course, was
one language of Bush in relation to the Gulf War.) To be
guiltless in this case appears not as projection, but as a
just measure of our own justified intervention in the real:
'we would feel acutely guilty if we did *not* unleash it'
(p. 102).

Again, at a late point in the book, Money-Kyrle talks
of the advance of conscience in the service of liberating
groups from oppression, which, although it may carry
unconscious projections (magnification of cruelty, scapegoating, disavowal of callousness at home), is none the
less evidence of what he calls 'different types of conscience' which have achieved 'many positive reforms to
humanise our culture' (the education of children and the
freeing of slaves) (p. 118). Guilt projection is therefore
the driving force of cultural humanization *and* the basis
of the destruction of all culture. It is incapable as a
concept of distinguishing between socially desirable and
socially undesirable effects.

I want to go back now to that image of truth as dictator
in its own home. For this is the image which Virginia
Woolf places at the heart of *Three Guineas*, her famous

essay on war.[22] For Woolf, the question of war is inseparable from that of gender, or sex. The 'fear which for-
bids freedom in the private house' simultaneously holds
down women and leads men to war (p. 162). That fear,
that lack of freedom, also gives the lie to the moral
superiority of the democratic world: ' "My husband insists that I call him 'Sir'," said a woman at the Bristol
Police Court yesterday when she applied for a mainten-
ance order . . . In the same issue of the same paper Sir
E. F. Fletcher is reported to have "urged the House of
Commons to stand up to dictators" ' (p. 200). For
Woolf, women are not innocent of war: 'Thus conscious-
ly she desired "our splendid Empire"; unconsciously she
desired our splendid war' (p. 46). (To paraphrase Lacan
on women and the phallus, 'they are not not in it not at
all, they are in it right up to the hilt.') But if at one level
women find themselves bolstering up the system that
maintains them ('our splendid Empire'), and then supporting war as one of the few opportunities to escape the
tyranny of the home ('our splendid war'), they none the
less – because they are regularly excluded from the great
fact of civilization – have a different take: 'What is this
civilisation in which we find ourselves?' (p. 73). Robbed
of all sensual being in the world, the successful professional man is a 'cripple in a cave' (p. 84); dominated by
the fear which drives him to dominate, he is 'an infant
crying in the night' (p. 161). Start with sexual difference
– it is the quickest way of calling the bluff on the superiority of the so-called democratic, civilized world, the
quickest way of severing, as Winnicott puts it, the moral
and military victory of war: 'What right have we, Sir, to
trumpet our ideals of freedom?' (p. 62).

Winnicott himself had a great deal to say about the
myth of freedom in relation to war. In 'Discussion of
War Aims' he writes: 'It is commonly assumed that we
all love freedom and are willing to fight and die for it.
That such an assumption is untrue and dangerous is

recognised by a few – who nevertheless fail, it seems to me, to understand what they describe. The truth seems to be that we like the idea of freedom and admire those who feel free, but at the same time we are afraid of freedom, and tend at times to be drawn towards being controlled.'[23] As Virginia Woolf put it in relation to that housewife from Bristol and Sir Fletcher's injunction to the House: 'This would seem to show that the common consciousness that includes husband, wife, and House of Commons is feeling at one and the same time the desire to dominate, the need to comply in order to keep the peace, and the necessity of dominating the desire for dominance – a psychological conflict which serves to explain much that appears inconsistent and turbulent in contemporary opinion' (p. 200).

According to Winnicott, freedom is something that has to be 'forced' (his word) on people; the trouble with freedom, unlike cruelty and slavery, is that it is not sexy enough: 'There is but little bodily gratification, and none that is acute, to be got out of freedom.'[24] Writing ten years later on 'The Meaning of the Word "Democracy" ', Winnicott suggests – although he does not himself make explicit the link to his earlier text – that this fear of freedom and the fear of woman might stand in the most intimate relation to each other: 'the tendency of groups of people to accept or seek *actual* domination is derived from a fear of domination by *fantasy woman*.'[25] '*One of the roots of the need to be a dictator can be a compulsion to deal with this fear of woman by encompassing and acting for her*'.[26] Which is why dictators demand not only obedience, but also love. Freedom may not be sexy, but fear of it is wholly determined by sex. Thus Bush on Hussein: 'Saddam is going to get his arse kicked' (an expression we hadn't heard that publicly since Bush used it, to considerable feminist objection, to describe his debate with Geraldine Ferraro during Reagan's second election campaign). The *Sunday Sport* headline of January 13,

1991, 'Saddam in Gay Lover Storm', is of course merely the flip side, or extension, of this. Compare, too, Saddam's comment that the ultimate evil of the West was demonstrated by the presence of American women in shorts in the desert – women in shorts, women baring their bodies in the desert, women at war.

There is, I want to suggest by way of conclusion, a very close link between this issue of sexuality and the problem of knowledge with which I began. Winnicott writes: 'with no more wars, males find themselves high and dry; yet they hate getting killed unless sure of the cause.'[27] The cause, however, is of course the problem. What is Winnicott saying about freedom if not that we think we are fighting for freedom, whereas the fear of freedom may be what drives us to war? If freedom is the cause we fight for, fear of freedom may also be the origin – the cause in its other sense – of war. What is Money-Kyrle describing if not the virtual impossibility of deciding who started it, or where it all began? If war, like the unconscious, troubles the concept of absolute truth, as well as the clear distinction between reality and fantasy, it troubles no less the category of cause. Fornari writes: 'war serves to defend ourselves against the "Terrifier" as an internal, absolute enemy . . . in this manner we arrive at the incredible paradox that the most important security function is not to defend ourselves from an external enemy but to find one' (p. xvii). So if we ask what causes war ('Why War?'), we find ourselves up against the problem of the cause. In his essay 'War and Individual Psychology', Jones quotes Nietzsche: 'Ye say it is the good cause that halloweth every war? I say unto you: it is the good war that halloweth every cause.'[28] This quote from the Iranian cleric Ayatollah Ali Meshkini graphically illustrates the problem: 'If war starts in the region, the Iranian people will regard America as the main enemy and aggressor and will definitely fight with this cause of corruption and crime, which trained warmongers such as Saddam.'[29] If war breaks out, he seemed to be saying, we will fight on the side of the effect to destroy the cause.

But Winnicott's comment – 'with no more wars, males find themselves high and dry; yet they hate getting killed unless sure of the cause' – links this problem of the cause and its certainty to the problem of sex. I don't think this is inadvertent, although when he talks of the 'mutual respect of maturing men who have fought each other' (war as a kind of initiation rite for boys), I am not sure.[30] Compare Winnicott's statement with this one from Clausewitz: 'logic sticks fast in this labyrinth . . . Why is the philosophical conception not satisfied? . . . What is the non-conducting medium that prevents the complete discharge?' (p. 368). (Remember that he is not even talking about the conduct of war, but about the challenge of war to knowledge, the failure of the theory to match up to its object or fulfil itself.) Likewise Freud, to go back to the exchange with Einstein, talks of the advance of war in terms reminiscent of the gradual completion, cohering, mastering of the polymorphous or partial drives: 'Hitherto, the unifications created by conquest, though of considerable extent, have only been *partial*, and the conflicts between these have called out more than ever for violent solutions' (p. 207). Unification becomes a necessary violence like, we might say, the subordination of a partial, multifarious, or even perverse sexuality to the dictates of a one-track, singular, and unified genital sex.

I am not, suggesting, however, that there is a monolithic and militarist culture grafted on to the body of the man, one with which all men automatically, and by dint of that body, cannot fail to identify. In fact, one of the remarkable features of Freud's own writings on culture is not just the ambivalence (eros and thanatos) of culture, but the way that, at several key moments in the theory, men's participation in culture is feminized by

Freud. Of course Freud regularly excluded women from the bounds of culture. But he also states that it is for fear of a loss of love that men submit to the authority of cultural law (the fear that he elsewhere makes the distinguishing mark of femininity, as opposed to the castration fear of the boy); and much as the oedipal injunction which lays down the law of sexual difference, so he describes the ethical sense as something which does not arise internally but is given – imposed – from the outside.[31] And compare this comment on culture: 'perhaps we may also familiarise ourselves with the idea that there are difficulties attaching to the nature of civilisation which will not yield to any attempt at reform,[32] with this famous comment about sexuality: 'we must reckon with the possibility that something in the nature of the sexual instinct itself is unfavourable to the realisation of complete satisfaction.'[33] Like sexuality, Freud hints, the law of culture is arbitrary, uncertain, incapable of completing itself. Thus Freud expels women from the bounds of culture (Woolf and other women of course turn this to their advantage) only to have his own account of the feminine and of the aporia of sexual difference return at the heart of his theorization of it. Only by acting as women – only if men, like women, fear a loss of love – will they internalize the cultural law in which their masculinity is so fiercely invested.

Which is why I want to end with something I will call 'the ethics of failure'. At an early stage in the controversy in the British Society, Susan Isaacs commented: 'We feel we ought to be better . . . because we see how much we fail; and this paradoxical but familiar fact tends to make us worse' (p. 59). War breaks out, uncontrollably, because – she seems to be suggesting – we are not willing to fail *enough*. Winnicott, in his first long intervention in the dispute, argued – after Freud – that scientific work would be possible only if 'we are not afraid to fail to cure' (p. 88). Knowledge will be possible only if we are willing to suspend the final purpose and ends of knowledge in advance. It is, in fact, remarkable how Jones, Money-Kyrle, and Glover (as well as Woolf) in their writing on war all propose not years, not decades, but millennia for the solution of the problem of war. According to Jones, Lord Davies asked him how much psychoanalytic research would be needed to bring war to an end, and when he answered a couple of centuries, Lord Davies said he would take a shorter cut and went for the League of Nations instead (the concept of interminability takes on whole new meaning here).[34] As if war is the place where the problem of the psychoanalytic cure – the idea that it is a problem – receives its most dramatic recognition.

Virginia Woolf proposes ridicule, censure, and contempt as the great antidotes to vanity, egotism, and megalomania, and then poverty, chastity, derision, and freedom from unreal loyalites (all mostly imposed on the female sex) as the conditions for women's entry into a world of professionalism which, without them, will inevitably lead to war (p. 90). Hang on to failure, hang on to derision – a failure and derision that would not invite a reactive triumphalism but pre-empt it – if you want to avoid going to war.

NOTES

First delivered as a Squiggle (Winnicott Foundation) Lecture, 19 January, 1991, two days after the outbreak of the Gulf War.
1   Sigmund Freud, 'Why War?' 1933 (1932), in *The Standard Edition of the Complete Psychological Works*, ed. and trans. James Strachey London: Hogarth, Vol. 22, pp. 195–215 (subsequent references are cited in the text). (Where two dates are given, the first is the date of composition, the second the original date of publication.) For an

indispensable account of the place and conceptualization of war in European culture from Clausewitz to Freud, see Daniel Pick, *War Machine: the rationalisation of slaughter in the modern age* (London and New Haven: Yale University Press, 1993).

2   Gertrude Stein, *Wars I Have Seen* (London: Batsford, 1945), p. 8 (subsequent references are cited in the text).

3   For a discussion of the First World War in relation to modernity, see Eric Leed, *No Man's Land – Contact and Identity in World War I* (Cambridge: Cambridge University Press, 1979).

4   Franco Fornari, *The Psychoanalysis of War* (Bloomington, Ind., and London: Indiana University Press, 1975), p. xviii (subsequent references are cited in the text).

5   Geza Roheim, *War, Crime and the Covenant*, Journal of Clinical Psychopathology Monograph Series, No. 1 (New York (Monticello): Medical Journal Press, 1945), pp. 113, 116 (subsequent references are cited in the text).

6   Freud, 'Thoughts for the Times on War and Death', 1915, in *Standard Edition*, vol. 14, p. 293 (subsequent references are cited in the text).

7   Freud, 'On Transience', 1916 (1915), in *Standard Edition*, vol. 14, p. 306.

8   Henri Barbusse, *Under Fire*, trans. F. Wray (London and Toronto: Dent, 1916), p. 332.

9   Karl von Clausewitz, *On War*, 1832, Pelican Classics Edition Harmondsworth: Penguin, 1982) (subsequent references are cited in the text).

10   Andrew Stephen, 'Who Blinked First?', *Observer*, 9 December 1990.

11   Roger Money-Kyrle, *Psychoanalysis and Politics, A Contribution to the Psychology of Politics and Morals* (London: Duckworth, 1951), p. 98 (subsequent references are cited in the text).

12   Freud, *The Future of an Illusion*, 1927, in *Standard Edition*, vol. 21, p. 34.

13   Ernest Jones, 'The Concept of the Normal Mind', *International Journal of Psychoanalysis*, 23, 1 (1942), p. 4; cited in Money-Kyrle, *Psychoanalysis and Politics*, pp. 98–9n.

14 Jones, 'How can Civilisation be Saved?', *International Journal of Psychoanalysis*, 24, 1 & 2, p. 4.

15 Edward Glover, 'Pacifism in Eclipse', in *War, Sadism and Pacifism, Further Essays on Group Psychology and War*, (London: Allen and Unwin, 1935), p. 133.

16 D. W. Winnicott, 'Discussion of War Aims', 1940, in *Home Is Where We Start From* (Harmondsworth: Penguin, 1986), p. 210.

17 Paul Wilkinson, A Way to Avoid the No-Win War', *Guardian*, 3 January 1991.

18 Joan Rivière, in *The Freud–Klein Controversies 1941–45*, ed. Pearl King and Riccardo Steiner, New Library of Psychoanalysis, vol. 11, (London and New York: Tavistock/Routledge, 1991), p. 110 (subsequent references are cited in the text).

19 Riccardo Steiner, Editorial Comments (2), in *ibid.*, p. 917.

20 Azar Gat, *The Origins of Military Thought from the Enlightenment to Clausewitz* (Oxford: Clarendon Press, 1989).

21 Money-Kyrle, 'A Psychological Analysis of the Causes of War', 1934, in *The Collected Papers of Money-Kyrle*, ed. Donald Meltzer (Strath Tay, Perthshire: Clunie Press, 1978), p. 137.

22 Virginia Woolf, *Three Guineas*, 1938 (Harmondsworth: Penguin, 1977) (subsequent references are cited in the text).

23 Winnicott, 'Discussion of War Aims', p. 214.

24 Ibid.

25 Winnicott, 'Some Thoughts on the Meaning of the Word "Democracy" ', 1950, in *Home Is Where We Start From*, p. 253; emphasis original.

26 Ibid.; emphasis original.

27 Winnicott, 'This Feminism', 1964, in *Home Is Where We Start From*, p. 193.

28 Jones, 'War and Individual Psychology', 1915, in *Essays in Applied Psycho-Analysis*, vol. 1, (London: Hogarth and Institute of Psycho-Analysis, 1951), p. 67.

29 'Sayings of the Week', *Observer*, 19 August 1991.

30 Winnicott, 'Discussion of War Aims', p. 220.

31 Freud, *Civilisation and its Discontents* 1930 (1929), in *Standard Edition*, vol. 21, p. 124.

32   Ibid., p. 115.
33   Freud, 'On the Universal Tendency to Debasement in
      the Sphere of Love', 1912, in *Standard Edition*, vol. 11,
      pp. 188–9.
34   Jones, 'War and Individual Psychology', Postscript, p. 76.

2   Margaret Thatcher and Ruth Ellis

An act of barbarism that is deeply *republic* [sic] (correction) *repugnant* to all civilised people.
Margaret Thatcher to the House of Commons after the execution of Farzad Bazoft, journalist, in Iraq, 15 March 1990.

It has been the strength of feminism to produce a recognition of the political importance of sexuality and subjectivity in the face of more traditional political or Marxist analyses which have consistently left them out of account. The dialogue between psychoanalysis and feminism belongs in that political space. But the very success of that intervention may in turn be in danger of producing an unintended consequence: that the domain of what is more easily and conventionally defined as the political can continue to be analysed as if it were free of psychic and sexual processes, as if it operated outside the range of their effects. The re-election of Margaret Thatcher to a third term and the resurgence of right-wing ideologies seemed the appropriate moment to take up this issue – a moment when those very processes revealed themselves more and more to be crucial determinants or at least components of the political scene, a moment when we found ourselves witnessing the pressure of fantasy on our collective political life. If Margaret Thatcher throws up this question, she also does so in a way which is especially difficult for feminism because she is a woman, one furthermore who embodied some of the worst properties of what feminism has identified as a patriarchal society and state. This very difficulty can, however, perhaps serve as a caution to what has become, in many discussions of psychoanalysis and feminism, an idealization of the unconscious, whether as writing or pre-oedipality, or both. This chapter attempts to situate Thatcher in the domain of what psychoanalysis calls the realm of symbolic possibility; that is, the general forms of psychic cohesion which societies engender and on which they also come to rely. For feminism the symbolic order is always gendered. The chapter is therefore an attempt to run two propositions together: that the symbolic order is gendered, and that right-wing ideologies thrive on and strain against the furthest limits of psychic fantasy. It then adds to these two a further consideration: how to analyse both these factors when it is a woman at the summit of political power who comes to embody them at their most extreme.

> Are women more apt than other social categories, notably the exploited class, to invest in the implacable machinery of terrorism? . . .
>
> The habitual and increasingly explicit attempt to fabricate a scapegoat victim as foundress of a society or countersociety may be replaced by the analysis of the potentialities of *victim/executioner* which characterize each identity, each subject, each sex. (Julia Kristeva, 'Women's Time'[1])

These quotations from Julia Kristeva raise the question of women and violence. They are taken from an article 'Women's Time' which has often been quoted as heralding a third stage of feminism which will follow feminism's demand first for equality and then for separation and difference. In this third stage, sexual difference itself will be exposed as a metaphysical category. If this is not the Derridean position to which it bears a striking resemblance, it is because of the concepts of subjectivity and psychic reality to which Kristeva holds and which here, as elsewhere in her writing, she pushes to a type of extreme. In this article, Kristeva's most explicit discussion of the history of feminism is conducted for a large part through an examination of the question of violence for women; that is, the way that women situate themselves in response to a crisis in what she calls the socio-symbolic contract, a contract to which they are subjected, from which they are also excluded, and which they can also embody in the worst of its effects. For Kristeva, that contract is founded on a moment of violence, the violence of primitive psychic separation which precipitates subjects into language and the violence of a social order which has sacrifice as its symbolic base. We can add to that the violence of sexual difference itself, meaning both the trauma of its recognition and the worst forms of its social enactment in the real. For Kristeva, it is feminism's importance that it confronts the furthest extremities, or perversion, of what it is that constitutes the social bond. Women can refuse that social bond (the feminism of difference) or they can take it on, in the two meanings of identification (the feminism of equality) and assault (terrorism). A third stage would idealize neither the social nor the concept of its antithesis, but would instead turn its attention to the violence of the subjectivity which upholds it. Far from heralding a new dawn, therefore, the deconstruction of sexual difference leads us straight back to the heart of violence itself, to 'the victim/executioner' in us all.

Why does Kristeva conduct her discussion of feminism in terms of this question of violence – a connection in her argument which, for the most part, has been ignored or overlooked? What leads her to produce such a dangerous proximity between women and terrorism and death? We can perhaps try to answer these questions not directly with reference to Kristeva, but by looking at that place within English culture where the issue of women, power, and violence presents itself with particular force. I am referring to Margaret Thatcher, whose re-election to a third term brought into special focus the question of what happens when it is a woman who comes to embody the social at its most perverse. The difficulty is that any discussion of Thatcher which relates specifically to her as a woman constantly risks a slide into misogyny (of which, it should be said, Kristeva has been accused). But something about Thatcher's place in the collective imaginary of British culture calls out for an understanding of what it is she releases by dint of being a woman and of the forms of fantasmatic scenario which she brings into play. Is there something in that scenario which touches on the most extreme edge of the social, of what it is that has to be secured and regulated to ensure the very possibility of our collective social life? And did Margaret Thatcher draw part of her imaginary power from the way that she operated, or appeared to operate, in that space? More fundamentally, can her re-election be used to understand something about the place of fantasy in our collective political life?

Discussion of the election result on the left came very close to acknowledging this as an issue of importance. In the first of what has become a set of key articles on Thatcher's third term, Stuart Hall argued in the July 1987 issue of *Marxism Today* that the Conservative victory needed to be understood not just in terms of material interest, but in terms of images and identifications. The Conservatives were unpopular in terms of policies, but had managed to mobilize a new ideological constituency. Political identities, he argued, are formed not just on the basis of 'so-called "real" majorities but on (equally real) "symbolic" majorities'.[2] The left weakens itself politically by failing to take images seriously, leaving the important field of these symbolic identifications to the right. Politics, Hall was effectively arguing, is not only, but also, a matter of fantasies, in which the way that people 'imagine' themselves occupies a crucial place. His analysis therefore picked up on a problem which has a history going back at least to the 1930s, when the left had to ask itself why, in the face of increasing political oppression, large sectors of people, including those who are most exploited, move not to the left but to the right. Thatcherism – and the analogy is more than gratuitous – forces us up against something which Wilhelm Reich was the first to call the mass psychology of fascism.

Hall's analysis was crucial for addressing the issue of fantasy and political identities. But it raised a problem for me – one that suggested the need to extend that basic insight – in so far as the argument about identification remained within the framework of rational calculation: 'far from this being a sign of voter irrationality, there are a number of quite "rational" reasons why there should be a trend in this direction.'[3] Avoiding the image of the irrational or, as Hall puts it elsewhere, the 'endlessly deceived, or endlessly authoritarian masses',[4] the article could be read as producing the counter-image of another: the always reasoned political subject. Subjects identify not with their immediate material interest, but with the place from which they can see themselves as potentially making good. The article was then criticized on the grounds that many voters hated the image of Thatcherism but voted for her policies as most likely to secure that good, as well as for a potential pessimism (if politics are determined by a kind of long-term fantasmatic version of individual self-interest, what is to prevent an eternity of Toryism?). It is crucial, however, that these criticisms not allow the political issue of identification and the image raised by Hall to be lost. For only if you are operating with a rationalist concept of fantasy will the dislike of Thatcher automatically dispense with the idea that something about her image is at work in the political processes that returned her to power. What if Thatcher was re-elected not despite the repugnance that many feel for her image, but also in some sense because of it? What if that force of identity for which she is so severely castigated somewhere also operates as a type of pull?[5]

That is not to argue that this is necessarily the case, but simply to point to the fact that the area of symbolic identifications, once it has been broached, cannot be halted at the level of the rational. One of the key characteristics of both identification and the image is their tendency to operate in a contradictory fashion, which means psychoanalytically that there is no stopping the potential range of their aberrant causes or effects. The attempt of the social order to secure its own rationality and its constant failure to do so may be one of the things that Thatcher brings most graphically into focus. If this is the case, any discussion of collective identifications which remains within the terms of the rational may find itself inadvertently reinforcing one of the most powerful myths carried by the image of Margaret Thatcher herself.

The centrality of Thatcher to the problem of this political moment therefore obliges us to take up the legacy of the debate about fantasy and the right. But it throws in a new factor for consideration: what might it be about a woman in power that brings us up against the furthest and most perverse – Kristeva's terms are 'irreducible and deadly' – extremities of the social bond?

Ruth Ellis was the last woman to be hanged in England. She died in 1955. She was brought back to public attention in 1983, at the time of the vote on capital punishment which Thatcher allowed in Parliament al-

most immediately after the election victory which secured her second term. Ruth Ellis was not the last person to be executed in England, but in the publicity over
the vote and the accompanying debate her image was
central. Film and photographs of protests at her hanging
appeared on television and in the Press; Renée Short
referred in the House to the 'judicial murder' of Ruth
Ellis as the event which had brought home to the
country as a whole the enormity of capital punishment.[6]
It was of course because Ellis was a woman that she
aroused this interest, which appeared more and more as
curiosity, both about the spectacle of hanging and also
about the sexual nature of her crime (she shot her lover).
The object of a voyeuristic attention (a film, *Dance with
a Stranger*, was made about her life in 1984), Ruth Ellis,
or rather the focus on her, seemed to be demonstrating
the power of spectacle, femininity, and violence and
their mutual association in public fantasy life. The protest at the hanging – the mobilization of Ellis for the case
against state violence – found itself repeating the drama
of the original event. Death by hanging became a symbol
of contention centring on two women: Thatcher, who
supported the restoration of capital punishment, and
Ellis, who was called up to demonstrate its inhumanity,
but who seemed equally to release something of that
peculiar pleasure which the idea of execution always
seems to provoke.[7]

In one sense there is no common point or even dialogue between these two women: from different historical moments and opposite ends of the social spectrum,
they stand respectively for criminality and the law.
(Thatcher was a barrister before, and during the early
stages of, her political career.) To this extent they could
be said to illustrate the emptiness of the category
'woman' as a totality which denies the crucial differences
of identity and class between women. To link them is
therefore to constitute a fantasy in itself.[8] Yet Margaret

Thatcher and Ruth Ellis were brought together at this historical moment in a scenario whose imaginary basis may well be what constitutes its importance and force. 'Victim' and 'executioner', they meet at that point of violence where the ordering of the social reveals something of the paradox on which it is based: the fact that civilization, as Freud puts it, 'hopes to prevent the crudest excesses of violence by itself assuming the right to use violence against criminals'.[9] René Girard makes this point the basis of his discussion of violence and the sacred: 'All the procedures that allow men to moderate their violence are analogous in that none of them are strangers to violence.'[10] That 'men' is of course eloquent, apparently expressive of the desire to 'protect' women from violence in both senses of the term. In that moment of symbolic encounter between Margaret Thatcher and Ruth Ellis, however, it was not men, but two women who stood for the violence which both Freud and Girard situate structurally on either side of the law. Drawing attention to themselves precisely *as* women, they could serve to gloss over that double and paradoxical location of violence; the perversion of the State in relation to violence could be transposed on to the perversity of the woman, its more troubling implications then siphoned off and ignored.

The 'perversity of the woman' refers here as much to Thatcher as to Ellis, for the woman supporter of capital punishment is as grotesque for the dominant stereotypes of femininity as for a feminist critique of the State as the embodiment of phallic power. We should not forget, however, that Thatcher initiated the debate on capital punishment after an election result secured by the Falklands victory. Her resoluteness over the machinery of war seemed to turn her from the most unpopular prime minister since the last World War to one guaranteed a return to power. In that second election, at least, there can be no doubt that one of the things which Thatcher

stood for was the desirability of war. We may therefore
be able to turn this episode to account by asking what
may the bizarre nature of the woman's position within
it reveal about the paradox in the definition and regulation of the limits of the social itself?

The trial of Ruth Ellis was described at the time as 'one
of the most one-sided legal battles ever to be fought in
the number one court'.[11] She was convicted, by all accounts, at the moment when she stated in court that she
had 'a peculiar feeling I wanted to kill him', repeating
on being questioned, 'I had an idea I wanted to kill
him.'[12] This supreme clarity on the part of Ruth Ellis
('she felt completely justified') destroyed any possibility
of reducing the charge from murder to manslaughter.[13]
Only if she had been out of control, 'the subject of such
emotional disturbance operating upon her mind so as
for the time being to unseat her judgement, to inhibit
and cut off those censors which normally control our
conduct,' might she have been found not guilty of the
charge.[14] Premeditation therefore signifies here the rationality of a subject who knows her own mind, meaning
that she knows – rather than simply experiencing as
something beyond her – that part of the mind controlled
by the censors which is normally cut off. In relation to
desires effectively acknowledged here as universal, Ruth
Ellis is a woman who knows too much.
   At the time of Ruth Ellis's trial, the defence of insanity
could be mounted only under the McNaghten Rules of
1843. These were applicable if 'the accused was labour-
ing under such a defect of reason, from disease of the
mind, as not to know the nature and quality of the act,
or, if he did know it, that he did not know that he was
doing wrong'.[15] The legal definition of insanity therefore
rests on something we could describe as a knowledge
relation. Those who are insane act not without reason,
but without that reason which should provide them with

correct knowledge of what they are doing. This is, as has often been pointed out, a legal rather than a medical account of insanity. The law adjudges the nature of the act, excuses those who are deficient in that knowledge, and condemns those who share that knowledge and act on it. The law therefore condemns the murderer to the extent that she or he can identify with its own adjudication. Thus Ellis's supreme rationality mimics the reason of the law.[16]

This rationality of Ruth Ellis clearly threatened a crisis of sexual difference. 'You will hear – and I am going to call a very eminent psychiatrist to tell you', the defence announces, 'that the effect of jealousy upon a female mind can so work as to unseat the reason and can operate to a degree in which a male mind is quite incapable of operating.'[17] Women, according to the psychiatrist's testimony, are 'inclined to lose some of their inhibitory capacity and solve their problems on a more primitive level. This is not applying to women in general, but if they do have hysterical reactions, they are more prone to hysterical reactions than men.'[18] When a man is hysterical, on the other hand, he is so in the service of self-interest, like the men in the firing line in the war whose hysterical paralyses ensured their removal from the front (the discussion of male hysteria was stopped by the judge). The problem with Ruth Ellis was that she was not 'hysterical *enough*' – lacking a 'sufficiently hysterical personality to solve her problems by a complete loss of memory'.[19] Showing no emotion, Ellis was described later by her counsel as having got herself into a 'stratosphere of emotion', as if some notion of her total strangeness had to be produced to cover the lack of hysteria, of the appropriate feminine affect.[20] It is a case in which a woman fails to mobilize a stereotype in her defence. She is outside the bounds of the law and of conventional expectation only by being not quite far outside enough.

What we see here is the way femininity is being used to draw a line around the limits of what a society will recognize of itself. Femininity, like insanity, is a type of mitigating circumstance. Subjects who commit murder must be feminine and/or out of control. The murderer who acts wilfully and in full knowledge of her or his emotions is rather like the psychoanalyst who, in defiance of the censors and in the name of forbidden knowledge, brings our guilty secrets to light.

Ruth Ellis was a problem for the court because her femininity did not come into play at the right point. Femininity failed to secure a limit-definition of violence: murder as the limit of what a society can recognize of itself, murder beyond the limit as the only form of murder it can accept. Because it did not guarantee this definition of violence, because it would not respect the existing conceptual boundaries, Ellis's femininity could appear only as an outrage, as something inappropriate and out of place – the peroxide she insisted on for her hair for her appearance in court, for example. If not essence, femininity can be only trapping or mere show.[21]

The trial of Ruth Ellis presents us with a unique combination of the terms of femininity, rationality, and violence in both their symbolic and concrete weight (the second as an effect of the first). It also forced their realignment in ways that I shall go on to describe. The woman who murders with reason (ambiguity intended) produces a particular form of crisis, doubling over with the fact of her sexuality that disturbing conflation of rationality with the most violent of crimes. In doing so, she provokes a sexualized version of the question produced by the category of 'reasoning madness' in nineteenth-century France: 'In what way rationality could be criminal, and how it all, crime and knowledge, could be "borne" by what was called the "social order".'[22] If rationality can be criminal, not, note, if crime can be rational: if murder can be reasoned – the question is almost asked – then what price the insight that reason might be murderous in itself?

What then happened in response to the case of Ruth Ellis is a realignment of the terms of criminality, reason, and madness on which the judgment had turned, terms organized so as to secure an image of the social but which the spectacle of the trial and execution had instead seemed to question or even undermine. Thus the year after her trial, the Conservative government was defeated on an opposition motion to abolish capital punishment (it had defeated such a motion just months before the trial, although the later vote was overturned in the Lords and capital punishment was not finally abolished until 1969). But the McNaghten Rules were altered by a new Homicide Act which introduced the category of 'diminished responsibility' – a borderline category in the legal definition of reason, since it is the only instance in law which recognizes a middle position between full responsibility for a criminal act and a total absence of responsibility. It was as if the trial and execution of Ruth Ellis had tested the limits of a set of key concepts through which we secure the 'sanity' of our collective social life. In doing so, the case led to a redefinition of violence: the violence not only of the criminal, but also of the due processes of the law.[23] The irony was that Margaret Thatcher would return to the issue of capital punishment, calling up the collective memory of Ruth Ellis, as part of an attempt to put back in place the very terms which that earlier moment had put so definitively under threat.

The McNaghten Rules of 1843 had required that the defence establish the insanity of the act. The concept of diminished responsibility applied more to the insanity of the person: 'such abnormality of mind (whether arising from a condition of arrested or retarded development of mind or any inherent causes or induced by disease or injury) as substantially impaired his mental responsibility for his acts or omissions'.[24] The Rules complete the pathologization and infantilization (feminization?) of the murderer, which locates criminality in the very nature of the criminal and her or his history. In Foucault's terms, this would bring the wheel full circle, from the idea dominant in the eighteenth century that the more aberrant the act, the more guilty the criminal, to the idea which emerged with the increasing psychiatrization of justice in the nineteenth century that only aberration is an excuse for violent crime.[25]

Unlike Foucault, however, I see this not just as the pathologization of criminality, but also as the criminalizing of pathology. By that I do not mean a simple reconstitution of the earlier institutional link between delinquents and the mentally ill, but rather a move by the legal system of recognition and denial: both murder and pathology are outlawed; but the effect is to bring murder into the realm of the psychic, thereby releasing the potential recognition that the psyche might be murderous in itself. Foucault himself acknowledges that – beyond the specific histories produced by these definitions, which they also reflect – we seem to be dealing with something universal, collective, a property of the social as such: 'the collective fear of crime, the obsession with this danger which seems to be an inseparable part of society itself'.[26] Psychoanalysis would recognize in such a collective obsession a way of disposing of a collective guilt. The guilt of the criminal establishes the innocence of the society; but, like all oppositions, it risks a potential identification between its basic terms.

The trial of Ruth Ellis, the changing legal account of responsibility which followed, and the debate about capital punishment which she helped to provoke all make it clear that the question of social regulation threw up a problem of delimitation in the fullest psychic sense of the term. This involved delimitation not only of the social, but also of the psychic, as well as of the boundaries and links between the two. It was a problem that had already been graphically underlined by the testimony of the Institute of Psycho-Analysis to the Royal Commission on Capital Punishment which had met from 1949 to 1952. Their question was what murder might mean to, or more exactly, in what sense we – that is, technically the non-murderers – might recognize ourselves in this most violent of crimes, not just at the level of spectacle, but in terms of the identification which it might uncover and provoke. Here 'identification' implies that crucial sense of an active self-recognition where what is at stake is a conflation of identities not just played out by the discourse, but positively sought after or desired.

In their strange encounter with the Commission, the analysts argued that most people react to murder as an unconscious threat to the security of their repressions. The murderer cannot be called 'abnormal' in so far as murder is potentially present in the very regulation of drives. For psychoanalysis, the subject's own aggression is an object of fear, and the child has two ways of preserving his fantasied world from its attacks. Either the aggression can be transformed into conscience, or it can be neutralized by the erotic drives. But both these solutions contain their own dangers. The first can lead to suicidal impulses if the aggression is turned against the self, and the second can lead to sexual murder if the sexual impulses find themselves eroticizing the very violence they were meant to control ('the presence of the erotic component shows clearly in the sexual nature of the crime'[27]).

Nor can the analysts predict with any certainty which of these outcomes is more likely to occur. What emerges from their testimony is a failure of discrimination between normal and abnormal at a psychic level as far as murder is concerned. The force of the psychoanalytic argument, its power of explanation, produces as its effect that, in relation to the most dangerous of crimes, the category of what is normal starts to fade and even disappear. It was a particular scandal of their testimony that one analyst found himself talking quite happily of the 'normal murderer' as the most important in psychoanalytic terms. This analyst was then hastily corrected by a colleague who insisted that between those who murder and those who don't there must finally be a difference in the impulses involved. The evidence of the analysts seemed, therefore, to repeat that mechanism of partial recognition and denial that they themselves had identified in the public response to the crime.[28]

The problem is of course the category of normality itself. What we can see here is a paradox inherent in psychoanalysis operating in the region of the law – that the concept of the unconscious at once dispenses with, yet still relies on, the concept of the normal mind. For Ernest Jones, writing in 1942 in an article entitled 'The Concept of the Normal Mind', it remains an ideal concept, and can be stated categorically not to exist, even if psychoanalysis can describe the conditions for its production.[29] Nor does he claim to know whether it might exist in the limited and clinical sense that he describes. In this context, the murderer merely highlights the problem, which has been accentuated with the understanding of infantile psychotic states developed after Freud, that the more you identify the aberrational and extravagant in the most fundamental workings of the mind, the harder it becomes to use those categories to secure a social classification – to secure the social itself. The trial and execution of Ruth Ellis, however, brought all this too close: 'The breakfast table is no place for a refresher course on the abnormal' – a beautiful parody of the link that psychoanalysis establishes between the crazy and the domestic, between psycho-pathology and everyday life.[30]

What then of capital punishment itself? What confusions does it in turn engender in relation to the public, the

criminal, and the State? For that account of the vicissitudes of the drives offered by psychoanalysis started with
the observation that capital punishment is the clearest
embodiment of the primitive mechanism whereby the
subject expels aggressivity only to experience it as returning from the outside. That is to say, if the murderer
threatens a lifting of repression, undoing the relative
comfort of a neurotic mechanism on which subjects and
statehood survive, then capital punishment acts out a
psychotic drama in which the libidinal impulses one
thought to be rid of return in the shape of God. This
may give its full meaning to the idea of capital punishment as the supreme embodiment of a penalty whose
enormity *matches* the hideousness of the crime. For the
Lancet, writing in 1955 after the execution of Ruth Ellis,
an execution whether actually seen or only imagined was
bound to be contagious in its effects: 'Small wonder if
the youngsters swallowing the poison find the idea of
violence dangerously attractive.'[31] It is an act of communal
violence which already operates by mimesis (from the
criminal to the punishment) and which then passes to
the public at large. The argument anticipates the debates
about violence which followed the Hungerford massacre
in 1987, except that in this instance the contagion was
presumed to stem from the violence of the State.

Clearly the issue of capital punishment poses one of
the greatest threats to the most basic of social differen-
tiations, because of this relation of mimesis between
punishment and crime. Each time the Conservative
Party returns to this issue in what became under Thatcher
the obligatory annual vote, it therefore places under
considerable strain the symbolic limits which a 'civilized'
society draws around itself. The motion on the first free
vote on hanging after the execution of Ruth Ellis read:
'This House believes that the death penalty no longer
accords with the needs or true interests of a civilized
society.'[32] If capital punishment is 'barbaric', however,

we should note that the desire for its restoration tends in the West to be a characteristic of extreme right-wing governments standing for the fullest authority of the State. It is a paradox expressive of the most fundamental regulation of the social that the government which most fully embodies that authority is closest to its symbolic limits, and therefore most likely to push it over the edge. As one Tory MP put it: 'It's a good red meat issue; it gives us something to chew on, but we won't swallow it.'[33] In the strictest sense, the issue of capital punishment under Thatcher set the limits to the anti-State rhetoric which she so consistently deployed. Specifically, in the 1950s, that free vote had found itself wedged between two imperatives: the distinction between the 'civilization' of England and the 'backwardness' of the colonies and the urgent necessity after Nazism to save the concept of a beneficent State.[34]

It none the less seems that, in strictly legal terms, capital punishment can be seen to represent the limits of judicial authority itself, challenging or exposing as a masquerade the very reason of the law. This is how David Pannick opens his *Judicial Review of the Death Penalty*:

> It was the optimistic belief of the eighteenth-century philosophers of the Enlightenment that all problems could be resolved, and all questions correctly answered, if only we could discover and apply the relevant formula. Leibniz dreamt of a 'logic machine' that would, without debate or delay, supply the right answer to any moral or political controversy. The Encyclopaedists worked at producing eighty-four octavo volumes that would provide information to settle any dispute. There remains only one forum where the Enlightenment philosopher would today feel at home: our courts of law.[35]

For Pannick, capital punishment best challenges this logic machine of the courtroom by demonstrating the essentially *hermeneutic* nature of the law, the difficulty it has in defining its own limits, and even the possibility that it might act contrary to its own form. The object of interminable dispute, capital punishment repeatedly shows the law passing beyond itself.[36] More crucially, according to the very constitution (written or unwritten) which appears to legitimate it, capital punishment may be contrary to the 'due process of the law'. Most of the criteria which could, technically, establish its constitutionality or not (that it is imposed in a 'cruel and painful manner', 'wantonly or freakishly', or by 'caprice or procedural irregularity') are not susceptible to absolute definition.[37] (Note how instability figures as the very content of the key terms.) Capital punishment brings the law up against the *arbitrary* – the arbitrary of its own practice, but through that, and in defiance of the enlightened rationality to which it still holds, the arbitrary as such. In strictly judicial terms, therefore, capital punishment represents that point where the law has the greatest difficulty in securing its own rationality. It provides a strange imitation or acting-out of the problem the law has in establishing the absence or presence of reason in the criminal it is required to judge.

In the case of Ruth Ellis, horror at the execution of a woman also played a crucial part in the reintroduction of the motion against capital punishment and in the subsequent passing of the Homicide Act. It is as if the thinness of the boundary between criminal and legal murder, the uncomfortable proximity between them, presents itself too starkly when it is a woman who is executed. It seems also that the spectacle of execution – 'seen or imagined' (*Lancet*) – is too powerful when it is a woman, because her status as spectacle in the more general culture threatens to turn this moment of a society's most precarious self-regulation into nothing but show (the classical and repeated ambiguity of the woman as spectacle, focus of a displaced anxiety which she always threatens to provoke).[38]

Returning to Margaret Thatcher, we can perhaps see now something of the extraordinary nature of having a woman in power who unequivocally supported the return of capital punishment, a woman who chooses to embody the State at that very point where it rests its authority on the right to kill, but does so by means of a language which is one of consistency, rationality, and control. One of the things that Thatcher presented us with is an inflated version of the rationality which can be the only basis for distinguishing between legal and illegal violence. For if the law partly allows for the murderer who is deemed to be out of her or his mind, punishing above all a violence which stems from a self-knowing calculation, it is also because violence as rational is the form of violence which it reserves to itself. It is her utter certainty of judgement which allowed Thatcher to release into our public fantasy life, with no risk of confusion, the violence which underpins the authority of the State. If femininity is opposed to violence according to one stereotype – women are not violent – Thatcher presented a femininity which does not serve to neutralize violence but allows for its legitimation.[39]

It is a grotesque scenario – one which mimics that of Ruth Ellis in reverse – where a woman who stands for a super-rationality writes violence into the law (or would do so), instead of being executed by it:

Allowing the repressed – the drive if you like, or the death drive to get to the point – to be spoken through language is perhaps one way of stopping it from erupting inside the code: for it is that codified, legitimated, eruption which precisely constitutes fascism.[40]

One of the key aspects of Thatcher's image, I would argue, is this symbolic legitimation and rationalization of violence. That this could be the case at the same time as the Conservatives mounted their official onslaught against media violence and crime – 'no procedure against

violence that is a stranger to it' (Girard) – merely demonstrates that structure of necessary antagonism which
inheres in rationality itself. Writing on American politics, Richard Hofstadter described this mechanism as
the 'paranoid style' which produces out of its own system an enemy of super-competence whose 'plots long
hatched and deeply premeditated' mirror its own supreme and deadly rationality in reverse.[41] Murderers
who premeditate are therefore the most dangerous because they too closely resemble the symbolic and psychic
structure written into the legal apparatus that comes to
meet them.

A brief look at Thatcher's rhetoric will confirm its investment in its own supreme logic and consistency, the way
that she elevated these concepts to the status of general
policy and object of desire. (The last chapter of Bruce
Arnold's *Margaret Thatcher: a study in power* is called 'The
Consistency of Rhetoric'.[42]) To take just one speech,
the New Year's message of 1984, and deliberately and
wildly extract from it the key images on which it turns:

> Our commitment remains as strong as ever . . . the
> defence of the realm and the rule of law. . . . We have
> already made considerable progress. . . . We have shown
> what can be done . . . this is only the beginning of the
> revival of Britain. . . . We have embarked on our second
> term with the same enthusiasm. . . . The British people
> now know that we are as good as our word and the rest
> of the world is beginning to know it too. . . . They know
> that this government will never hesitate to stand up for
> Britain's interests. We shall persist. . . . We want people
> in all walks of life to set their hopes high and to carry
> them through into reality. . . . We shall not be afraid . . .
> people need a government which follows a consistent
> and coherent policy and sticks to it . . . we shall continue
> to protect the value of your money. We shall continue to
> control public spending. . . . This government already
> has a reputation for consistency. . . . No one can accuse

this government of complacency. Far from losing our way, we are just getting into our stride. We have stayed right on course. We believe what we say. We say what we believe.[43]

I am not sure that it is necessary to pick out the repeated and central terms of consistency, persistence, and sameness, the refusal of any possible gap between reality and intent (which passes to her subjects 'who set their hopes high and carry them through into reality'), and then, as the inevitable corollary for those who see in this form of rhetoric a denial of the precariousness of language itself, the insistence on the utter coherence of the word ('We are as good as our word. . . . We believe what we say. We say what we believe'). We can call it an inflation and parody of government as reason, an appropriation into the pure *form* of reason of an earlier idealist and more radical tradition which rested its hopes on the idea of a rational State.[44]

It is this quality of consistency and logic that was picked up by commentators on Thatcher's style, whether 'for' ('We will have one of the most logical governments this country has ever had'[45]), or 'against':

The picture of consistent certainty is a complete one. The fact that it is so free of doubt is unnerving. The fact that it is so well remembered is puzzling. The fact that it is so freely given, and yet in so limited and circumscribed a form, is faintly frightening. . . . The self-assurance, the assured recollection and presentation of self, in one who keeps no diary, retains no personal papers, deals always and emphatically in the present, is itself a kind of consistency.[46]

Compare Hofstadter: 'It is nothing if not coherent, far more coherent than the real world, no room for mistakes, failures, ambiguities, if not rational intensely rationalistic.'[47] The conviction politician by her own definition,

Thatcher made of her own logic, and of logic itself, a type of personality and political cult. The image is uncannily close to that of Ruth Ellis ('She felt completely justified') standing in the dock 'firm, erect and unafraid' (for one correspondent, this in itself was enough to condemn her[48]). The two women, therefore, present the image alternatively of an acceptable and a threatening form of reason in excess – unless it is the case that, according to a logic which is proper to reason, the acceptable form of reason is not opposed to the threatening, but depends on it.

For Hofstadter, it is precisely that super-rationality which takes precedence over, and then releases, the paranoid mode. This is Thatcher:

> We must become aware of the way in which our daily lives, our own thinking, may have become affected, become tainted without our ever realising it, by the ceaseless flood of Socialist and pseudo-Socialist propaganda to which we have been exposed for so long. . . . The decline of contemporary thought has been hastened by the misty phantom of Socialism. . . . Socialism has lured [people's] conscience into thinking that the steamroller which is about to flatten them is a blessing in disguise.[49]

> The British character has done so much for democracy, for law, and done so much throughout the world that if there is any fear that it might be swamped people are going to react . . . the moment the minority threatens to become a big one, people get frightened.[50]

Power in the adversarial mode: Thatcher seems to be repeating here one of the fundamental psychic tropes of Fascism, which acts out this structure of aggressivity, giving name and place to the invisible adversary which is an inherent part of it, and making fear a central component of strategy. 'People get frightened . . . we are not here to ignore people's wishes.' It does not take much to reorganize the semantics of that sentence and to read it as stating that fear in itself is an object of desire. The Falklands War, therefore, simply brought to its logical conclusion a rhetoric whose basic terms were already firmly in place. The film of the Black Audio Film Collective *Handsworth Songs*, made in 1986, makes the link explicit: 'Between Thatcher's "swamping" speech and the Falklands expedition, lies another melodrama of consent: *the war of naming the problem*, the rush to discover the unclubbables, the drug barons, the new black, the black of disorder and mayhem' (my emphasis). The message seems to be, as is the case with paranoia: we have every reason to be frightened, we have everything firmly under control. It is on the back of this that Thatcher reopened the question of capital punishment, which repeats this message with explicit reference to the violence on which its structure depends ('a vehicle for political capital, a scapegoat to illogically appease our society's sense of guilt, fear, passion and vengeance'[51]). In 1986, the first report of the new Conservative Research Department, taking over from the Centre of Policy Studies, argued that retribution is the very meaning of the law. (Compare this, however, with Willie Hamilton in the House of Commons: 'Retribution did not solve the problem . . . in desperation the party of law and order put forward these debates to prove its virility.'[52])

Commenting on the sacrificial nature of the social order as described by anthropologists, Kristeva writes: 'But sacrifice orders violence, binds it, tames it.'[53] It also, however, *repeats* it, or binds it in the form of what Girard calls a 'violent unanimity', scapegoating its victim in order to expel violence out into the real and so end it. If this mechanism is the basis of social cohesion, it is the characteristic of a right-wing ideology such as this one not to threaten the social, but to act out its most fundamental symbolic economy. Or, rather, it threatens the social by making that economy too blatant – the object of a renewed investment by the very drives it was intended to regulate or keep underground.[54]

In this context, it seems to me that it is limiting to talk of images and identifications in relation to politics as if what we are dealing with belonged to a straightforward economy of desire. Desire may well be the necessary term, but only if we define it as something which includes not irrationality – what is at stake here is not some rational/irrational dualism – but a logic of fantasy in which violence can operate as a pole of attraction at the same time as (to the extent that) it is being denied. If this logic is 'deadly and irreducible', it is so only in so far as it repeats a paradox inherent to the organization of the social itself. One of the things that Margaret Thatcher was doing, or that was being done through her, was to make this paradox the basis of a political identity so that subjects could take pleasure in violence as force and legitimacy while always locating 'real' violence somewhere else – illegitimate violence and illicitness increasingly made subject to the law. There is, however, always the risk for any right-wing ideology which plays on this scenario that, in the very place where violence and the illicit seem most effectively to have been abolished, they will return: witness the call for the legalization of incest and the songs in praise of the Yorkshire ripper at the conference of the Federation of Conservative Students in 1986.

To return to the question of the woman. In 'Women's Time', Kristeva describes the woman terrorist as the woman who, too brutally excluded from the socio-symbolic, counter-invests the violence she has experienced and takes arms against the State. She also describes the woman who identifies with and consolidates power because she brings to it the weight of the investment consequent on her struggle to achieve it. Without accepting Kristeva's terms as an explanation for women's political activity (it is never clear whether this is a causal analysis or one which crucially describes the affective and unconscious repercussions for women of their participation in political life), we can none the less recognize in Thatcher a hybrid of both these positions: a consolidation of power which is also a violence not of counter-investment, but the violence which underpins power as such. Blatantly drawing on this violence, Thatcher legitimated and encoded it (the real risk of Fascism), but she also laid bare the presence of violence at the heart of the socio-symbolic order. Certainly because she is a woman, she appeared to do both these things – which merely articulate a paradox at the heart of right-wing ideology – separately and together, in the form of an extreme. We can call her an object of fantasy – castrating mother, punitive superego, would be the psychoanalytic terms – only if we stress that the scenario she embodies goes way beyond her to take on the furthest parameters of our psychic and social life.

And Thatcher's own femininity, the way she presents herself as a woman (or not)? We can only note the contradictions: from denial ('People are more conscious of me being a woman than *I* am of being a woman'[55]), through an embracing of the most phallic of self-images (the iron lady), to the insistence on her femininity as utterly banal (the housewife managing the purse-strings of the nation). Predictably these images are mirrored and exceeded by the more or less misogynistic images which she provoked: 'doubtful whether any male PM would have actually seen that Falklands thing through to the end', 'in practice as sentimental as a Black Widow'.[56] It is none the less the case that Margaret Thatcher does deliberately choose to situate herself in the place of such an ambiguous sexual self-fashioning. The paranoid structure which I am describing here no

doubt thrives on this ambiguity of a femininity appealed
to and denied, a masculinity parodied and inflated. It is
the worst of a phallic economy countered, and thereby
rendered permissible, by being presented as masquerade.[57]

When Reich wrote *The Mass Psychology of Fascism* in
1933, he described Fascist ideology as mystical and irrational, opposing it to the rationality of a revolutionary
ethic which would be based on a shared, democratic
organization of sexuality and work. Fascism was repressive and distortive of body and mind, engendering
a pathological sexuality and form of thought. Under-
neath that distortion, Reich saw an ideally untrammelled
genitality and mental clarity. It has frequently been
pointed out that both of these conceptions effectively
dismantled the two poles of Freudian psychoanalysis on
which Reich claimed his work was based: an infantile
sexuality characterized above all by its perversion and
an unconscious which stood for an irreducible splitting
of the mind. More important, perhaps, Reich's idea of
pure rationality – of rationality *as* purity – rejoined at
crucial moments the Fascist ideology to which he opposed it.[58]

Although Thatcherism cannot be equated with Fascism (given the preservation of democratic government,
the support of the free market, the rhetoric – at least –
of the rolling back of the State), there are of course
points of connection that can be made (the glorification
of nationhood, the assault on homosexuals, the destruction of local government, and the increasing centraliza-
tion – despite the rhetoric – of State power). More
important, the retributive violence of her ethical abso-
lutism, as I have described it here, echoes a central
component of what Reich and others have described.
What Thatcher seems to have demonstrated is a taking
off, a relative autonomy, of certain psychic tropes be-

yond their historically attested political and economic base. Crucially, the phenomenon of Thatcher suggests that our understanding of the libidinal undercurrents of political processes can no longer be restricted to the historically recognized moment of Fascism alone – the place to which the possibility of a dialogue between psychoanalysis and politics has traditionally been consigned.

In this context, Reich's analysis, his stress on the irrationalism of Fascist discourse, has left us with a difficulty to which everything I have been describing in this chapter seems to return. It is not the irrationality of Thatcher's rhetoric that strikes me as the problem, but its supreme rationalism, the way that it operates according to a protocol of reason elevated to the status of a law. In this case, we cannot counter that ideology with a greater rationality without entering into one of the predominant fantasies of the ideology itself. This is not of course to argue that the idea of rationality has not been historically mobilized by the left, and to positive effect; but rather that, as a concept, it is inadequate for dealing with the specific force of right-wing ideologies at that point where they harness fantasy to reason, giving reason to what I want to call the flashpoints of the social, the very point where reason itself is at its least secure. If we want to think about the place of fantasy in public life today, we need therefore to avoid or qualify two conceptions: the one that describes fantasy as a projection of individual self-interest (the 'rational' reasons identified by Stuart Hall), but equally the one that sees fantasy as an unbridled irrationalism without any logic, a conception which turns fantasy into a simple counter-image of the law.

For Reich irrationalism meant sexual pathology and perversion, but that was because of the normative, if liberationist, concept of genital sexuality to which he held – normative *because* liberationist, we might argue today. He could therefore argue that the aggressivity mobilized by Fascism stemmed from drives which in an ideal world would move effortlessly into love, work, and health. Gradually the concept of infantile sexuality was replaced by that of adolescent desire, which Fascism rendered pathological because its repressive dictates stopped this desire from fulfilling itself. For Reich, Fascism mobilized above all pre-genital forms of sexuality, but he considered that in a Socialist society they would naturally dissipate themselves. But if one no longer believes in this normative account of sexuality, then what form of sexuality can one oppose to that which is mobilized by the right? Even if today we would stress more than Reich did the phallocentric organization of these fantasies, we would still surely recognize that right-wing fantasy also draws on some of the earliest formations of the drives. That seems to place under considerable strain two recent ways of attempting to politicize psychoanalysis: the appeal, especially by a feminist and gay politics, to early sexuality for the pre-oedipal and non-normative possibilities which it appears to permit, which means ignoring the aggressive components of the early drives; or an appeal to a developmental model which recognizes early aggressivity and then seeks reparation from an ego which will gradually organize the drives which support it into sexual and psychic health.

The problem with the first position is its idealization of early psychic life. The problem with the second is not just that it entails a normative concept of sexual development, but also that the category of the ego, far from being independent of the political fantasies which it is being called on to avoid, is deeply implicated in them. Thus the authors of *The Authoritarian Personality*, written after the war as part of an attempt to predict the psychic possibility of Fascism in America, called on the ego as both solution to, and cause of, authoritarianism:

It is the ego that becomes aware of and takes responsibility for nonrational forces operating within the personality. This is the basis for our belief that the object of knowing what are the psychological determinants of ideology is that men can become more reasonable.

Measurement of antidemocratic trends: . . . overemphasis on the conventional attributes of the ego.[59]

This simply means that it is not possible to fix the ego unequivocally on either side of the political divide – any more, indeed, than American democracy: 'It has frequently been remarked that should fascism become a powerful force in this country, it would parade under the banners of traditional democracy.'[60] The problem reproduces itself almost exactly in Klaus Theweleit's *Male Fantasies*, which attributes the fantasies of the German Freikorps to the fragmentary nature of the ego which these soldiers seem to display, and then almost immediately locates some of the most pernicious forms of Western logic in the defenders of the 'bourgeois ego struggling to stave off their own demise'.[61]

If, therefore, we recognize in right-wing fantasy a mobilization, and specific economy of aggressivity and its defence; if we allow that it is through the category of rational identity that this economy authorizes (codifies, legitimates) itself, then the political case for a non-normative, pre-oedipal sexuality, as much as for an ego which guarantees normality and reparation, seems to collapse. A key component of the sexuality some of us thought to oppose to the law suddenly appears – and in the worst forms of the social imaginary – enshrined within it. And the ego, which others have invested as the site of our psychic and social health, confronts us in the shape of the worst form of social authority that knows only its own reason and truth. If, as Kristeva suggests, one solution is to let these fantasies be spoken so as to prevent their social legitimation, their acting out in the very framework of the law (the case for psychoanalytic practice), then this can only be on condition that it does not lead into the no less troubling fantasy of a total knowledge and control of the mind. The alternative presents itself with startling clarity at the end of Deborah Cameron and Elizabeth Frazer's 1987 study of the male sexual killer, *The Lust to Kill*, when, recognizing the problem of female violence, they argue for nothing less than a total reconstitution of desire.[62]

I should perhaps stress here that psychoanalysis gives us no absolute or consistent theory of violence which could adequately describe it as much in its genesis as in its effects. It is described by Klein as an instinct, by Lacan as a structure inherent in intersubjectivity, by Kristeva as both cause and result of the precipitation of subjects into linguistic form. Nor should we forget Freud's insistence that it is always already attached to the fantasies which it appears to provoke. Rather, the point is to notice that if psychoanalysis is the intellectual tabloid of our culture ('sex and violence' being its chief objects of concern), we have recently privileged – sought, indeed, to base the politicization of psychoanalysis on that privilege – the sex over the violence. (Barbara Ehrenreich makes a related point in the Foreword to *Male Fantasies*.[63])

A question remains about the status of the woman – about that difficult position which Thatcher occupies and, I must acknowledge, in which I have positioned her, thereby repeating what I see as the problem of the way she functions as both authority and fantasy. For anything that might be said about the power which she concretely exerted, with effects that I think most of us would recognize as devastating, starts to join in and be complicit with the forms of projection which, precisely because of that strange and unique position she occupies as a woman, she provokes. Writing on the link which Freud thought he had established between femininity and death, Kristeva comments in *Histoires d'amour*, published four years after 'Women's Time':

> In Freud's later writing, [a paternal] position emerges which resolves the feminine share of subjectivity, by leaving to it the operative place of hatred and death promoted to the status of driving forces of the law. A scandal? Misogyny? Women analysts, starting with Melanie Klein, will recognize here an unconscious truth: their own?[64]

We can reformulate this question in the terms of her own earlier article, and insist on its social implications and determinants – that this association of women with hatred and death is expressive of their peculiar relation to the social in so far as it is grounded symbolically on both. But even if we do so, the question still remains as to whether this is something projected on to the woman or something which corresponds to women's psychic experience as such. Because of the power which she concretely had in reality, Thatcher forces us up against the limits of this problem. Another way of putting this would be to say that Thatcher is both a fantasy and a real event.

For a feminism which has argued for the perversity and even deadliness of the social, and then called it male, Thatcher presents a particular difficulty and anxiety which has perhaps been operating in the form of a taboo. In the scenario I have tried to outline here, the fact that Thatcher is a woman allowed her to get away with murder.

To return finally to the beginning of this chapter, I should stress that none of this is to deny the 'rational' reasons why people may have voted for Thatcher, nor indeed to give to anything I have described here the status of single political determinant or cause. It is, however, to point to a realm no less politically important (perhaps even more important) for not being containable in these terms.

POSTSCRIPT (August 1992)

It was perhaps inevitable that when Margaret Thatcher
resigned as the leader of the Conservative Party in November 1990, it would be represented – and apparently
experienced by her and her followers – as something
between a political assassination and a palace *coup*, as if
she were being confronted, and framed in effigy, by one
version of the language of violence, not to say execution,
on which she herself had often seemed to thrive: 'a
political assassination which it will be hard to forgive';
'She picked up the pistol after all'; 'The great oak has
been brought down'; 'Those who live by the sword shall
perish by the sword'; 'It was like when Kennedy was
shot. I suppose we'll all remember this.'[65]
Margaret Thatcher was of course neither murdered
nor assassinated, but it seemed as if no other language
could quite capture or do justice to whatever it was that
her own dramas of self-imagining had released. The
sexual sub-text of this was explicit: Thatcher as a woman
who, *as* woman, had managed to elevate phallic power
to new heights: 'Boudicca [Boadicea] riding a Chal-
lenger tank'; 'The heroine expired in the night . . . many
hands have an interest in keeping [the stage] erect' – a
basically violent and paranoid structure, as feminism
has long argued, which relies on an antagonist to keep
itself up: 'Her thrust fizzled because it lacked a black-
and-white enemy.'[66] Ironically, but confirming the basic
point, the man who has replaced her – his benign grey-
ness is famous – offers self-effacement as the model
of masculinity in power. Perhaps it is only a woman
leader today who can claim so literally to embody the
phallus.
The question then arises of what is left of Thatcher
and/or Thatcherism. When, the following year, Thatcher
announced her decision to stand down from parliament,

the *New Statesman* was quick to insist that Thatcherism
was a chimera and largely a creation of one part of the
intellectual left.[67] Certainly the fact that the fourth Conservative election victory took place under John Major's
leadership suggests that whatever it is that guarantees
the triumph of Conservatism cannot be located in
Thatcher's psycho-political agenda, her triumphalism,
alone. But while it may be true to say that Thatcher was
'as much a creature of Thatcherism as its creator' (on
the day after her resignation, the *Independent* listed all
the men who had 'made' her), yet it still seems to be the
case that Thatcher effected a decisive shift in the British
collective imagination, that she managed at some level
to fulfil her best (worst) ambition: to 'change, not only
the priorities of politicians, but the national soul'.[68] As
Eric Hobsbawm argues:

> What difference did Thatcher make? Negatively, prob-
> ably quite a lot, even if some of the more dangerous and
> irresponsible changes of the Eighties can be reversed –
> notably the excessive centralisation of state power and
> state direction, and the downgrading and destruction
> of lesser collective autonomies . . . The atmosphere of
> Thatcherism, that conglomerate of egoism, political serv-
> ility and moral blindness will not be so easy to elimin-
> ate.[69]

When the *New Statesman*, for example, argues that
social attitude surveys show that there is no evidence of
a public opinion shift in favour of State intervention and
tax cuts[70] (there were a plethora of such polls during the
election all suggesting support for increased public
spending and hence a Labour victory), it is ignoring
what the concept of 'attitude' is precisely unable to
grasp. And that is the set of convictions which hover
somewhere between an articulable belief and a fantasy
in which collective self-imaginings take shape. That
fourth election victory has if anything confirmed, rather

than contradicted, the argument that it is in the crucible
of subjective identities that political histories are forged
– the issue not one of immediate or the most obvious
forms of self-interest, but of how subjects 'envision'
themselves. As if the fantasy component and legacy of
Thatcherism could ride over all the material evidence
(the worst recession, the decline if not collapse of health
and educational provision, since the war). The difference today seems to me to reside in the fact that it
has become harder to separate out what Hobsbawm calls
the egoism and moral blindness from valid social and
material aspirations; just as in Eastern Europe we are
being presented with the split and coalescence of legitimate claims to national self-determination and autonomy with the absolutes of ethnic purification and hatred.
How to distinguish them may be one of the most important political questions of today.

It seems to me far too easy, then, to say that what
Thatcher carried psychically has now gone away; too
easy to load on to her something which, in the course of
her administrations, seemed at moments out of control
if not mad. If Thatcher thrived on the ideology and
mechanism of the scapegoat (the victim to be expelled),
it would be a strange irony now to see ourselves as
innocent of that process because we have so entirely
lodged it in her: 'Is she going off her rocker? The inhabit-
ants of the bar divide evenly between the "I've always
said she was barking mad anyway" school and those who
drool at the prospect of Maggie going publicly beserk
and being escorted away in kindly fashion by men in
white coats . . . We are simply waiting for Krakatoa to
erupt.'[71] Which is not to say that Thatcher did not operate in that space of fantasy where terrors are evoked,
paradoxically but effectively, as part of a message and
strategy of reassurance and control. Nor to suggest that
what she enacted could not be described as politics in the
paranoid mode. But what matters in all this is the struc-

ture or underside of *legitimate* power which Thatcher laid bare at its most extreme.

In a small news item tucked away at the bottom of the front page on the day of Thatcher's resignation, the *Independent* reported that one of the last things she had done before resigning was to double the British presence in the Gulf. It is notorious that the Gulf War – or at least the buildup to it – was partly a result of her egging Bush on ('Don't be a wimp, George'). In the last few weeks, Thatcher has been the first and the loudest to call for military intervention in Bosnia, echoing without qualification the strongest anti-Serbian rhetoric, in the face of the mounting evidence that this is not in any simple sense a one-sided situation, that the Serbs are becoming racial parodies and psychological scapegoats for a crisis in which they are not the sole agents of violence and in which Western Europe (past and present) has, at the very least, played its part. It does not seem to me to be a time when dismissal of Thatcher and her psychic agendas is appropriate. The risk is that, like any good – or rather bad – act of repression, the extent to which we require her to bear the burden will be in exact proportion to the grotesqueness with which those agendas return.

NOTES

Written after the Conservative Party's third election victory, 1987; published in *New Formations*, 6 (Winter 1988), pp. 3–29.
1 Julia Kristeva, 'Women's Time', trans. Alice Jardine and Harry Blake, in *Feminist Theory, A Critique of Ideology*, ed. Nannerl O. Keohane, Michelle Z. Rosaldo, and Barbara C. Gelpi (Chicago: University of Chicago Press, 1981; Brighton: Harvester, 1982), pp. 47, 52.

2   Stuart Hall, 'Blue Election, Election Blues', *Marxism Today* (July 1987), p. 33. An edited version was published as 'When It's the Only Game in Town, People Play It', *Guardian*, 6 July 1987; see also correspondence, 8 July.

3   Ibid., p. 31.

4   Hall, 'The Toad in the Garden: Thatcherism among the theorists', in *Marxism and the Interpretation of Culture*, ed. Cary Nelson and Lawrence Grossberg (Urbana, Ill. and Chicago: University of Illinois Press, 1988), pp. 35–73; the phrase was used by Hall specifically in response to a question about Wilhelm Reich (p. 72). These articles are just two from a series by Stuart Hall which, together with those by Sarah Benton (see n. 5 below), represent for me the most sustained and valuable critique of Thatcherism overall. See also 'The Great Moving Right Show', in *The Politics of Thatcherism*, ed. Stuart Hall and Martin Jacques (London: Lawrence and Wishart, 1983), pp. 19–39.

5   Sarah Benton makes this point in her analysis of Thatcher, 'The Triumph of the Spirit of War', when she talks of Thatcher as 'loathed with a rare passion', while also commenting on the way that Thatcher has been able to feed on the (feminist) insight that 'hitherto private feelings and fantasies can, once uttered, strike an unexpected public response' (*New Statesman*, 29 May 1987, p. 14).

6   *The Times*, 14 July 1983.

7   The strange relation between women and hanging in classical Greece is examined by Eva Cantarella. 'Dangling Virgins: myth, ritual, and the place of women in ancient Greece', in *The Female Body in Western Culture*, ed. Susan Suleiman (Cambridge, Mass., and London: Harvard University Press, 1986), pp. 57–67.

8   In fact it is the points of connection and difference that are so striking. The two women were born within a year of each other (Ellis in 1925, Thatcher in 1926). Ellis's father came from a successful and respected middle-class family which had made its money out of weaving. His own father was a musician (a cathedral organ player), and he himself was a cellist and cinema musician until the

advent of speaking pictures drove him down the social scale into unemployment, and then work as a porter, caretaker, and chauffeur. Her mother was a Belgian-French refugee. Ellis could be said to have tried to make her way as a woman back up that scale by working as a model and then a club hostess. In that post-war period which was so decisive for the two women, therefore, Ellis had strong aspirations to social mobility not dissimilar in kind, although unlike in trajectory, Thatcher's own. As James Donald put it, they can be seen to represent the 'seedy' and 'golf club' sides of the petty bourgeoisie, and have in common the same iconography of meticulous artificiality and precision (on Ellis's hair in court, see p. 51).

9 Sigmund Freud, *Civilisation and its Discontents*, 1930 (1929), in *Standard Edition*, vol. 21, p. 112. Cf. also: 'Thus we see that right is the might of a community. It is still violence, ready to be directed against any individual who resists it; it works by the same methods and follows the same purposes. The only real difference lies in the fact that what prevails is no longer the violence of an individual but that of a community' ('Why war?', in *Standard Edition*, vol. 22), p. 205.

10 René Girard, *La Violence et le sacré* (Paris: Grasset, 1972), p. 41.

11 Laurence Marks and Tony van den Bergh, *Ruth Ellis: a case of diminished responsibility?* (London: Macdonald and Jane's, 1977), p. 105; for a full account of the trial, see Jonathan Goodman and Patrick Pringle, *The Trial of Ruth Ellis* (Newton Abbot: David and Charles, 1974).

12 Marks and van den Bergh, *Ruth Ellis*, p. 87.

13 Dr Duncan Whittaker, psychiatrist, quoted in ibid., p. 104. Cf. also Ellis's defence counsel's later remarks: 'She had got into a very calm state of mind . . . in which she thought everything she did was right and justified . . . that there was no other course open to her' (p. 127).

14 Opening statement by the judge, cited in ibid., p. 117.

15 Quoted in *Royal Commission on Capital Punishment, 1949–52* (London: HMSO), p. 3.

16 The French newspaper *Le Monde* commented at the time of the trial: 'English law does not at the moment recognize

any intermediate stage between the rational and balanced being who kills in perfect awareness of what he is doing and the total lunatic who is not conscious of his own acts. As everyone knows, the Englishman is – or believes himself to be – a creature of sang-froid, and the legal system in force supports this fiction' (cited in Marks and van den Bergh, *Ruth Ellis*, p. 134).

17   Ibid., p. 118.

18   Ibid., p. 125.

19   Cited in Goodman and Pringle, *Trial of Ruth Ellis*, p. 119.

20   Cited in Marks and van den Bergh, *Ruth Ellis*, p. 127.

21   In a review of *Myra Hindley: inside the mind of a murderess* (London: Angus and Robertson, 1988), Helen Birch points to the analogies that can be drawn between Hindley and Ellis, on the question of both their 'sanity' and their 'femininity', when commenting on the public obsession with Hindley, compared with other women this century who have murdered children: 'Hindley, on the other hand, is viewed as sane – "a calculated pretty cool operator" in the words of the prosecution . . . the story goes that she sat impassive throughout the trial, in smart clothes, full make-up, with newly dyed hair. There are echoes here of the case of Ruth Ellis. . . . Feminists have since argued that one of the reasons Ellis was sent to the gallows was because, in the eyes of the all-male jury, her appearance did not match the line of her defence' (*New Statesman*, 18 March 1988), p. 25.

22   Alexandre Fontana, 'The Intermittences of Rationality', in *Pierre Rivière*, ed. Michel Foucault (Harmondsworth: Peregrine, 1978), p. 273: 'Is it possible for a criminal to keep his reason entire or lose it for an instant and then recover it? Was he aware of what he was doing? Did he harbour delusions about a single subject only, keeping the remainder of his faculties intact? Was only one of his faculties affected to the exclusion of all the others? . . . Reasoning madness and monomania were the flaw, the twilight zone, the point of opacity in the system'; first published in French in *Moi, Pierre Rivière, ayant égorgé ma mère, ma soeur, et mon frère . . . un cas de parricide au XIXe siècle* (Paris: Gallimard, 1973).

23 The defence counsel later said that he was convinced that the trial had led to the new law of diminished responsibility (cited in Marks and van den Bergh, *Ruth Ellis*, p. 127). The authors open their book with this statement by Muriel Jakubait, sister of Ruth Ellis, to whom the book is dedicated: 'When any child is murdered in England today, I am the subject of attack. They say that if it weren't for my sister, we would still have the death penalty . . . and then that child would have lived.' Cf. also Goodman and Pringle: 'There is little doubt that the execution of Ruth Ellis played a major part in bringing about the abolition of capital punishment' (*Trial of Ruth Ellis*, p. 77).

24 Cited on the opening page of Marks and van den Bergh, *Ruth Ellis*.

25 Michel Foucault, 'About the Concept of the "Dangerous Individual" in Nineteenth-Century Legal Psychiatry', trans. Alain Baudot and Jane Couchman, *International Journal of Law and Psychiatry*, 1 (1978), pp. 1–18.

26 Ibid., p. 12.

27 'Memorandum submitted by the Institute of Psycho-Analysis', 23rd day, Thursday, 1 June 1950, in *Royal Commission on Capital Punishment*, p. 546.

28 Dr Carroll ('We would stress the need to cover the normal murderer') was interrupted on this point by Dr Gillespie ('It depends on what you mean by "normal", because if one assumes most people have murderous impulses but very few people give way to them and so become murderers, then statistically speaking the murderer cannot be called normal'). Roger Money-Kyrle then added: 'In a precise way [normal] would mean a very high degree of integration of personality. I think we at the Institute would all agree that a normal person in that sense would very rarely commit a murder' (ibid., p. 548). The memorandum also states that this outcome will depend on 'the relative strengths of the aggressive and loving impulses . . . determined by both inborn factors and environmental experience, especially during the first months and years of life' (p. 546). See also n. 29 below.

29 Ernest Jones, 'The concept of the Normal Mind', *International Journal of Psycho-Analysis*, 23, pt 1 (1942),

pp. 1–8. See also Ernest Jones, *Hamlet and Oedipus* (New York: Norton, 1949; Anchor edition, 1954), where he states that psychoanalysis confuses the division 'which until our generation (and even now in the juristic sphere) separated the sane and responsible from the irresponsible insane' (p. 76). Arthur Koestler and C. H. Rolph quote this passage from the Commission in their campaigning book *Hanged by the Neck: an exposure of capital punishment in England* (Harmondsworth: Penguin Special, 1961): 'There is no sharp dividing line between sanity and insanity . . . the two extremes shade into one another by imperceptible gradations. The degree of individual responsibility varies equally widely; no clear boundary can be drawn between responsibility and irresponsibility. Likewise crimes of passion shade without a sharp division into crimes due to mental disease' (p. 136). Roger Money-Kyrle, who spoke at the Commission in defence of the category of 'normality', quotes Jones's article on 'The Concept of the Normal Mind' in his book *Psychoanalysis and Politics, A contribution to the Psychology of Politics and Morals* (London: Duckworth, 1951), where he makes much more explicit the relation of the concept of the 'normal' to 'rationality': 'For if the "normal" is equivalent to the "rational", and if there is a type of conscience common to normal people which differs from the consciences of abnormal people, then this type is an attribute of rationality' (p. 19).

30   Letter from R. C. Webster, Todmorden, Lancashire, cited in Marks and van den Bergh, *Ruth Ellis*, appendix 3, p. 143.

31   'The Death Penalty', *Lancet* (23 July 1955), reprinted in Marks and van den Bergh, *Ruth Ellis*, appendix 3, 138–40.

32   Cf. also the correspondence on the execution of Ruth Ellis: '[Capital punishment] is *not* rational: it is barbaric'; 'the barbaric penalties of execution'; 'the medieval savagery of the law'; all in Marks and van den Bergh, *Ruth Ellis*, appendix 3, pp. 147, 128, 129.

33   Cited in 'Another Defeat Expected for Pro-Hanging Lobby', *Independent*, (27 May 1988). For an 'aesthetic'

defence of capital punishment, or rather a defence of capital punishment *as* aesthetic, however, see Walter Berns, *For Capital Punishment, Crime and the Morality of the Death Penalty* (New York: Basic Books, 1979): 'Can we imagine a world that does not take its revenge on the man who kills Macduff's wife and children? . . . Can we imagine a world that does not hate murderers? To ask these questions is to ask whether we can imagine a world without Shakespeare's poetry . . . punishment may be likened to dramatic poetry or the purpose of punishment to one of the intentions of the great dramatic poet' (p. 168).

34 The distinction is not as straightforward as it seems however; see Hannah Arendt's discussion of the concept of *raison d'état* in Postscript to *Eichmann in Jerusalem* (Harmondsworth: Penguin, 1977 (1963; 1965)), pp. 290–1.

35 David Pannick, *Judicial Review of the Death Penalty* (London: Duckworth, 1982), p. 1.

36 See also Mark Cousins, '*Mens rea*: a note on sexual difference, criminology and law', in *Radical Issues in Criminology*, ed. Pat Carlen and Mike Collinson (Oxford: Martin Robertson, 1980): 'Certain forms of traditional jurisprudence can unify [the law] as the expression of an unfolding rationality. Legal positivism could represent it through the unity of a command of a sovereign. Pashukanis will reply to this by making it the space of rights of the subject of possession. But each of these positions requires to be supported theoretically, and each of them will face analytic problems of where the boundaries of the unity lie, where law suddenly passes beyond itself' (p. 115). Cousins is reviewing Carol Smart, *Women, Crime and Criminology* (London: Routledge and Kegan Paul, 1976), a feminist critique of the category of the woman criminal. The point about the limits of the law was made quite explicitly with reference to Ruth Ellis: 'Judges have often pointed out that the courts are courts of law, *not* courts of morals. The McNaghten rules are really based on moral theology, which assesses human acts on the basis of gravity of the act, knowledge of the agent, and volition of the agent' (R. C. Webster, cited in Marks and van den Bergh, *Ruth Ellis*, appendix 3, p. 143).

37   Pannick, *Judicial Review*, p. 65; he is describing specific-
     ally the American and Indian judiciary. The other two
     criteria are 'That it is mandatory for a defined offence'
     (this would rule out the attempt in England to make the
     death sentence mandatory for terrorism), and 'That it is
     grossly disproportionate to the offence' (this immediately
     comes up against the problem of proportionality: 'One
     must be careful not to assume "the role of a finely tuned
     calibrator of depravity, demarcating for a watching world
     the various gradations of dementia" ' (p. 145), quoting
     Godfrey vs *Georgia* [1980]). All these difficulties have not
     prevented courts from claiming that they have provided
     the means to 'promote the evenhanded, rational and con-
     sistent imposition of death sentences under law': *Jurek* vs
     Texas, cited on p. 179.

38   'Not since the condemnation of Mrs Edith Thomson in
     1923 had such a storm of public protest been aroused
     against the hanging of a woman' (Duncan Webb, *Line up
     for Crime* (London: Frederick Muller, 1956), p. 203).
     The horror, however, was clearly ambivalent: 'Children
     in a school near the prison are described by one of their
     teachers as being in a ferment: "Some claim to have seen
     the execution from a window, others spoke with fascin-
     ated horror of the technique of hanging a female" ' ('The
     Death Penalty', p. 140).

39   It is a stereotype which, specifically in relation to capital
     punishment, is written into the history of the law; see
     William Blackstone, *Commentaries on the Laws of England*,
     facsimile of the first edition of 1765–9, vol. 4 (Chicago
     and London: University of Chicago Press, 1979): 'Was
     the vast territory of all the Russias worse regulated under
     the late Empress Elizabeth, than under her more sanguin-
     ary predecessors? Is it now, under Catherine II, less
     civilised, less social, less secure? And yet we are assured,
     that neither of these illustrious princesses have, through-
     out their whole administration, inflicted the penalty of
     death' (p. 10).

40   Julia Kristeva, in discussion at the colloquium 'Psych-
     analyse et politique', Milan, 1973, published as *Psychana-
     lyse et politique* (Paris: Seuil, 1974), p. 40.

41 Richard Hofstadter, *The Paranoid Style in American Polit-
    ics and Other Essays* (London: Cape, 1966), quoting Bar-
    nuel (p. 12). In a series of articles starting in 1984, Sarah
    Benton has commented on the 'cultivated paranoia' on
    which the Conservative Party relies: 'Press a placid Tory,
    who wants nothing more than a world in which there is
    no argument, no interference with the natural way of
    doing things, no disturbing questions on war, economics
    or sex, and out comes a flow of nightmare fears and
    anecdotes . . . [they feel part of] a mystical national good.
    Such a belief can only derive coherence from the conjur-
    ing up of the Alien, a force whose shape you never quite
    see but which lurks in every unlit space ready to destroy
    you; and is incubated, unnoticed, in the healthy body
    politic' ('Monsters from the Deep', *New Statesman*, 19
    October 1984, pp. 10–12). Benton was arguing here that
    the Brighton bomb fulfilled these persecutory fantasies;
    compare Tebbit, quoted in *The Times*, (19 December
    1984), as saying that the bomb was not an 'isolated
    incident' but 'part of an irrationality that had crept into
    politics and society'. See also Benton, 'The Triumph of
    the Spirit of War', and 'What are They Afraid of?', (*New
    Statesman*, 11 March 1988), pp. 14–15.
42 Bruce Arnold, *Margaret Thatcher: a study in power* (Lon-
    don: Hamish Hamilton, 1984), pp. 269–74.
43 Printed in full in *The Times*, 31 December 1983; compare
    also this comment from the *Observer*'s leading article, (29
    May 1988): 'She is a woman who not only says what she
    means but, to a degree unusual in politicians, actually
    means what she says.'
44 The most important examination of this concept of ra-
    tionality is Herbert Marcuse's *Reason and Revolution:
    Hegel and the rise of social theory* (London: Routledge and
    Kegan Paul, 1969 (1941)).
45 Ernle Money, *Margaret Thatcher, First Lady of the House*
    (London: Leslie Frewin, 1975), *Margaret Thatcher*, p. 134.
46 Arnold, *Margaret Thatcher*, p. 271.
47 Hofstadter, *Paranoid Style*, pp. 36–7; see also N. McCon-
    aghy, 'Modes of Abstract Thinking and Psychosis', *Amer-
    ican Journal of Psychiatry*, 117 (August 1960), pp. 106–10

(this article is cited by Hofstadter), and also Robert Waelder, 'The Structure of Paranoid Ideas', *International Journal of Psycho-Analysis*, 32 (1951), pp. 167–77, especially on why the paranoiac correctly fears, and must therefore fight off, the defeat of his or her own system: 'It is a fight in which all the initial advantages are with the paranoiacs, but which they are bound to lose, because of their lack of elasticity, unless they can turn initial advantages into complete victory' (p. 167 n.). This description by Hofstadter sounds uncannily like Thatcher: 'The passion for factual evidence does not, as in most intellectual exchanges, have the effect of putting the paranoid spokesman into effective two-way communication with the world outside his group – least of all with those who doubt his views. He has little real hope that his views will convince a hostile world. His effort to amass it has rather the quality of a defensive act which shuts off his receptive apparatus and protects him from having to attend to disturbing considerations that do not fortify his ideas. He has all the evidence he needs; he is not a receiver, he is a transmitter' (p. 38).

48   Letter from L. Webb, cited in Marks and van den Bergh, *Ruth Ellis*, appendix 3, p. 132.

49   Speech to the Junior Carlton Club, 4 May 1976, quoted in Patrick Cosgrave, *Margaret Thatcher: a Tory and her party* (London: Hutchinson, 1978), p. 215.

50   Remarks made during an interview on *World in Action* (Granada TV, January 1978), quoted in Penny Junor, *Margaret Thatcher: wife, mother, politician* (London: Sidgwick and Jackson, 1983), pp. 116–17; when challenged on this speech by Kenneth Harris in an interview in the *Observer*, Thatcher replied, 'I *never* modified it! I stood by it one hundred per cent. Some people have felt swamped by immigrants. They've seen the whole character of their neighbourhood change. I stood by that statement one hundred per cent' (*Margaret Thatcher Talks to the* Observer, published as a separate booklet, January 1979).

51   From *State* vs *Dixon*, 1973, cited in Pannick, *Judicial Review*, p. 71n.

52 *Confidence in the Law*, Conservative Study Group on Crime, Conservative Research Department, vol. 1 (January 1986). William Hamilton, speaking in the debate on capital punishment in the House of Commons, reported in *The Times*, 14 July 1983.

53 Kristeva, 'Women's Time', p. 47.

54 See Georges Bataille, 'The Psychological Structure of Fascism', in *Visions of Excess: selected writings 1927–1939*, ed. with an introduction by Allan Stoekl, trans. Allan Stoekl with Carl R. Lovitt and Donald M. Leslie Jr (Minneapolis: University of Minnesota Press, 1985), pp. 137–60. In a very different, recent article specifically on the Conservative Party and violence, Frank Burton argues, within a Foucauldian framework, that the Conservative rhetoric of coercion is deceptive, and merely expresses a 'rationalization of the administration of justice'; but he does acknowledge that the free vote on capital punishment does not quite fit into this frame. ('Questions of Violence in Party Political Criminology', in *Radical Issues in Criminology*, ed. Carlen and Collinson, pp. 123–51).

55 Harris, *Margaret Thatcher Talks to the* Observer.

56 John Nott, interviewed on the BBC *Panorama* programme *300 Days*, which marked Thatcher's becoming the longest-serving prime minister this century (4 January 1988); Robert Harris, '*Prima donna inter pares*', *Observer*, 3 January 1988.

57 On the question of Thatcher as a woman, see Beatrix Campbell, 'To Be or Not To Be a Woman', in *The Iron Ladies: why do women vote Tory?* (London: Virago, 1987), ch. 9, pp. 233–47, and Benton, 'Triumph of the Spirit of War'.

58 Wilhelm Reich, *The Mass Psychology of Fascism*, trans. Theodore P. Wolfe, 3rd edn (New York: Orgone Institute Press, 1946); retrans. Vincent R. Carfagno (New York: Farrar, Straus and Giroux, 1970; Harmondsworth: Penguin, 1975).

59 T. W. Adorno, Else Frenkel-Brunswick, David J. Levinson, and R. Nevitt Sandford, in collaboration with Betty Aron, Maria Hertz Levinson, and William Morrow, *The Authoritarian Personality*, Studies in Prejudice series,

ed. Max Horkheimer and Samuel H. Flowerman (New York: Harper and Row, 1960; Science Editions, 1964), vol. 2, p. 228.

60   Ibid., p. 50; compare, however, the last lines of the book: 'If fear and destructiveness are the major emotional sources of fascism, eros belongs mainly to democracy' (p. 976).

61   Klaus Theweleit, *Male Fantasies*, vol. 1, trans. Stephen Conway in collaboration with Chris Turner and Erica Carter (Minneapolis: University of Minnesota Press; Cambridge: Polity Press, 1987), pp. 208, 219.

62   Deborah Cameron and Elizabeth Frazer, *The Lust to Kill* (Cambridge: Polity Press, 1987): '*We* insist that there can be a vision of the future in which desire will be reconstructed totally' (p. 176).

63   Barbara Ehrenreich, Foreword to Theweleit, *Male Fantasies*, p. xii.

64   Julia Kristeva, *Histoires d'amour* (Paris: Denoël, 1983), p. 121n; trans. Leon S. Roudiez, *Tales of Love* (New York: Columbia University Press, 1987).

65   *Daily Telegraph*, *The Times*, *Daily Mail*, *Independent*, 23 November 1990.

66   Colin Hughes, 'The Woman who Transformed Britain', *Independent*, 23 November 1990; Ross McKibbin, 'Diary', *London Review of Books*, 6 December 1990, p. 25; Hughes, 'Woman who Transformed Britain'.

67   'The End of an Error', Editiorial, *New Statesman*, 5 July 1991, pp. 4–5.

68   Hughes, 'Woman who Transformed Britain'.

69   Eric Hobsbawm, 'What Difference Did She Make?', *London Review of Books*, 23 May 1991, pp. 3–6.

70   'End of an Error'.

71   R. W. Johnson, 'The Human Time Bomb – Is the Former Prime Minister Going off her Rocker?', *New Statesman*, 22 March 1991, p. 10.

Part II The Death Drive

3 'Where Does the Misery Come From?' Psychoanalysis, Feminism, and the Event

A classical political dichotomy, not without relevance for feminism, is captured by the question Wilhelm Reich placed at the heart of his dispute with Freud in a conversation with Kurt Eissler in 1952: 'From now onward, the great question arises: *Where does that misery come from?* And here the trouble began. While Freud developed his death-instinct theory which said "The misery comes from inside," I went out, out where the people were.'[1] We can immediately recognize the opposition that is central to Reich's complaint: between a misery that belongs to the individual in her or his relation to her- or himself, which is also, in Freud's theory of the death instinct, a species relationship, and a misery that impinges on the subject from the external world and that therefore refers to a social relationship. Here, the dynamic is not internal to the subject, but passes between the subject and the outside, an outside that has direct effects upon psychic processes, but is seen as free of any such processes itself. And we can see too the easy slide from that opposition to another that so often appears alongside it in political debate: the opposition between misery conceived as a privatized, internalized *Angst* (the product of a theory that, like the psyche it describes, is *turned in on itself*) and the people, 'out where the people were,' – that is, where it is really happening, with the people.

These people who are outside, the place from which Reich claims to speak, have, therefore, two different meanings. They are outside psychoanalysis, seen as a socially delimiting and self-blinding institution, but also – and this second meaning follows from the first – they themselves only *have* an outside, since whatever they are and suffer is a direct effect of a purely external causality and constraint. Reich's question to Freud, with its dichotomy between inside and outside, thus contains within it two more familiar versions of the opposition by means of which politics is pitted against psychoanalysis: the opposition between public and private (the people versus analytic space) and between social and the psychic (social oppression versus the drive to death).[2]

In Reich's case, as we know, these views resulted in the gradual repudiation of any concept of psychic dynamic and the unconscious in favour of the notion of a genital libido, dammed up or blocked off by a repressive social world, a natural stream that 'you must get back into its normal bed and let it flow naturally again' (p. 44). This essentially pre-Freudian and normative concept of sexuality reveals the most disturbing of its own social consequences in Reich's attacks on perversion, homosexuality, Judaism, and women, together with the inflation of his own sexual prowess which accompanied them: 'It is quite clear that the man who discovered the genitality function in neurosis and elaborated the orgastic potency question could not himself live in a sick way' (p. 104). This moment lays down the terms of the most fundamental political disagreement with psychoanalysis, which then finds one of its sharpest representations in a much more recent and more obviously feminist political debate in relation to Freud, whose underlying issue perhaps becomes clear only through a comparison between the two moments. Kurt Eissler has the distinction (dubious, fortunate, or unfortunate, depending on which way you look at it) not only of having conducted that interview with Reich in 1952, but also of later becoming the key figure within the analytic institution in what has come to be known as the Jeffrey Masson dispute, personally giving Masson access to the archives through which he mounted his critique of Freud. Masson's critique – in which he challenges Freud on the relinquishment of the seduction theory of neurosis in favour of fantasy and the vicissitudes of psychic life – is expressed quite unequivocally in terms of the same dichotomy between inside and outside: 'By shifting the emphasis from an actual world of sadness, misery, and cruelty to an internal stage on which actors performed invented dramas for an invisible audience of their own creation, Freud began a trend away from the real world that, it seems to me, is at the root of the present-day sterility of psychoanalysis and psychiatry throughout the world.'[3] If the dichotomy appears this time as a feminist issue, it is because the aggression of the outside world has been stepped up and sexually differentiated, and is now conceived of in terms of seduction, mutilation, and rape.

The similarities between these two moments are, I think, striking. We can point to the inflated view of sexual prowess, which in relation to Masson – the famous and now legally contested reference to his thousand and one nights[4] – merely mirrors in reverse the grotesque image of masculinity which runs through the whole book. What the two have in common is the utterly unquestioned image of sexual difference whose rigidity is, I would argue, the real violence and, in Masson's case – with a logic to which he is of course totally blind – leads directly to it. Reich also had his image of sexual violence, only the other way round: the misogyny-cum-vampirism worthy of Henry James's *The Sacred Fount* which can be detected in his observation that he has frequently observed couples in which the man is 'alive', the woman 'somehow out', inhibiting then drawing off, by implication, his vitality and power (p. 117). But most important is that we can detect behind these two moments (the Reich and Masson disputes) this question of violence, which presents itself today as an explicitly feminist political issue, but which was already there in the dispute over the death drive at the centre of the earlier political repudiation of Freud.

It is this issue of violence, and with it that of the death drive, which has become a key issue for any consideration of psychoanalysis in relation to feminism today. Clearly, the question of sexual violence is crucial to feminism (violence is, of course, also a political issue in a much more global sense). It is central to the discussion of pornography, to take just one instance. Reich himself spoke of the pornographic drives, although for him they were not part of genital sexuality but the effect of a deviation from it. But Masson's book can, I think, be read as a key pornographic text of the 1980s, as well as a text on pornography, much the same way as we can, or have to, read Andrea Dworkin's writing on pornography, a form of feminism to which Masson now explicitly claims allegiance.[5]

For isn't the argument finally that psychoanalytic theory, by ignoring the pressing reality of sexual violence, becomes complicit with that violence and hands women over to it? Isn't the argument therefore that theory itself can cause death? And isn't that merely one step on from Reich's insistent relegation of all death to the outside, which then, in a classic inversion, leads directly to this persecutory return, for which psychoanalysis is held accountable? Reich himself was clearly operating in some such terms as these: '[Freud] sensed something in the human organism which was deadly. But he thought in terms of instinct. So he hit upon the term "death instinct." That was wrong. "Death" was right. "Instinct" was wrong. Because it's not something the organism wants. It's something that happens to the organism' (p. 89).

Where to locate violence? This was the question sensed in all its difficulty in that earlier political debate. It is worth looking back at that moment to see how it was played out. What then emerges is that violence is not something that can be located on the inside or the outside, in the psychic or the social (the second opposition, which follows so rapidly from the first), but rather something that appears as the effect of the dichotomy itself. I want to suggest that feminism, precisely through its vexed and complex relationship with psychoanalysis, may be in a privileged position to recast this problem, refusing the rigid polarity of inside and outside together with the absolute and fixed image of sexual difference which comes with it and on which it so often seems to rely. But I also want to suggest why the feminist undoing of this polarity needs to be different from other deconstructions that might be, and have been, proposed, especially because of the form of feminism's still, for me, necessary relationship to psychoanalysis itself.

So where does violence go if you locate it on the outside? In Reich's case, in a structure reminiscent of foreclosure, it returns in a hallucinatory guise. His insistence on the utter health of the subject brings murder in its train:

> In order to get to the core where the natural, the normal, the healthy is, you have to get through the middle layer. And in that middle layer there is terror. There is severe terror. Not only that, there is murder there. All that Freud tried to subsume under the death instinct is in that middle layer. He thought it was biological. It wasn't. It's an artefact of culture. It is a structural malignancy of the human animal. Therefore before you can get through to what Freud called Eros or what I call orgonotic streaming or plasmatic excitation, you have to go through hell. . . . All these wars, all the chaos now – do you know what that is to my mind? *Humanity is trying to get at its core, at its living, healthy core. But before it can*

> *be reached, humanity has to pass through this phase of*
> *murder, killing and destruction.* (p. 109)

This is apocalyptic – a kind of hideous, born-again anticipation of that vision of a necessary hell put forward by some of the most extreme proponents of the New Right. It expels terror into the outer zone, and then brings it back as a phase of human development, a catharsis whose purgatorial nature is not concealed by the concept of cultural artefact through which Reich tries to bring it to ground. Horror in Reich's argument operates at two levels: it is the product of culture (something that happens to the organism), and it is part of a vision (something his own language so clearly desires). But that link between two absolute outsides – one relegated to something called culture and the other to the nether depths of all humanity and all history – is not, I suspect, unique to Reich.

Against these rigid extremes, what Reich could not countenance was contradiction – the contradiction of subjectivity in analytic theory and the contradiction that, if it has any meaning, is the only meaning of the death drive itself. For a theory that pits inside and outside against each other in such deadly combat wipes out any difference or contradiction on either side: the subject suffers, the social oppresses, and what is produced, by implication, is utter stasis in each. At one level Freud's concept of the death drive was also about stasis – the famous return to the inorganic which indeed hands the concept over to biology and determinism alike. But if we follow the theorization through, deliberately avoiding the *fort-da* game through which it is most often rehearsed, it is the oscillation of position, the displacement of psychic levels and energies, which the concept of the death drive forces on the theory, the problem it poses in relation to any notion of what might be primary or secondary, which is striking. Challenging Freud on the concept of masochism, Reich commented: 'When I asked him whether masochism was primary or secondary, whether it is turned-back sadism or aggression or a disturbance of aggression outward, or whether it's a primary death instinct thing, Freud, peculiarly, maintained both' (p. 89). The ambiguity of the concept is the concept itself. In the chapter 'The Classes of Instinct' in *The Ego and the Id*, Freud addressed the question of whether ambivalence – the transposition of love into hate and its reverse – throws his new dualism of the life and death instincts into crisis. Doesn't the shifting of one form of affect into another suggest a form of energy characterized by nothing other than the form of its displacements? And doesn't that in turn throw into question our understanding of the instinct as such: 'The problem of the quality of instinctual impulses and of its persistence throughout their various vicissitudes is still very obscure.'[6]

What Reich therefore misses in his biology/culture opposition is that the theorization of the death instinct shows the instinct itself at its most problematic. For it gives us Freud articulating most clearly the concept of the *drive*: that is, a drive that is only a drive, because of its utter indifference to any path it might take. Freud uses the erotic cathexis and its indifference to the object as the model for this dynamic; but in a twist that mimics the very process he describes, the reference to eros leads him straight into the arms of death:

[This trait] is found in erotic cathexes, where a peculiar indifference in regard to the object displays itself. . . . Not long ago, Rank published some good examples of the way in which neurotic acts of revenge can be directed against the wrong people. Such behaviour on the part of the unconscious reminds one of the comic story of the three village tailors, one of whom had to be hanged because the only village blacksmith had committed a capital offense. Punishment must be exacted even if it doesn't fall upon the guilty.[7]

This utterly random *drive to* punishment links up with the concept of a *need for* punishment, the very concept Reich so criticized because it contradicted the earlier libidinal theory, which had stated that sexual desire does not seek punishment but fears it (the theory of repression). It was this concept of a need for punishment which upset Reich's conception of a purely extraneous causality (suffering as an external event). Freud summed it up in his observation in 'The Economic Problem of Masochism', written immediately after *The Ego and the Id*: 'It is instructive, too, to find, contrary to all theory and expectation, that a neurosis which has defied every therapeutic effort may vanish if the subject becomes involved in the misery of an unhappy marriage, or loses all his money, or develops a dangerous organic disease.'[8] Of course, if it weren't all so deadly serious, what is most noteworthy about this, as with the story of the village tailors, is the utter comedy of it all.

In following these arguments, I should make it clear that I am not suggesting simply that the psychic dimension be prioritized over the cultural and biological determinism of Reich (which turn out finally to be the same thing within Reich's own theory, since the concept of cultural repression depends on that of a pre-ordained genital drive). For to argue in these terms leads almost inevitably to the reverse dualism of Janine Chasseguet-Smirgel and Bela Grunberger's book on Reich, which opposes to Reich's refusal of internal factors, psychic processes that they directly and with unapologetic reductionism make the determinant of social life. Also, although they insist on the difficulty of the internal factors and on that basis criticize Reich's glorification of the id, they do so in terms of a reality-differentiating ego, which has to succumb to the constraints on instinct offered by the real world; they thereby hand the concept of psychic conflict over to that of adaptation to reality – which might explain the defence of maturation, Oedipus, and sexual difference, not to mention the dismissal of all politics as reality-denying, which seems to follow.[9] The book ends with two quotations '*Wo es war soll ich werden*' ('Where id was, there ego shall be': Freud) and '*Wo ich war soll es werden*' ('Where ego was, there id shall be': roughly Reich), the first the much contested, much interpreted statement presented unproblematically as the 'goal of the analytic process' (p. 237). The statement '*Wo es war soll ich werden*' was of course the phrase retranslated by Lacan from Strachey precisely because of the normative ethics of ego and adaptation it implied.[10] The implication is that Reich wanted to replace ego with id, whereas the objective of analysis should be the reverse. Faced with this, one might concede that Reich had an important point.

But what emerges instead in looking at Freud's theory of the death drive is precisely the impasse it produces in Freud's own thought around this very issue of location and dualism, to which I would want to assign both more and less than Derrida, who makes of it in *La Carte postale* the exemplary demonstration of the impasse of theorization itself (of metalanguage, knowledge, and mastery),[11] thereby evacuating the specific dynamic – of masochism, punishment, and the drive to death – which has historically been, and still is, I would argue, the point of the political clash. For the failure to locate death as an object, the outrageous oscillation which this failure introduces into causality and the event, signals for me something that has a particular resonance for a feminism wishing to bring the question of sexuality on to the political field: and that is that a rigid determinism by either biology or culture, by inside or outside – an outside that then turns into man posed in his immutable and ahistorical essence as man – simply will not do. Wasn't it precisely to bypass both these causalities (of culture and biology) that Juliet Mitchell turned to psychoanalysis in the first place?[12] Then the question was posed in terms of how to understand the origins of femininity and sexual difference (where does sexual difference come from?). To which I would merely add that the question of determinism reveals itself today as the issue of violence and its location (determinism also as a form of violence).

Like Reich before him, Masson insists on the externality of the event, only this time he calls it 'man'. He is perhaps useful only to the extent that he anthropomorphizes the inside/outside dichotomy, turning it unmistakably into an issue of whether it is our (women's) or their (men's) fault. It seems to be the inevitable development of the basic dichotomy, since a reality split off into a realm of antagonism cannot finally be conceptualized as anything other than violence, or perhaps even rape. But to ask for a language that goes over to neither side of this historical antagonism, and to suggest that we might find the rudiments of such a language in the very issue of the death drive, is merely to point to something that is in a way obvious for feminism – the glaring inadequacy of any formulation that makes us as women either pure victim or sole agent of our distress. The realm of sexuality messes up what can be thought of in any straightforward sense as causality. Precisely, then, through its foregrounding of sexuality, feminism may be in a privileged position to challenge or rethink the dualities (inside/outside, victim/aggressor, real event/fantasy) which seem to follow any rigid externalization of political space.

There is, however, another discourse, with its own relation to feminism and to psychoanalysis, which has quite explicitly addressed this polarity of inside and outside, aiming to undo these polarities in which it also locates a violence. This is a violence not against women but against something that can be called 'the rhetoricity of language', in so far as the binary is always the point at which, under the impact of an impulse to mastery and control, the oscillation and randomness of language is closed off. Not only in Derrida's writing, but also in Shoshana Felman's book on madness and the literary thing, Barbara Johnson's essay on Poe, Lacan, and Derrida, and Samuel Weber's reading of Freud, the specific polarity of inside and outside appears as the stake of their discourse. One quotation from each of the last three can serve as illustration:

> To state that madness has well and truly become a commonplace is to say that madness stands in our contemporary world for the radical ambiguity of the inside and the outside, an ambiguity which escapes speaking subjects who speak only by misrecognising it. . . . A discourse that speaks of madness can henceforth no longer know whether it is inside or outside, internal or external, to the madness of which it speaks.[13]

> The total inclusion of the 'frame' is both mandatory and impossible. The 'frame' thus becomes not the borderline between the inside and the outside, but precisely what subverts the applicability of the inside/outside polarity to the act of interpretation.[14]

> The specific problem posed by anxiety is that of *the relation of the psychic to the nonpsychic*, or in other words, *the delimitation of the psychic as such.* But if anxiety poses this problem, its examination and solution are complicated by the fact that anxiety itself both simulates and dissimulates the relation of psychic to nonpsychic, of 'internal' to 'external.' . . . [Freud's attempt] is intended to put anxiety in its proper place. But his own discussion demonstrates that *anxiety has no proper place.* . . . The psychoanalytic conception of the psychic can neither be *opposed* to the nonpsychic nor *derived* from it; it cannot be expressed in terms of cause and effect, outer and inner, reality and unreality, or any other of the opposing pairs to which Freud inevitably recurs.[15]

And at the conference on feminism and psychoanalysis held at Normal, Illinois, in May 1986, Barbara Johnson said in discussion: 'For pedagogy, aesthetics, therapy, you have to have a frame, and if you have a frame, what you get is pedagogy, aesthetics, therapy (which doesn't mean that you can do without one).' Now there are obvious differences among these statements and of course among the individual writers; but, none the less, a number of important links – both among them and in relation to what I have been describing – can be made. First, the problem of externality, delimitation, as a problem that encompasses the object – whether madness, literary enunciation, or anxiety – also includes the very theorization through which that object can be thought. The impossibility of delimiting the object becomes, therefore, the impossibility for theory itself of controlling its object – that is, of knowing it. Felman asks, 'How can we construct the theory of the essential misprision of the subject of theory?' (p. 221). Barbara Johnson: 'If we could be sure of the difference between the determinable and the undeterminable, the undeterminable would be comprehended within the determinable. What is undecidable is precisely whether a thing is decidable or not' (p. 488). And Weber: 'Such a *reality* [the "real essence of danger"] can never be fully grasped by theoretical "insight," since it can never be seen, named or recognised as such' (p. 59).

Second, and as an effect of this, the characterization of the object shifts into the field of its conceptualization or the impossibility of its conceptualization, so that, in Felman's case, for example, madness becomes precisely *la chose littéraire*, the very *thing* of literature (not *a* literary thing), because literature is the privileged place in which that tension between speaking madness and speaking of madness, between speaking madness and designating or repressing it, which is also the distinction between rhetoric and grammar, is played out. The object becomes the very structure of representation through which it fails to be thought, the impasse of conceptual thinking itself. The classic and dazzling instance of this theorization has to be the moment when Barbara Johnson reads Oedipus as a repetition of the letter purloined from the abyssal and interminable interior of Poe's story, instead of seeing the letter as a repetition of an oedipal fantasy it necessarily and always reproduces (the basis of Derrida's critique of Lacan, in whose reading of the Poe story he locates a classic psychoanalytic reduction) (p. 488).

Third, the shifting of the object into the very form and movement of representation brings with it – cannot, finally, avoid – its own meta-psychology. This appears in the category of grammar that Felman sets against rhetoric: the misrecognizing subject that thinks – has to think in order to speak – that it knows itself, has to ignore, as she puts it, that radical ambiguity between inside and outside that madness gives us today. But it is in the theorization of the death drive, the vanishing-point of the theory, that the meta-psychology of this reading of psychoanalysis becomes most clear. In Weber's reading of Freud's key text on the death drive, *Beyond the Pleasure Principle* (1920), what turns out to be driving the very impulse to death is narcissism, the binding and mastery that Weber identifies not only in the concept of the death drive but also in the very process through which Freud tried to formulate it, 'the narcissistic striving to rediscover the same: an aspect of speculation Freud was ready to criticize in others, but which he sought to justify in his own work' (p. 129). It is this emphasis on narcissism which saves the death drive from that intangible, generalized, and ultimately transcendent realm of the unfathomable to which the insistence on the failure of conceptualization could so easily assign it. Against this possible reading, which he attributes to Gilles Deleuze, Weber sees in the death drive 'just another form of the narcissistic language of the ego' (p. 129). It is a kind of self-accusatory ego psychology, one that laments and undoes its own categories and status even as it gives them final arbitration over psychic life.

Something similar goes on in Derrida's own reading of this same text by Freud (Derrida and Weber refer to each other[16]) through the concept of the *'pulsion d'emprise,' 'pulsion de puissance'*. At a key moment in Derrida's speculation on this most speculative of Freud's writings, this drive emerges as being for Freud the very motive of the drive itself: 'The holding, appropriating, drive must also be the *relation to itself* of the drive: no drive not driven to bind itself to itself and to ensure its self mastery as drive. Hence the transcendental tautology of the appropriating drive: the drive as drive, the drive of drive, the pulsionality of the drive.'[17] The concept appears in a term Freud offers almost as an aside in his discussion of the *fort-da* game: *Bemachtingungstrieb*. Freud's 'transcendental predicate' for describing the death drive is for Derrida, as for Weber, the term through which Freud's own meta-conceptual impulse is best thought.[18]

The concept of the death drive has of course been central to Derrida's reading of Freud since 'Freud and the Scene of Writing', when it hollowed out Freud's theory at its weak points of binarism through its *unheimlich* presence (as binding and repetition) inside the very process of life. We could in fact say that it is through the theorization of the death drive that Derrida ultimately thinks the relationship between the proper and that *différance* which subverts any causality, any dichotomy of inside and outside, all forms of language mastery in which he locates the violence (his word) of the metaphysical act.[19] Barbara Johnson, too, draws 'The Frame of Reference' to a close through the categories of narcissism and death (the inverted message that forces the subject – and reader – up against an irreducible otherness) (p. 503). Let's call deconstruction, for the moment at least, another way of dealing, another '*savoir-faire*', with the death drive itself (using and reformulating Catherine Millot's description of psychoanalysis as a *savoir-faire* with the paternal metaphor) that manages over and again to assert itself at the heart of theoretical and political debate.[20]

Let's note too, for all the distance between them, how the two very different articulations in relation to the death drive that I have been describing come uncannily close; how Derrida seems to pick up, or rather produce from within his own theorization, something of the terms present in Reich and, later, Masson: narcissism as phallogocentrism and the hymen as counter-image, with the relation between them formulated as rupture. Couldn't this also be seen as a grotesque recasting of the world (now Western metaphysics) under the sign of a massive violation, if not rape? 'Perpetual, the rape has always already taken place and will nevertheless never have been perpetrated. For it will always have been caught in the foldings of some veil, where any or all truth comes undone.'[21] No rape because the hymen is the point where all truth is undone; but always already rape, because always truth, logos, presence, the violence of the metaphysical act.

The act is metaphor or figuration for Derrida; for Masson, figuration, or fantasy, is the act (fantasy is a denial of the reality of the act). The difference can be seen in the opposite political effects: deconstruction of a sexual binary in language, which then seems, in Derrida's discourse at least, condemned to repeat it, or refusal of language itself in favour of the event. For what is at stake in Masson's rejection of fantasy if not representation as such, the idea of a discourse at odds with itself with no easy relation to the real? And isn't that also the key to the radical feminist critique of pornography, which sees the image as directly responsible for the act? But by setting figuration against the act in my own discourse, I am only too aware of the risk of reintroducing that inside/outside dichotomy which is so often the guarantor of political space. It is a question that has of course been put many times, not least by feminists, to deconstruction itself:

> This raises an important question which should not be overlooked although we haven't the space to develop it to any extent here: the complicated relationship of a practical politics to the kind of analysis we have been considering (specifically the 'deconstructive' analysis implicit in your discussion). . . . Just how one is to deal with the inter-relationship of these forces and necessities in the context of feminine [*sic* – I think this should be 'feminist'] struggle should be more fully explored on some other occasion. But let's go on to Heidegger's ontology.[22]

The slip – 'feminine' for 'feminist' – is beautifully expressive of the problem being raised: the absorption of the political (feminist) into the space of representation (feminine). Or, as Derrida would insist – as indeed he goes on to insist in the same interview – with reference to a concept like 'hymen' or 'double chiasmatic invagination of the borders', these terms are present in his own writing as a trope not reducible to the body of the woman as such, at once anchored in and taking off from the recognizable historical reference they inevitably invoke (p. 75).

Crucially however, in both these positions, the problem of how to locate violence and the act brings with it – is inseparable from – the question of how to locate sexual difference. It needed feminism, of course, to make the point.

In three stages, therefore, feminism has returned to and recast the controversies at the heart of the 1920s and 1930s political debate with Freud[23]: first, the issue of phallocentrism, which came originally from within the analytic institution and, in its largely clinical formulation, was at that time marked by the total absence of any political consciousness or critique (it was this criticism that was remade for radical feminism by Shulamith Firestone and Kate Millett in the late 1960s); second, the attempt to use psychoanalysis as a theory of ideology, which had characterized the political Freudians of Berlin.[24] The key figure here is Otto Fenichel, who tried to use psychoanalysis in relation to Marxism without losing, like Reich and the culturalists, the unconscious and sexuality; without sacrificing, like the Vienna and British orthodox analysts, the political challenge to social and sexual norms (Juliet Mitchell's intervention in 1974 is almost an exact retranscription for feminism of this aim). And finally now, the issue of the death drive, of a violence whose outrageous character belongs so resolutely with its refusal to be located, to be simply identified, and then, by implication, removed (possibly the only meaning of the persistence, or immutability, of the death drive of which it has so often been politically accused). Perhaps one reason why this issue has returned is that, faced with the hideous phenomenon of right-wing apocalyptic and sexual fantasy, the language of interpellation through which we thought to understand something about collective identification is no longer adequate. At the point where fantasy generalizes itself in the form of the horrific, that implied ease of self-recognition gives way to something that belongs in the order of impossibility or shock.

That this is now a key issue for feminism can be read across the very titles of two texts of contemporary feminism: Andrea Dworkin's *Pornography: men possessing women*, with all that it implies by way of a one-sided (which means outside of us as women) oppression, violence, and control, and the Barnard papers on sexuality, *Pleasure and Danger*, whose ambiguity allows us at least to ask whether the relation between the two terms is one of antagonism or implication, whether there might be a pleasure *in* danger – a dangerous question in itself.[25] In her opening essay, the editor, Carole Vance, puts the question like this: 'The subtle connection between how patriarchy interferes with female desire and how women experience their own passions as dangerous is emerging as a critical issue to be explored' (p. 4). In this formulation, although danger is still something that comes from outside – patriarchy makes female desire dangerous to itself – the terms of femininity, passion, and danger have at least started to move. If the deconstructive way of undoing the sort of dichotomy I have outlined leaves me unsatisfied, therefore, it is not just because of the return of the basic scenario of difference, but because I cannot see how it can link back to this equally pressing question for feminists – which is how we can begin to think the question of violence and fantasy as something that implicates us as women, how indeed we can begin to dare to think it at all.

It is the problem increasingly at the heart of Kristeva's work, the concept of abjection (already posed as horror and power), which has led inexorably to the question of feminism and violence, 'to extol a centripetal, softened and becalmed feminine sexuality, only to exhume most recently, under the cover of idylls amongst women, the sado-masochistic ravages beneath'.[26] In Kristeva's case, this difficulty has produced in turn the no less problematic flight into a paternally grounded identification and love.[27]

The question then becomes: what could be an understanding of violence which, while fully recognizing the historical forms in which it has repeatedly been directed toward women, none the less does not send it out wholesale into the real from which it can only return as an inevitable and hallucinatory event? How can we speak the fact that violence moves across boundaries, including that of sexual difference, and not only in fantasy. For only by recognizing that boundaries already shift (not *can* be shifted – the flight into pure voluntarism) can we avoid the pitfalls of a Masson (women as utter victim to the event). And only by seeing this as a problem for subjects who recognize and, in so doing, misrecognize themselves and each other as sexual beings can we seize this problem at the level of what is still for feminism an encounter between the sexes. For psychoanalysis, this difficulty is precisely the difficulty of sexuality itself, or of the death drive, which might be a way of saying the same thing. It is a point of theoretical and political difficulty still unresolved today.

NOTES

Originally presented at subsequent references are 'Feminisms and Psychoanalysis', a conference held in Normal, Illinois, 1986, published in *Feminism and Psychoanalysis*, ed. Judith Root and Richard Feldstein (Ithaca, NY: Cornell University Press, 1989).

1 Wilhelm Reich, *Reich Speaks of Freud. Conversations with Kurt Eissler*, ed. Mary Higgins and C. M. Raphael (New York: Farrar, Straus, and Giroux, 1967), pp. 42–3, (subsequent references are cited in the text).

2 The key text in which Freud introduced the concept of the death drive is *Beyond the Pleasure Principle*, 1920, in *The Standard Edition of the Complete Psychological Works*, ed. and trans. James Strachery (London: Hogarth), vol. 18.

3 Jeffrey Masson, *The Assault on Truth, Freud's Suppression of the Seduction Theory* (New York: Farrar, Straus, and Giroux, 1984), p. 144.

4 In 1983 Janet Malcolm interviewed Jeffrey Masson, and used the material as the basis for two articles published first in the *New Yorker* and then as a book, *In the Freud Archives* (New York: Knopf, 1984). Masson subsequently sued Malcolm. The reference here is to his statement that he had slept with a thousand women.

5   Chris Reed, 'How Freud Changed his Mind and Became a Chauvinist', Guardian Woman, *Guardian*, 20 February 1985. Masson had also published a long article in the radical feminist journal *Mother Jones*.

6   Freud, *The Ego and the Id*, in *Standard Edition*, vol. 19, p. 44.

7   Ibid., p. 45.

8   Freud, 'The Economic Problem of Masochism,' in *Standard Edition*, vol. 19, p. 166.

9   Janine Chasseguet-Smirgel and Bela Grunberger, *Freud or Reich? Psychoanalysis and Illusion*, trans. Claire Pajaczkowska (London: Free Association Books, 1985), see esp. p. 10.

10 Freud, 'The Dissection of the Psychical Personality,' in *New Introductory Lectures*, in *Standard Edition*, vol. 22, p. 80; Jacques Lacan, 'L'Instance de la lettre dans l'inconscient; ou, La raison depuis Freud,' in *Écrits* (Paris: Seuil, 1966), p. 524; trans. Alan Sheridan, 'The Agency of the Letter in the Unconscious; or, Reason since Freud', in *Écrits: a selection* (New York: Norton, 1977), p. 171.

11 Jacques Derrida, *La Carte postale: de Socrate à Freud et au-delà* (Paris: Flammarion, 1980) trans. Alan Bass, *The Post Card: from Socrates to Freud and beyond* (Chicago: Chicago University Press, 1987).

12 Juliet Mitchell, *Psychoanalysis and Feminism* (London: Allen Lane, New York: Random House, 1974).

13 Shoshana Felman, *Writing and Madness*, trans. Martha Noel Evans and Shoshana Felman (Ithaca, NY: Cornell University Press, 1985), pp. 12–13; originally published as *La Folie et la chose littéraire* (Paris: Seuil, 1978) (subsequent references are cited in the text).

14 Barbara Johnson, 'The Frame of Reference: Poe, Lacan, Derrida,' *Yale French Studies* 55/56 (1977), p. 481, (subsequent references are cited in the text).

15 Samuel Weber, *The Legend of Freud* (Minneapolis: University of Minnesota Press, 1982), pp. 50, 58–9 (subsequent references are cited in the text).

16 Derrida, *La Carte postale*, p. 400n.; Weber, *Legend of Freud*, p. 172n.

17 Derrida, *La Carte postale*, p. 430 (my translation).

18 Ibid., pp. 430–2. Although very close, there does seem to be a difference between Weber's and Derrida's theorization here. For Weber the death drive becomes a manifestation of the drive to mastery; for Derrida the *'pulsion d'emprise'* is the category through which the death drive is thought by Freud, but it is always exceeded by the death drive, 'at once the reason and the failure, the origin and the limit of power'. Hence in Derrida's commentary, the last word, so to speak, is given to rhythm: 'Beyond opposition, the rhythm' (pp. 432, 435).

19 Derrida, 'Freud et la scène de l'écriture', in *L'Écriture et la différence* (Paris: Seuil, 1967), pp. 293–340; trans. Alan Bass, *Writing and Difference* (Chicago: University of Chicago Press, 1978), pp. 196–231.

20 Catherine Millot, 'The Feminine Super-Ego', *m/f* 10 (1985); pp. 21–38.

21 Derrida is commenting on Mallarmé: Jacques Derrida, 'La Double Séance', in *La Dissémination* (Paris: Seuil, 1972), p. 260; 'The Double Session', trans. Barbara Johnson, in *Dissemination* (Chicago: University of Chicago Press, 1981), p. 292.

22 Jacques Derrida and Christie V. McDonald, 'Choreographies', *Diacritics* 12 (Summer 1982), pp. 66–76.

23 For a fuller discussion of this history, see Jacqueline Rose, 'Introduction – Feminism and the Psychic', in *Sexuality in the Field of Vision* (London: Verso, 1986), pp. 1–23.

24 See Russell Jacoby, *The Repression of Psychoanalysis: Otto Fenichel and the Political Freudians* (New York: Basic Books, 1983).

25 Andrea Dworkin, *Pornography: men possessing women* (New York: Perigree, 1981); Carole S. Vance, *Pleasure and Danger: exploring female sexuality* (Boston and London: Routledge and Kegan Paul, 1984).

26 Julia Kristeva, *Histoires d'amour* (Paris: Denöel, 1983), p. 349.

27 I discuss these shifts in Kristeva's work more fully in 'Julia Kristeva – Take Two', in *Sexuality in the Field of Vision* (London: Verso, 1986), pp. 141–64.

4 Shakespeare and the Death Drive

The conference at which the paper that forms the basis of this chapter was first presented had the title 'Shakespeare and Eros', and I chose to talk about Shakespeare and death. If this should seem perverse, it is a perversion which, in relation to both the field of sexuality and the writing of Shakespeare, has as I will be arguing, an inner logic. *Measure for Measure* is one of the plays by Shakespeare which brings the two instances (of eros and death) forcefully together, although not in the perhaps familiar and more predictable sense of death as a facet of eroticism – that is, an eroticism tinged with an intrinsic violence and morbidity because it belongs to the realm of excess (a reading associated with the great 'erotic' drama of Shakespeare's *Antony and Cleopatra* and to some extent with *Romeo and Juliet*). In *Measure for Measure*, the association between eros and death is more complicated, passing as it does through an explicit discussion of the enactment of just and unjust law. What is at stake in *Measure for Measure* in not a fusion of the two terms, but their interchangeability, a question precisely of *measure*: whether death and eros can be exchanged for each other; whether, finally, either of them can be put in the scales.

The question of exchangeability is there of course from the very beginning, when Claudio's death is the punishment for a sexual offence, and then immediately again in the barter that Angelo tries to establish between that death and the sexual act with Isabella. But that basic exchange (death for sex and sex for death) is rapidly confused with a number of others, which force the relation between the two way beyond the terms of the central and structuring dramatic event. If illegal sexuality *leads to* death as its legitimate punishment, death is also, in the form of illegitimate violence or murder, its *equivalent*. Angelo justifies the sentence on Claudio in these terms:

> It were as good
> To pardon him that hath from nature stolen
> A man already made, as to remit
> Their saucy sweetness that do coin heaven's image
> In stamps that are forbid.
>
> (II. iv. 41–45)[1]

The illicit and illegitimate production of life is the same as the illegitimate taking of it, which lines up death on the side of life, as well as inadvertently drawing together – since Claudio is to be executed – the law's enactment of violence and murder. In this context, the problem of justice in the play is no longer that of just measure (the *mean* of its fair application), but is rather that of the symbolic basis and contradictions in the concept of legal justice itself, of the paradox, as Freud put it, that 'civilisation hopes to prevent the crudest excesses of brutal violence by itself assuming the right to use violence against criminals'.[2] To put it another way, Angelo is guilty long before the emergence of his desire for Isabella, because the law is only ever the embodiment – and enactment – of a collective guilt, or crime.

This reversibility, or mutual implication, of terms which propose themselves as opposites comes to be at the heart of Freud's theorization of the death drive.[3] It is also, through the principle of demonic and unpleasurable repetition, what leads him to a recognition of its force. The death drive is identified by Freud in that moment when the child seeks to master absence by staging the recall of the lost object, but finds it can only do so by first making the object disappear. This locks the child into the structure of representation, but, more crucially, allows the child to achieve its aim only by repeating the very moment it is designed to avoid. This process of uncanny and self-defeating repetition Freud opposes to eros; but commentators have been quick to point out that it contradicts the most fundamental psychoanalytic understanding of sexuality to try and preserve eros from these effects.[4] Pleasure and unpleasure, for example, are inseparable in psychoanalysis because, through repression, what was once desired comes to be feared. That reversal can then be seen as not radically distinguishable from the game of the infant in which what is most feared becomes the object of a demonic repetition and desire.

In Freud's account the death drive comes increasingly to stand for that contradictory repetition, a drive whose object is finally indifferent, subordinated as it is to the force of the mechanism itself. Nothing illustrates the perversity of this mechanism more clearly than the unconscious relation which can hold between punishment and crime:

> Not long ago, Rank published some examples of the way in which neurotic acts of revenge can be directed against the wrong people. Such behaviour on the part of the unconscious reminds one of the comic story of the three village tailors, one of whom had to be hanged because the only village blacksmith had committed a capital offence. Punishment must be exacted even if it doesn't fall upon the guilty.[5]

If we take these two statements of Freud together – that the law embodies the very crime it punishes, and that it may strike at random even where there is no crime –

then the law starts to look uncannily like that principle of blind repetition which characterizes the death drive itself. Such a definition is effectively proposed in Barnaby Riche's *The Adventures of Brusanus, Prince of Hungary,* given by Bullough as one of the sources of the play:

> They make themselves guilty of great injustice, who beeing appointed of God to persecute the wicked with the swoorde drawne, will yet keep their handes cleane from bloude, whereas the wicked in the meantime commits all manner of sin, and that uncontrolled: and it is no less cruelty to punishe no offence, than not to forgive any.[6]

Of course, in this instance any seeming extravagance is cancelled by being placed within the framework of what would be an ideal administration of the law. *Measure for Measure* also, through the trajectory of the narrative, defines the problem in terms of an ideal standard, turning it into an encounter between different moral subjects so that what are being examined are the qualities that make an individual the fitting bearer of justice. But what if the problem is not moral, but formal? If it is fundamentally irreducible to something which can be managed by a benign statehood, indicating that there is something wilder at play? Then we might start to see how the contradictions at the heart of the very definition of legality spread across the play's whole field of signification, constantly confounding, even as it establishes, the precious distinctions which the law orchestrates and arbitrates into place. The law can be narrativized, but, like death and sexuality, there is always something which escapes.

I want to come at this question now through a consideration of the explicit discussion of death in Shakespeare's play. One of the most striking things about *Measure for Measure* is the way that it seems to bring about something which could be called a 'putting into discourse' of death. If I wanted to talk about 'Shakespeare and the Death Drive' in the context of a conference on eros, it is also because the question of sexuality has been so privileged over that of death in both traditional and more radical readings of the play. But in *Measure for Measure*, sex is not just set against death, it is wedged into a discussion of the morality of death which is of equal importance to, and is finally inseparable from, the representation of sexuality itself. In fact, death takes on the status of a desired object no less than sexual pleasure. Thus, while the narrative is driven by the attempt to forestall the death of Claudio (a death which is felt to be excessive), death insists across the whole fabric of the drama (not just *this* death as excessive, nor death *as* excess, but a kind of superfluity *of* death). Juliet describes her life as a 'dying horror' when she is told that Claudio is to die; Isabella comments when told the story of Mariana: 'What a merit were it in death to take this poor maid from the world'; Angelo threatens Isabella that, if she relents, Claudio's death will be drawn out 'to a ling'ring sufferance' (an added piece of viciousness which, as J. W. Lever comments in his Introduction to the Arden edition, is nowhere in any of the sources of the play).

Alongside this morbidity, we can place the status of death as object of exchange, not just between Claudio, Angelo, and Isabella, but in its comic, or low, version in the transition of Pompey from 'unlawful bawd to lawful hangman', which echoes the point about legality, sexuality, and murder that I have already made. It is as if death can be avoided only in the form of its repetition, which means – in psychoanalytic terminology – that death becomes an object of desire. Isabella states this most clearly, in a speech which has caused some awkwardness for those insisting (whether for or against) on her sanctity:

> . . . were I under the terms of death,
> Th'impression of keen whips I'd wear as rubies,
> And strip myself to death as to a bed
> That longing have been sick for, ere I'd yield
> My body up to shame.
>
> (II. iv. 99–103)

Lever comments: 'The image is more obviously suited to an Antony or Claudio than to the chaste Isabella, but its occurrence here is psychologically revealing', meaning – we gather from the Introduction – that it reveals that 'strongly sexed ardour and impetuosity' which will find its 'true destiny' in her marriage to the Duke.[7] Lever is right, of course, that the passage is extraordinary, and indeed that it appears out of place. More crucially, it also produces a dramatic confusion of the alternatives which it seems to propose. The passage seems to say that Isabella would prefer death to sexual dishonour, but the choice is in fact between sexual dishonour and the sexualization of death. Like Angelo producing proximity (between the administration of justice and murder) where there should be antagonism, Isabella manages to confuse the opposition between honourable death and dishonour on which she stakes her moral ground. This constant destabilization, and the central place of death within it, suggests that even if, technically, the central act of barter is a body for a life (that of Claudio), it is simultaneously a body for a death. Furthermore, as we will see, death and the body are not always, or necessarily, opposed. As Erasmus puts it, citing St Paul, in the *Ars Moriendi*, 'Who shall deliver me from the body of this death?'[8]

Before going on to discuss the two famous speeches in Act III in which this crisis of representation in relation to death is most manifest, a number of other points should be made. For there is another fundamental contradiction on this subject of death which runs right across the play. In the struggle over Claudio, death is punishment, and the basic argument is that this punishment is unreasonable. Claudio should not have to relinguish his right to life. In the case of Barnardine, however, there is no questioning of the sentence, but the problem of execution is that Barnardine is not ready for death. Neither Barnardine nor Claudio 'deserve' to die, but that 'deserve' has two different and potentially contradictory meanings: worthiness (implying death as something noble) and refusal (implying death as something one has the right, for as long as possible, to resist). The Duke, as we will see, will try to resolve this contradiction by preparing Claudio for death, but he can precisely do so only by a form of generality which brackets out any distinction between death as fair or unfair. At the same time, Barnardine is busily signalling that very distinction by his presence elsewhere in the play. Clearly, at one level the difference between Claudio and Barnardine turns on the question of readiness for death, but it is too easy simply to oppose them in these terms. 'Unfit to live or die', Barnardine represents together what are meant to be two mutually exclusive terms, since the story which revolves around Claudio implies that you merit one or the other, but not both. The law, and the dynamic of Shakespeare's drama in so far as it precisely narrativizes the law, would in fact be pointless if there was no absolute distinction between the granting and the withholding of human life.

The question then emerges as to *which* death is at issue, or what could be a specification of death. 'No need of a signifier', writes Lacan, 'to be dead or to be a father, but without the signifier there would be no knowledge whatsover about either of these two states of being'.[9] Rereading (he called it returning to) Freud's oedipal myth, Lacan sees in its symbolic staging of the death of the father the basic tie between death and paternity as the unavoidable indices of the structure of symbolization itself. That which can *only* be signified turns the subject '*en abîme*' into the endless flight of signification. According to this reading, it is language that drives the subject to death. *Measure for Measure* does not, therefore, only *signify* death (a contradiction in terms, as well as being the classic psychoanalytic reduction); it *stages* it. To see Shakespeare's play in this way is to see it as one discourse – psychoanalysis is another – in which the necessity and impossibility of naming death are played out. Death and sexuality come together again here in relation to this concept of representation in so far as the sexual drama between Isabella and Angelo takes the form of, or is precipitated by, a putting of sexuality into speech. For it is the speech of the woman which is represented in the play as the initial and dangerous sexual act.[10]

It is worth grounding these remarks in contemporary discourses by looking at some of the theorizations of death at the time when Shakespeare was writing, not least because some of these are so explicitly and strangely evoked in the famous speeches about death in Act III of the play. Chapter 1 of 'The First Book of Death' in Coverdale's *Treatise of Death* – 'Declaring What Death Is' – lists the four types of death to which man is subject as:

> natural death which separates the soul from the body; spiritual unhappy death when the grace of God 'for our wickedness's sake is departed from us'; ghostly blessed death here in time when 'the flesh being ever, the longer the more, separated from the spirit, dieth away from his own wicked nature'; everlasting life and everlasting death.[11]

The second and third – 'spiritual unhappy death' and 'ghostly blessed death' – are in turn contrasted with ghostly blessed life and ghostly unhappy life, the first living unto God, the second being the continual and wilful breaking forth of the flesh. Rather than going into the theological issues at stake here, I simply want to point to this cataloguing, naming, distributing, and redistributing of death. What we are presented with can only be called a combinatory, where a number of terms circulate around a set of fixed points (this is precisely what death *is*). The point of the combinatory is at once to set up distinct oppositions and to move the terms around. The principle is that anything can be exchanged for or compared with anything else, but the distinctions between the various states are absolute. The possibility of sliding from one to another is then interpreted as the moral trajectory (ascent or descent) of man.

We can contrast this account with Erasmus's *Ars Moriendi* or *Preparation for Death*, which belongs to a whole discourse on the art of dying well, on which – it is generally assumed – Shakespeare based the Duke's speech.[12] In the *Ars Moriendi* – Erasmus's and more generally – the opposition between spiritual and natural death takes a different form. There is a similar classification of four types of death, with a 'transmuting death' which involves, like Coverdale's 'ghostly blessed death', a dying away from the flesh. Preparedness for natural death is precisely such a transformation; but in Erasmus's text, it becomes the basis for a total denegation of life. This is preparedness rather than preparation, although Sister O'Connor sees the genre as a practical guide to the business of dying, 'a method to be used in that all important and inescapable hour'.[13] Erasmus's text makes it clear, however, that something far more dialectical is at stake, in which to be ready for death is to refuse life, and even to be repelled by it. Preparedness, at least, is as much as a positive looking forward, a totally negative rereading or looking back. This has the effect of asserting, by way of negation or refusal, the intense physicality of life:

> Let us recollect throughout all the stages of life, the uncleanness of our conception, the hazards of the womb, the pangs of birth, the many ills of infancy, the accidents to which childhood is liable, the vices which defile youth,

the cares which harass manhood, the wretchedness of old age.[14]

Death is, in fact, everywhere in the very life to which it seems to be opposed (death is not unforeseen because 'it lurks on every side'); it is also present in man's daily self-deception when he sees as pure something abominable in the eyes of the Lord. Death is therefore imperfect vision, the failure of representation as well as the failing and repulsion of the flesh. Finally, death is the very significance of the human: 'Nay the very name of *man* recalls the very idea of death, so that *man* and *mortal* signify the same thing.[15] This, then, is the form of discourse on death which Shakespeare puts right into the middle of the play. We should note that this 'putting into discourse' of death is something which appears nowhere in any of the sources in which (this is the case in both Cinthio and Whetstone) the sister relents finally in the face of the argument of her brother (it is therefore assumed by implication that death is a greater ill than sexual dishonour, although other forms of calculation on keeping it secret and the possibility of marriage also come into play). But nowhere else is there a discourse on the *desirability* of death. Shakespeare therefore completely muddles the moral stakes, not just by having Isabella refuse Angelo, but by introducing immediately prior to the scene with her brother a speech which makes the spiritual case for death. Critics who castigate Isabella for her sexual inhumanity (that's putting it mildly) could usefully have borne that in mind. The issue of Isabella's sexuality is therefore packed around with a debate about the very value and meaning of human (meaning sexual) life.

Let's now look at the Duke's speech and at Claudio's reply:

Be absolute for death: either death or life
Shall thereby be the sweeter. Reason thus with life:

If I do lose thee, I do lose a thing
That none but fools would keep. A breath thou art,
Servile to all the skyey influences
That dost this habitation where thou keep'st
Hourly afflict. Merely, thou art Death's fool;
For him thou labour'st by thy flight to shun,
And yet run'st toward him still. Thou art not noble;
For all th'accommodations that thou bear'st
Are nurs'd by baseness. Thou'rt by no means valiant;
For thou dost fear the soft and tender fork
Of a poor worm. Thy best of rest is sleep;
And that thou oft provok'st, yet grossly fear'st
Thy death, which is no more. Thou art not thyself;
For thou exists on many a thousand grains
That issue out of dust. Happy thou art not:
For what thou hast not, still thou striv'st to get,
And what thou hast, forget'st. Thou art not certain;
For thy complexion shifts to strange effects
After the moon. If thou art rich
For, like an ass whose back with ingot bows,
Thou bear'st thy heavy riches but a journey,
And death unloads thee. Friend hast thou none;
For thine own bowels which do call thee sire,
The mere effusion of thy proper loins,
Do curse the gout, serpigo, and the rheum
For ending thee no sooner. Thou hast nor youth, nor age,
But as it were an after-dinner's sleep
Dreaming on both; for all thy blessed youth
Becomes as aged, and doth beg the alms
Of palsied eld: and when thou art old and rich,
Thou hast neither heat, affection, limb, nor beauty
To make thy riches pleasant. What's yet in this
That bears the name of life? Yet in this life
Lie hid moe thousand deaths; yet death we fear
That makes these odds all even.

(III. i. 5–41)

Ay, but to die, and go we know not where;
To lie in cold obstruction, and to rot;
This sensible warm motion to become

A kneaded clod; and the delighted spirit
To bath in fiery floods, or to reside
In thrilling region of thick-ribbed ice;
To be imprison'd in the viewless winds
And blown with restless violence round about
The pendent world: or to be worse than worst
Of those that lawless and incertain thought
Imagine howling, – 'tis too horrible.
The weariest and most loathed worldly life
That age, ache, penury and imprisonment
Can lay on nature, is a paradise
To what we fear of death.

(III. i. 117–31)

This is Lever's commentary, which is worth giving in full:

Superficially the Duke's homily to Claudio, 'Be absolute for death', might seem to be a statement of 'doctrine' by Holy Church in the guise of a friar. Its catalogue of the vanities of life recalls the spiritual exercise of the *ars moriendi*. Similarly Claudio's reflections on the afterlife, 'Ay, but to die', suggest the *contemplatio mortis* which formed the second part of the exercise. Considered more closely, both speeches are subtle distortions, and the 'doctrine' is to be found in neither. The Duke's description of the human condition eliminates its spiritual aspect and is essentially materialistic and pagan. By Christian teaching, man's breath, far from being 'Servile to all the skyey influences', came to him from God. His nobility and valour, happiness and certainty, were not 'nurs'd by baseness', but were spiritual qualities permeating natural life. The self was no Lucretian amalgam of 'grains / That issue out of dust', but an immortal soul. Even on the natural plane, though riches, health and friendship may prove illusory, offspring was to be seen as a consolation and blessing. Moreover, Claudio's reflections form an equally heretical counterpart. Lucretian in its concept of both soul and body resolved after death into the four elements, it adds to this the pagan superstition, derided by Lucretius, of the afterlife as a state of eternal affliction. Reacting against the call to be 'absolute for death' out of disgust for life, Claudio is 'absolute for life' through horror of the world to come.[16]

Lever continues, however, that none of this should be taken as the 'expression of ultimate cynicism or despair', since neither speech, he insists, provides an objective viewpoint for judging the events of the play. At this point in the play, 'when all principles seem to be lost and the significance of authority, virtue and life itself is called into question, the Duke intervenes'. What Lever is arguing here – and in this he is merely following the play's own narrative logic – is that the Duke is there to bring about not only a dramatic, but also a symbolic, resolution. This is also taken to imply a reconciliation of the mortal and immortal life of man which falls somewhere between the extremes of these two speeches, although such a concept is nowhere articulated in the play. Lever's increasing judgement on Isabella (her 'strongly sexed ardour and impetuosity', her 'hysterical diatribe') appears in this context as at least partly a transposition on to her moral trajectory of the disturbance posed to harmonious interpretation by the play's extravagant discourse on death. If, as Lever suggests, what is put into crisis by Act III of the drama is the 'significance of authority, virtue and life', then the end of the play restores the first two to their socially and symbolically appropriate position but in fact says absolutely nothing about the third.[17] This may be because what is released by that moment in Act III is not susceptible to this (to any) dramatic resolution.

The problem of the speeches is not only, it seems to me, a violation of doctrine to be lifted out of the content of what they appear to say, but also resides in the movement of the language and their form. If the discussion of death is finally unmanageable and has to be forgotten, it is because what it generates is not so much heresy as illegibility. Or, to use the words of Angelo at another point of the drama, it speaks against the thing it says.

Let's take the proposition of the Duke's speech to be, as Lever puts it, a 'contempt of death through a contempt of life'. Let's also note that it takes the form of a judicial argument whose structure corresponds to the rhetorical principles laid out in Tully's *Ad Herennium*, described by T. W. Baldwin in *Shakespere's Smalle Latine and Lesse Greeke* as a 'complete outline of the formal oration at its most formal as applied to judicial causes'.[18] The Duke therefore speaks dramatically as friar, formally as rhetorician or even lawyer. The argument for death passes through the defiles of legal speech. We can see the Duke's speech as a condensation of legal and religious discourse in which death is demonstrated as pure rhetoric, even as the possibility of holding death to the formalities of language is being put to the test.

Both the Duke's and Claudio's speeches talk of death, one 'for', the other 'against' – that is, one on the side of death, the other on the side of life. Both can only make the case for death or for life however, in terms of the element to which it is opposed, and in both cases the second element could be said to usurp the place of the first. The Duke argues for the superiority of death over life (a relation of comparison implying difference), but does so in terms of the presence of death inside life (a relation of identity or identification). But if death is present to life, thereby turning life into an always already of death, then we should also expect to find that life is there in the place of the very death that appears so utterly to negate it. This will be the indirect logic of Claudio's speech, but not before the Duke has also demonstrated something of its self-defeating perversity.

'Be absolute for death', the opening proposition of the Duke that the rest of his speech will set out to demonstrate or confirm: 'absolute', glossed by Onions as 'positive, perfectly certain, decided', but which also carries the meanings of 'unconditional or unrestricted', as well as 'complete, finished, perfect'. What the proposition proposes, therefore, is a totality of being, unconditionally and perfectly on the side of death. But the clause which follows, 'either death or life / Shall thereby be the sweeter', is immediately ambiguous as the correct formulation for the logical meaning would be 'or . . . or', signifying 'both of the two', not 'either . . . or', signifying 'one or the other'. It must be both if the Duke succeeds in his case, which is to demonstrate the desirability of death to the subject who lives now – that is, the desirability of death to life. Both death and life must be the sweeter if the Duke's speech is to do its work, not one or the other which allows their re-differentiation, the possibility that life will assert itself – against such a logic – as precisely sweeter than death (the whole point of Claudio's speech, whose possibility has therefore already been released in advance here).

Note then that the Duke does not only reason, he instructs his addressee *how* to reason; that is, the *ratio* of his discourse takes the form of a lesson in oratory in which it is not Claudio who is to be persuaded of the argument, but life itself ('Reason thus with life'). The discourse therefore shifts: from Claudio as the one addressed to Claudio as the hypostasized subject of speech, who is thereby absorbed into its enunciation and already differentiated from (more than or greater than?) life because it is life that he is presumed to address. That 'I' –, 'If I do lose thee, I do lose a thing / That none but fools would keep' – is the Duke first, but, more important, already Claudio as 'man', privileged syntactically by his distance from the object 'life', which precisely only 'fools' would keep. These lines Baldwin classifies as the 'Reason' of the argument, which, according to Cicero, 'by means of a brief explanation subjoined, sets forth the causal basis for the proposition, establishing the truth of what we are arguing', for which he gives the example of Ulysses' motives in killing Ajax: 'Indeed he wished to rid himself of his bitterest enemy, from whom, with good cause, he feared extreme danger to himself.'[19] The Duke's opening, we could also argue, has established the terms of an opposition, if not enmity, between life and man. Life is that which man is well rid of, meaning both that he does not in fact possess it and that he is better off without it – propositions which could be said to cancel each other out, but which the confirmations of the rest of the speech will then set out to prove.

It is the body of the confirmations which Lever concentrates on in his account of the speech as excessive (pagan, heretical) in its total denegation of life. In the very first of these confirmations there is another potential slippage, since the sentence is syntactically ambiguous. Either 'skyey influences' is the subject of the verb 'afflict': this is the meaning one lends most readily to the sentence: life is a breath servile to all the 'skyey influences' hourly rained down upon human habitation. Or breath is the subject of 'dost afflict', at the mercy of 'skyey influences', but also active and hourly afflicting human habitation in its turn. This second meaning makes life the persecutor of life. As do the later lines:

> For thine own bowels which do call thee sire,
> The mere effusion of thy proper loins,
> Do curse the gout, serpigo, and the reheum
> For ending thee no sooner,

which seem to start as a list of the body's effusions, cursing the illnesses that afflict it, before turning in that last line to reveal that 'bowels' signifies offspring who wish their parent dead. That concentrated repulsion of the body to itself then leaves the sacrilege of the infant suspended over a body which would already seem to have no possible reason to live.

It is the gist of these meanings that Lever lifts out of the speech – what he calls its pagan and materialist slant: breath subject to 'skyey influences' rather than to God, all the accommodations of life as 'nurs'd by baseness', without spiritual worth, the self a mere amalgam of grains issuing out of dust with no soul, and finally off-spring as a curse. Note too that to say that death is *no more* than sleep is to go way beyond the familiar trope of death as the *image* of sleep. It is, as Baldwin puts it, an 'Abominably unChristian sentiment', and he describes the lengths to which critics have then had to go to absolve Shakespeare of such a charge.[20] All this in the mouth of a friar (who is of course no friar but a Duke in disguise). We could say that the force of this rhetorical persuasion – the utter repulsion it engenders in relation to life – is finally self-defeating. For it there is no spiritually redeeming aspect to life itself, then from where can the repudiation of life in the name of the spirit be spoken? How can what is valuable and preferable in death itself be known if death already and so totally subordinates life to its cause? Be 'absolute' for death, reasons the Duke, because death is *already* absolute, a tautology which abolishes the condition of reason itself.

Yet the contrary message is also allowed for in the speech; that is, that life and man are inseparable, and it is one at least suggested by the form of its enunciation. Gradually and imperceptibly the words of the Duke shift back to addressing not life but Claudio, or at least man – man unvaliant and afraid, who shuns and fears death, strives for what he has not got and forgets what he has, borne down by riches he has to discard at the end of his journey, and cursed by his child. And if it is possible to slide from life into man according to an almost imperceptible and unmarked elision, then hasn't the whole discourse drawn life and man back together, producing their structural inseparability, even as it drives the contrary message to death? This is man in so far as he lives, holding – against all the odds – on to life. And the address of the speech, moving from life to man, passes us along the lines of a similar identification. Choose death over life, because life is so worthless; but who can argue and who receive such a case? Either death absorbs life, putting life beyond all reason, or life as man will continue to set his face against death. The Duke concludes:

> What's yet in this
> That bears the name of life? Yet in this life
> Lie hid more thousand deaths; yet death we fear
> That makes these odds all even.

If I read this (following Lever) as death the great equalizer between men, it is only because the other meaning – that death is the great equalizer between life and death – cannot work, since death is itself one of the two uneven terms. Rhetorically, the question remains at least suspended as to whether, in the wager of life and death, the ratio of odds and evens can ever be made to come out.

Briefly, then, on Claudio's speech, the speech on the horror of death which comes in delayed reply to the Duke (Claudio's immediate response is to concur), but also in response to Isabella's horror of sexual shame. Claudio has therefore to make his horror worse than that horror, as well as to make death more repellent than anything that can be charged against life. The problem again is that the horror of death can be described only from the position of a sentient and knowing consciousness whose palpable self-presence to the death it fears makes that death both more and less total in its effects. F R. Leavis praised this speech for its 'vividly realised particular situation . . . the imagined experience of a given mind in a given critical moment that is felt from the inside – that is lived – with sharp concrete particularity'.[21] What the speech gives us precisely is Claudio *living* his death. Thus Leavis makes of death the emblem of poetic vividness and the self-achievement of aesthetic form. Taking this one step further, death becomes the most vivid of representations because, as that which can by definition subsist only within representation, it always signals the self-referentiality of art. Thus death comes to stand for that moment when the category of fiction most fully recognizes itself – like Claudio invoking the 'worse than worst', imaginings of a 'lawless and incertain thought' – imaginings which he thereby classifies as aberrational, even as he projects himself so totally into their place. Between the vivid particular and the lawless 'incertain' (Leavis of course omits the second), we can grasp something of what is involved in Claudio's (in any) representation of death.

I want to go back to Freud at this point for two reasons. First, because it seems to me that *Measure for Measure* plays out so graphically the inseparability of the two principles Freud himself tried to differentiate under the headings of eros and death. But it does so by first positing their antagonism via the operations of the law. Second, because the repeated failure of that differentiation (which the speeches of Act III give us in a particularly acute form) reveals itself as a property of discourse; that is, of a constant destabilizing of language for which death itself may well be the ultimate signifier (since there can only ever be a signifier for death), but which inheres in the very structure and process of all language in so far as it endlessly produces its objects with reference to itself. According to this reading, death is not only the end of life but is also figured (it is above all figured) in this internal hollowing out of language which only ever rests on so 'lawless and incertain' a base.

Measure for Measure has always called up an anxiety about representation or aesthetic form. Leavis himself was involved in a dispute about the play in the pages of the English literary journal *Scrutiny*, which tried in the

1930s and 40s to capture the very meaning of culture for the literary high ground.[22] Faced with that play by Shakespeare which Coleridge described as the 'most painful – say rather, the only painful' – part of his works, Leavis went to great lengths to establish the non-ambiguity of the work, the utter resolution of all its terms. To argue anything different, he wrote, would be to suggest that 'Shakespeare shows himself the victim of unresolved contradictions, of mental conflict, or uncertainty'.[23] The defence of Claudio's speech was made in the context of a critique of the equivalent speech by Beatrice in Shelley's *Cenci* ('nothing but wordy emotional generality'), as part of a demand, therefore, that language should always root itself in the particular if it is not to take off into an extravagant surplus of words.[24] Walter Pater also, in his essay on *Measure for Measure*, sees in the play a problem of aesthetic purpose, something lacking in the expected *finish*, while also arguing that the whole has the 'unity of a single scene'. For Pater, the tension of the writing leaves the reader suspended, looking out for the traces of the nobler hand which leaves 'its vestiges, as if accidentally or wastefully, in the rising of the style'.[25] In both cases, *Measure for Measure* threatens something by way of supplementarity, excess, or waste, throwing into question, if only momentarily, the critic's attempts to locate in Shakespeare – as the greatest of English writers – the self-fulfilment of aesthetic form. *Measure for Measure* shows the literary institution destabilized by too much play of the signifier, by something which is not containable finally by the necessary cohesion of high art.

   Neither death nor sexuality escape from these effects. (One could argue – psychoanalysis does argue – that they are in turn only ever produced by them.) In *Measure for Measure* the presence of both death and sexuality as the subjects of the drama constantly bind back the language into the apparent referentiality of theme. But they do so only partly, and only ever with momentary success. This binding back could also be described as one of the chief objectives of the State, which uses its measuring out of death and sexuality to blind its subjects to the arbitrary foundation of the law. 'Any statement of authority has no other guarantee than its very enunciation', writes Lacan, 'and when the Legislator (he who claims to lay down the Law) presents himself to fill the gap, he does so as an imposter.'[26] The State may constitute its deviants in order to legitimate its authority – there is no concept here of sexuality as inherently transgressive – but to make this important point (as Jonathan Dollimore does in his critique of a potentially Bakhtinian reading of the play[27]) runs the risk of setting up the State as the originator and arbiter of all the effects of the signifier itself. If the transgressors are products of the State's endless need for the renewal of its authority, the logic also works the other way around – transgression is an intrinsic property of the State.

Finally again on eros. It is of course the positive term of the binary I have operated with here. Separated from its opposite, it becomes the term of festivity, the celebration of humanness which, in conjunction with Shakespeare, becomes the celebration of a culture that knows its own endurance, its perpetually self-renewing worth. For that reason I have introduced the other concept of repetition that Freud located in the demonic insistence of the drive. And I have tried to describe the perversion of a language that would repress that demonism into the articulation of artistic form. Which is to say that the fiercest, and in some ways primary, repression aims not for eros, but for death. That repression, I would argue, has been carried out particularly fiercely in relation to Shakespeare, who has been required over and over again to bear the weight of a culture which continues to validate its objects, not wishing to see in them just one rendering of the precariousness (the imposture) of institutions, nor that of the subjects who recognize themselves in those institutions, nor that of the language through which all of this seems to be secured – above all, not wishing ever to see a possible end to our persistent validation of Shakespeare (and of course I have to include myself in that here), which would indeed signal for a whole literary establishment nothing short of a symbolic death.

NOTES

Originally presented at 'Shakespeare and Eros', Taormina Arts Festival, 1987, and published in *L'Eros in Shakespeare*, ed. Alessandro Serpieri and Keir Elam (Parma: Pratiche Editrice, 1988), pp. 29–46.

1 All references are to the Arden edition of *Measure for Measure*, ed. by J. W. Lever (London: Methuen, 1967).

2 Sigmund Freud, *Civilisation and its Discontents*, 1930 (1929), in *The Standard Edition of the Complete Psychological Works*, ed. and trans. James Strachey (London: Hogarth), vol. 21, p. 112.

3 Freud, *Beyond the Pleasure Principle*, 1920, in *Standard Edition*, vol. 18.

4 See Moustapha Safouan, *Echec du principe de plaisir* (Paris: Seuil, 1979), and Jacques Derrida, *La Carte postale, de Socrate à Freud et au delà* (Paris: Flammarion, 1980) trans. Alan Bass, *The Post Card* (Chicago: Chicago University Press, 1987).

5 Freud, *The Ego and the Id*, 1923, in *Standard Edition*, vol. 19, p. 45.

6 Barnaby Riche, *The Adventures of Brusanus, Prince of Hungaria*, 1592, in G. Bullough, *Narrative and Dramatic Sources of Shakespeare*, vol. 2 (London: Routledge and Kegan Paul; New York: Columbia University Press, 1968), p. 528.

7 Lever (ed.), *Measure for Measure*, pp. 60n., xciv.

8 Erasmus, *On Preparation for Death* trans. Jacob Henry Brooke Mountain, (London: Joseph Masters, 1866), p. 8.

9   Jacques Lacan, 'D'une question préliminaire à tout traite-
     ment possible de la psychose', in *Écrits* (Paris: Seuil,
     1966), p. 556; trans. Alan Sheridan, 'On a question pre-
     liminary to any possible treatment of psychosis', in *Écrits:
     A Selection* (London: Tavistock, 1977), p. 199.
10   I discuss this in 'Sexuality in the Reading of Shakespeare:
     "Hamlet" and "Measure for Measure" ' in *Alternative
     Shakespeares*, ed. John Drakakis, New Accents (London:
     Methuen, 1985), pp. 95–118.
11   Coverdale, *Treatise on Death*, in *Remains*, ed. Parker
     Society (Cambridge: Cambridge University Press, 1846),
     pp. 47–8.
12   See also Christopher Sutton, *Disce Mori (Learn to Die)*,
     reprinted from the first edition of 1600 (London: SPCK,
     1846); and William Caxton. *The Book of the Craft of
     Dying, and other early English Tracts Concerning Death*,
     ed. Frances M. M. Comper (London: Longmans, Green
     and Co., 1917); Lever gives a list of related works on
     p. lxxxvii of his Introduction to *Measure for Measure*.
13   Sister Mary Catherine O'Connor, *The Art of Dying Well*
     (New York: Columbia University Press, 1942), p. 5.
14   Erasmus, *On Preparation for Death*, p. 22.
15   Ibid., pp. 41, 61.
16   Lever, Introduction to *Measure for Measure*, pp. lxxxvii–
     lxxxviii.
17   Ibid., pp. lxxxviii, lxxx, xciv, lxxxviii.
18   T. W. Baldwin, *Shakespere's Smalle Latine and Lesse
     Greeke*, (Urbana, Ill. University of Illinois Press, 1944),
     vol. 2, ch. 33, 'The Rhetorical Training of Shakespeare:
     Tully's Rhetoric', p. 96.
19   Cicero, *Ad C. Herennium*, Loeb Classical Library (Lon-
     don: Heinemann; Cambridge, Mass.: Harvard University
     Press, 1956), pp. 108–9.
20   Baldwin, *Shakespere's Smalle Latine*, vol. 2, pp. 601–2.
21   F. R. Leavis, 'Shelley', in *Revaluation* (London: Chatto
     and Windus, 1959), p. 226.
22   L. C. Knights, 'The Ambiguity of "Measure for Meas-
     ure" ', *Scrutiny*, vol. 10, no. 3 (1942), pp. 222–33, and
     F. R. Leavis, 'The Greatness of "Measure for Measure" ',
     pp. 234–47. For a full historical account of *Scrutiny*, see

Francis Mulhern, *The Moment of 'Scrutiny'* (London: New Left Books/Verso, 1979).

23 Leavis, 'Greatness', p. 240.

24 Leavis, 'Shelley' p. 227.

25 Walter Pater, 'Measure for Measure', in *Appreciations* (London: Macmillan, 1922), p. 171.

26 J. Lacan, 'Subversion du sujet et dialectique du desir dans l'inconscient freudien', in *Écrits*, p. 813; trans. 'Subversion of the subject and dialectic of desire', in *Écrits: A Selection*, p. 311.

27 Jonathan Dollimore, 'Transgression and Surveillance in "Measure for Measure" ', in *Political Shakespeare, New Essays in Cultural Materialism*, ed. Jonathan Dollimore and Alan Sinfield (Manchester: Manchester University Press, 1985 pp. 72–87).

Part III Returning to Klein

5   Negativity in the Work of Melanie Klein

Analytic theory has treated the two instincts in an unusual manner: the libido is the first-born and privileged
child, the destructive instinct is the latecomer, the stepchild. Libido was recognised as such from the first; the
other instinct, its adversary, went under various dis-
guises, and had several names before its true identity was
established.

  Paula Heimann, *Freud – Klein Controversies 1941–45*

If we stick to Freud's elaborated categories . . . we are
able to conceive the primitive psychical make-up of an
infant and the elaborate organisation of an adult personality as a lawful continuity.

  Hedwig Hoffer, ibid.

For anyone attempting to follow the tracks of the psyche
across the terrain of contemporary political life, it is hard
to avoid Melanie Klein. The new brutalism of Thatcherism in the 1980s and the Gulf War, with its renewed and
absolute moral antinomies for the West, are just two
instances where some seemingly irreducible negativity,
bearer of a violence sanctioned – if only momentarily –
by State and subjects, appears to rise up to the surface
of political consciousness, setting the parameters of our
being-in-the-social, confronting us with something at

the limits of psyche and social alike. High priestess of psychic negativity, Melanie Klein pushed the institution of psychoanalysis in Britain – and, some would argue, her child patients – close to the edge. In the tradition of Freud, she saw her task as one of excavation, as the retrieval of something which even Freud, she argued, had barely been able to approach. Thus outmanoeuvring the father of psychoanalysis, while claiming her unswerving loyalty to and continuity with his project, she assigned to him as much the role of represser as uncoverer of the hidden repressed. And yet, in the recent and continuing turn to psychoanalysis in the humanities, Klein – compared with Freud – has received relatively little attention. Why, then, has there been no rereading of Melanie Klein?[1]

In the context of the humanities, the idea of rereading has become something of a commonplace. Without assuming that a writer has necessarily been read before, it refers instead to a strategy of reading which heads past the most immediate or professionally received meanings of the writer, straight for the points of creative tension in her or his works. This way of reading 'otherwise' is interested in the moments when writing slips its moorings, when it fails – as all writing must fail, it is suggested – its own tests of coherence, revealing – the analogy with analysis is intentional – its 'other' scene. In relation to psychoanalysis, this way of reading, often described as 'deconstructive', takes on a particular weight. Less interested in a general instability of language, it places itself instead *inside* the psychoanalytic project, aiming to demonstrate the triumph of the unconscious over all attempts at hermeneutic or therapeutic control. In a recent discussion on 'Melanie Klein Today', organized in London as part of a series aiming to promote dialogue between psychoanalysis in the clinic and psychoanalysis in the academy, Elizabeth Bott Spillius, editor of two volumes of contemporary analytic essays on Klein, argued that Klein was not a theorist in the strict sense of the term.[2] What happens if we read her comment not as a statement *against* theory, but as suggesting that Klein does theory *otherwise*, that Klein produced a theory which, because of what it was trying to theorize, could not, by definition, contain or delimit itself? Another way of putting this would be to ask whether Klein's writing is a monolithic, singular text; or, can she be read as producing in her writing something as intractable, as creatively unmasterable, as what many readers have become accustomed to discovering in Freud?

In the humanities, a post-Lacanian orthodoxy has blocked access to Klein. In a reading of which it should theoretically, according to its own tenets, be more suspicious, this orthodoxy has accused her of taking apart – but only to resolder more rigidly – body, psyche, and speech; it has imputed to her something of a psychic and sexual fix. Klein's ego is too coherent; it eventually takes all conflict and phantasy under its control. Her concept of the instinct is reductive; deriving all mental operations from biological impulses Klein leaves no gaps, no space for the trials and errors of representation, in the mind. Her account of sexuality is coercive; sexual difference, and hence heterosexuality, is given in advance by the knowledge which the bodies of girl- and boy-children are assumed, from the beginning, to have of themselves.[3] And yet, alongside these criticisms, we have to place the no less fervent rejection of Klein for proposing something so negative that it is incapable of assimilation by human subjects, by theory. Especially in the United States, Klein's work has been rejected on account of its violence and negativity. It is a critique which, as we will see, was at the centre of the fierce dispute which, in England too, was originally aroused by her work.

Far from offering reassurance, these reactions suggest, Melanie Klein disturbs. That disturbance, largely responsible for the rejection of Klein in analytic circles in the United States, has been mirrored in recent feminist debate. Searching for an alternative femininity free of the dictates of patriarchal, oedipal law, one feminism has turned to the preoedipal relation between mother and girl-child only to find Klein's account of early psychic processes standing in its way.[4] Too negative, this account blocks the new identification, troubles the ideal. Against the idyll of early fusion with the mother, Klein offers proximity as something which devours. Is there a way of linking the two criticisms – Klein as too safe and too dangerous, Klein as taking too much under, letting too much slip out of, control?

It is in the context of these issues that I want to return here to the earliest disagreement over Melanie Klein's work in England, which threatened to divide the psychoanalytic institution and has left its traces on the organization of the Institute of Psycho-Analysis to this day. The focus for this was the 'Controversial Discussions', relatively unknown outside analytic circles, which took place at the scientific meetings of the British Psycho-Analytic Society between 1943 and 1944, centring on the disagreement between Anna Freud and Melanie Klein. In this instance, the theoretical issue reveals itself unmistakably as an issue of the psychoanalytic institution and its continuity. As if in response to the dictates of unconscious time – amnesia as the first stage in allowing something to return – this moment of psychoanalytic history has gradually and recently come back to the fore of debate. In 1991, the full edition of the 'Controversial Discussions' was published as Volume 11 of the New Library of Psychoanalysis, a monumental feat of editing running to over 900 pages and including all the original papers and the ensuing debates (prior to this, only a selection of the papers had been available in a 1952 edition itself reprinted in 1989).[5] Articles have been written on the subject; two books have appeared on the institutional vicissitudes of psychoanalysis in Britain –

Freud in Exile and an anthology of articles *The British School of Psychoanalysis – The Independent Tradition* (the independents were those who chose to affiliate with neither party to the dispute).[6] Within feminism, a sometimes celebratory (Klein as 'mother' of a new second-generation psychoanalysis), sometimes critical (Klein as sexually normative) attention has produced something, if not quite, in the order of a 'return' to Melanie Klein.[7]

More oddly, this originating moment of local institutional dispute had its highly successful passage across the London stage. Nicholas Wright's play *Mrs Klein* played to packed houses in 1988 at the Cottesloe Theatre, and then transferred to the West End.[8] Vicariously, the play offers the spectacle of three women – Melanie Klein, her daughter Melitta Schmideberg, and Paula Heimann – battling it out over the legacy of Klein's work. Femininity becomes the site on which the vexed question of affiliation and institutional continuity is explored. It is a shocking play, not least of all, as one student commented, because of the terrible way analysts are seen to behave. Now this story of dreadful behaviour on the part of analysts has of course been told over and over again in relation to Freud; for some thinkers, it has become the key to the analytic institution itself (Roazen, Roustang, Derrida, Grosskurth[9]). But this has been seen to date as an affair strictly between men. The affair involved here, by contrast, is strictly between women, between mothers and daughters (literally and metaphorically), which might suggest another reason for looking at it again.

It is a point worth making in relation to a book like François Roustang's *Dire Mastery*, one of the more nuanced, less simply accusatory readings of the historic trials of psychoanalytic affiliation and descent. Roustang traces what he sees as the psychotic fantasies underpinning the institution and its (patri)lineage, and locates these fantasies on more than one occasion in an unconscious image of femininity which, he argues, that same institution refuses and on which it relies. Yet, he never makes the link from there to the work of Melanie Klein – theoretician of the psychotic in all of us and, together with Anna Freud, the first woman inheritor, contester, and transmitter of the legacy of Freud. When Jacques Derrida asks in a final essay in his book on Freud: 'Who will analyse the unanalysed of Freud?' ('*Qui paiera à qui la tranche de Freud?*'; more exactly, 'Who pays the price for the unanalysed slice of Freud?'), it is tempting to answer, 'Melanie Klein'.[10] Similarly, Julia Kristeva has argued that Freud's obsessional return to the oedipal narrative was a way of rationalizing his own more psychotic discovery of a negativity which he both theorized and effaced. Freud, she suggests, thus repeated in his own intellectual trajectory that process of flight from, disavowal, and semi-recognition of something murderous and unmanageable which, at the end of his life, he read in the story of Moses.[11] What all this points to is a residue – theoretical, institutional, sexual – of the Freudian institution, in which Melanie Klein, or more specifically the controversy over her work, occupies a crucial place.

Two issues arise centrally from this moment of analytic history, both with relevance for how we think about psyche and the social (the psyche as social) today. The final two essays in this book will address each of them in turn. First, the concept of psychic negativity in Klein: What is it? Is it an instinctual reductionism, with biology the final court of appeal for what is most troubling in the mind? Or is it something else, perhaps closer to, even if crucially distinct from, the negativity which Lacan places at the heart of subjectivity – not as instinctual deposit, but as the price that all human subjects pay for the cruel passage of the psyche into words? Secondly, what was at stake in the row over child analysis between Anna Freud and Melanie Klein? Central to the psychoanalytic institution is the problem of how to transmit knowledge of – which must mean educating – the unconscious without effacing the force of the unconscious as such. What happens when this problem turns into the question of whether one can, or indeed should, analyse a child? It is the point where the institution comes up against its own subjective origins, or rather the fantasy of its own origins, its own infancy – an infancy which, according to its own theories, it must both relinquish and repeat. It is also one of the points where the issue of power in the analytic scenario reveals itself most starkly, since the analyst's intervention in the mind of the child seems to be disputed according to the alternatives of education or violation, moral control or abuse. Clearly a matter of psycho-politics, because it touches on the limits of the psychoanalytic institution in its dealings with its own outside. But if the issue of psychic negativity can be included under the same heading, it is because it also seems to bring us up against a limit: the limit of what a society, of what a subject, can recognize of itself. It does so, however, in a way which is absolutely unassimilable to that idea of transgressive liberation which has been the most frequent radical political version of Freud (what would a 'liberation' of unconscious negativity mean?).

In the context of Klein's work, the dialogue between psychoanalysis and politics therefore shifts. As it does, we can see just how tightly the institutional and disciplinary boundaries and points of affiliation have recently and restrictively been drawn. Instead of the dialogue between psychoanalysis and literature or film, for example, we find psychoanalysis in confrontation with pedagogy and the law. Instead of the unconscious as the site of emancipatory pleasures, we find something negative, unavailable for celebration or release. One could argue that it has been too easy to politicize psychoanalysis as long as the structuring opposition has been situated between an over-controlling, self-deluded ego and the disruptive force of desire; that this opposition has veiled the more difficult antagonism between superego and unconscious, where what is hidden is aggression as much as sexuality, and the agent of repression is as ferocious as what it is trying to control. Much of the psycho-political colouring of the past decade suggests that the political import of psychoanalysis may reside in what it has to say about the passage across the social of thanatos as much as eros (not the unconscious which the social denies, but the unconscious which it sanctions and pursues). By seeing the unconscious as the site of sexual or verbal free fall, the humanities have aestheticized psychoanalysis, by-passing other points of (greater) friction, both internal to psychoanalytic thinking and in the historically attested confrontations between psychoanalysis and its outer bounds. Could it be that the humanities, inadvertently repeating a legacy of which they have been unaware, have, like psychoanalysis itself, preferred the 'legitimate heir' over the 'stepchild'?

The 'Controversial Discussions' were originally published in 1952 in a collection edited by Joan Rivière under the title *Developments in Psycho-Analysis* (Volume 43 of the Hogarth International Psycho-Analytical Library). The book included three of the original papers; 'The Nature and Function of Phantasy' by Susan Isaacs, 'Certain Functions of Introjection and Projection in Earliest Infancy' by Paula Heimann, and 'Regression' by Paula Heimann and Susan Isaacs. It also included an introduction by Rivière, additional papers by Heimann and Rivière, as well as four papers by Klein, including a revised version of the paper which she herself delivered to the scientific meetings in March 1944.[12] In what follows, I concentrate on the papers by Isaacs, Rivière, and Heimann. Apologias for, and defences of, Klein's work, they speak for Klein, although not in her voice, hovering in that hybrid space of identification where bodies and psyches at once recognize each other as separate and get too close (whether identification as incorporation necessarily destroys its object will be one of the issues of theoretical dispute). Less well known than Klein's own writings, these papers offer perhaps the clearest account in Kleinian writing of negativity in the process of emergence of the subject, as the passage through which subjects come to be. What is also remarkable about them is their degree of theoretical self-elaboration, or self-consciousness about theory, which means that they read very differently from that extraordinary direct lifting of theory out of the act of interpretation which more than one commentator has remarked on in relation to Klein.[13] Taken in conjunction with the responses now made available with the 1991 publication of the full text of the debates, these documents provide a unique opportunity to examine *in statu nascendi* the founding, theoretically, of a school. It should be stressed, then, that this is an analysis of one key moment of self-representation in a body of evolving thought, not an account of what Kleinianism has become, in theory and practice, today.

One reason for the self-elaboration of these papers is that they are presented, had to be presented, in terms of an argument for their own legitimacy, their right to contest areas of Freudian orthodoxy even as they claim to be developing from the true letter of his text. In Britain, Melanie Klein was to find herself at once the heiress and usurper of Freud – brought to England by Ernest Jones in 1926, twelve years before Freud himself arrived in 1938 accompanied by Anna Freud. Recently published correspondence shows Freud, long before his arrival, troubled by a number of Klein's theoretical innovations (on the superego, on the sexual development of the girl), but even more concerned about the critiques of his daughter by Klein and her supporters, which he took as a personal affront.[14] When Anna Freud arrived, therefore, she took up a position which was at once laid down – she was the daughter of the founding father of psycho-analysis – and occupied or contested in advance. Who, we might ask in this context, is the legitimate child?

It follows that Klein and her followers could only partially base their claims for authority on their fidelity to Freud. In his Preface to the 1952 collection, Ernest Jones writes: 'What is certainly illegitimate is the Pro-crustean principle of assessing all conclusions with those reached by Freud, however great our respect for the latter can and should be.'[15] Joan Rivière opens her General Introduction with this quotation from Freud: 'I have made many beginnings and thrown out many sug-gestions . . . I can hope that they have opened up a path to an important advance in our knowledge. Something will come of them in the future.'[16] Given what we know of Freud's vexed relation to filiation and legacy, we al-ready have to view this with caution, as something of a rhetorical strategy, a calling up of Freud against Freud. Freud is being invoked here as permitting – demanding even – a future for his discipline which goes beyond his own name (something of a self-cancelling proposition in itself). But it allows Rivière to argue that, while Freud's central discovery was the world of unconscious phant-asy, 'there are many problems to which he did not apply it', which have subsequently been brought nearer to a 'solution' by Klein ('her consistent awareness of its sig-nificance').[17] And she continues: 'The circumstances under which his work began and was carried through, i.e. its origin in medicine, no doubt affected his outlook,' leading him to concentrate on the differences between 'normal' and 'morbid' mentality at the expense of general laws and to an overestimation of the 'force of the reality principle'.[18]

The case for Melanie Klein rests, therefore, on this image of her as inheritor of the Freudian 'truth' (Rivière's word), one which the limits of Freud's own scientific training made him unable fully to pursue. What is already clear is that this truth, in the name of which Rivière speaks for Klein, does not belong to an order of scientifically verifiable knowledge. In the heat of the discussions, Susan Isaacs replies to her critics: 'Dr Friedlander refers to the fact that Mrs. Klein's views as to mental life is "inferred knowledge" as of course it is.'[19] Critiquing the Kleinian concept of phantasy, Marjorie Brierly states: 'if we persist in equating mental functions with our subjective interpretations of them, we forfeit our claim to be scientists and revert to the primitive [sic] state of the Chinese peasant who interprets an eclipse as the sun being swallowed by a dragon.'[20] To which Paula Heimann replies: 'The science of psychology is not to be equated with the science of astronomy. What *we* are studying is *not* the solar system, but the mind of the Chinese peasant, not the eclipse but the belief of the peasant concerning the eclipse. How do such beliefs arise? . . . And further, how does the knowledge that the sun is *not* swallowed by a dragon develop in the mind of peasants and philosophers?'[21] For Heimann, psychoanalysis makes no distinction between peasants and philosophers. The unconscious conditions of all knowledge and belief systems are what need to be explained. As Rivière later puts it, citing Bacon: 'There is a superstition in avoiding superstition.'[22] The dispute about the transmission of the Freudian legacy thus appears as a dispute about the possibility of objective knowledge and (thinly veiled behind the first) the scientific supremacy of the West.[23]

These, then, are the grounds of the first opposition to Klein; the second Rivière attributes to Klein's idea of a destructive instinct and a psychotic part in all human subjects: 'The concept of a destructive force within every individual, tending towards the annihilation of life, is naturally one which arouses extreme emotional resistance; and this, together with the inherent obscurity of its operation, has led to a marked neglect of it by many of Freud's followers, as compared with any other aspect of his work'; '[in] the very early phases of mental life . . . she finds in operation mental mechanisms (splitting, projection, etc.) closely similar to those of the psychotic disorders, another aspect of her work which arouses strong emotional resistance.'[24] Thus the argument about fidelity to, and divergence from, Freud carries the weight of psychosis and death – precisely the discoveries which Kristeva argued were rationalized by Freud. (Note too the link between destruction and obscurity as if destruction were conceivable only if it can be fully – scientifically – mastered or grasped.) It is, however, another classic rhetorical move, where opposition or resistance to a theory is seen to belong inside, or be tributary of, what it is that the theory itself invokes. But we should perhaps ask what a legacy can be in this context, how an institution can perpetuate itself, when what it offers as the true content of that legacy is death? Death, after all, as Paula Heimann puts it in her paper on introjection and projection, is the one thing which the mind cannot expel.[25] It is in this context with all its institutional ramifications, that the 'Controversial Discussions' offer their account of what is meant by the destructive impulse or the death instinct in the work of Melanie Klein.

The first thing that becomes clear is that the concept of the death instinct or impulse is in no sense a biologistic concept in the work of Klein.[26] It was the Anna Freudians who insisted on the biological status of the concept (the principle of conservation and the return to the inanimate state) in order precisely to keep it outside the range of analytic work. The objections to the centrality accorded to the concept by Klein rested, therefore, not on her biologizing of the concept (instinctual reductionism) but on the opposite, on the way she assigned to it psychic significance, made it part of the phantasy life of the child. Whether the child could inhabit a world of meanings would be another central issue in the dispute over Klein's work. To site Isaacs: 'The word "phantasy" serves to remind us always of this distinctive character of meaning in mental life'; Michael Balint: ' "Phantasy" suggests "meaning" '; Barbara Lantos: 'This pleasure we call auto-erotic . . . organ pleasure . . . and intellectual pleasure – they all are the same in so far as they are pleasures in themselves, that is to say: pleasures without meaning'; Edward Glover: 'And so we come back once more to the dispute over "meaning" and "implicit meaning".'[27]

Death for Klein was *meaning*, which also meant that death *had* meaning for the infant. When Freud argues that the infant could have no knowledge of death, this does not preclude the possibility, Rivière argues, that the child 'can experience feelings of the kind, just as any adult can feel "like death", and in a state of great anxiety often does'.[28] What seems to be going on here, if we look closely at the passage, is not an undiluted appeal to feeling, but rather the suggestion that feeling itself is simile ('feel "*like* death" '), that the most severe anxiety the child can feel opens up the path of indirect representation by putting it at a fundamental, at *the* most fundamental, remove from itself. Thus the child's anxiety becomes the foundation for the first experience of 'as if': 'We surmise that the *child feels as if* '; ' "He behaves as if", to my mind, is the same thing as saying "He has phantasies . . .".'[29]

It is this fundamental negativity which these papers put at the basis of subjectivity. This is a moment of infancy when, if an ego can be postulated, its powers to integrate mental processes are weak. The problem for Klein's critics was that conflict was seen to arise before there was an ego there to manage it: 'According to the theory of the English school of analysis, introjection and projection, which in our view should be assigned to the period after the ego has been differentiated from the outside world, are the very processes by which the structure of the ego is developed.'[30] Edward Glover, in his long critique of Klein published in the first volume of *The Psychoanalytic Study of the Child* in 1945 argued that, unlike the customary teaching which overestimates the primitive ego, there is an underestimation of the primitive ego in Klein.[31] Two common recent theoretical assumptions about Klein therefore fall to the ground: her biologism and the pre-given category of the ego. If Klein was objected to, it was precisely because she was seen as bringing the death drive under the sway of a subject, as making the death drive constitutive of a subject, who is not yet enough of a subject for death to be mastered or controlled.

The third point of dispute was the early relation to the object (these are the three basic points of disagreement which Rivière lists in her Introduction). For the Anna Freudians, the infant – again posited in essentially biological terms – is narcissistic and auto-erotic, pure pleasure-seeker under the sway of the erotogenic zones. One way of describing the Freudian position, then, would be as a plea to keep pleasure out of the reach of meaning, to leave pleasure *alone*: 'Does Isaacs think – as we do – that there are activities just carried out for the sake of auto-erotic pleasure without any phantasies being attached to them . . . just for the sake of the organ-pleasure which is gained?'[32] For the Kleinians, the child relates to the object from the start, meaning not that the child has some inherent capacity for relatedness, the version of object-relations which has become best known, but that even in the state of auto-eroticism there are bits and pieces of objects – fragments of introjects, objects that are not quite objects – inside the mind. Objects without propriety, neither fully appropriated nor whole: 'Miss Freud speaks of object relationship "in the proper sense". I do not think there is a "proper" sense.'[33]

No ownership, therefore, and no agent of control. At each stage, the infant and its world seem to emerge *in absentia, or at a loss*. It is by withholding that the external world comes to be. Rivière writes: 'painful experience does much to bring about the recognition of an external object.'[34] The infant oscillates between 'seeking, finding, obtaining, possessing with satisfaction' and 'losing, lacking, missing, with fear and distress'.[35] In this scenario, and despite references to satisfaction obtained, the emphasis is far more frequently on the negative pole. For the loss of the object forces a breach in the primitive narcissism of the subject, a breach which, in a twist, then produces the object as its effect: 'the ego's need to dissociate itself from the unpleasure is so great that it *requires an object* upon which it can expel it . . . For such an experience of unpleasure is too intense to be merely "killed", hallucinated as non-existent. Narcissistic phantasy would thus in itself lead to object-relations, and these object-relations will at first be of a negative order.'[36] Note again that reference to death in the instigation of the object, an experience of unpleasure so intense that it cannot be 'killed', cannot be negatively hallucinated. And note too how different this is from the more familiar idea of hallucination ('narcissistic phenomenon *par excellence*'[37]) – not in this case something desired, but something instead which fails to be effaced. The lost object is not, therefore, only the hallucinated object of satisfaction; it is also and simultaneously an object which, because of this failure of negative hallucination, is required – is actively sought after – *in order to be bad*. In these papers from the 'Controversial Discussions', the genesis of the famous Kleinian bad object is nothing less than the genesis of the object itself.

Rivière will qualify her account in her 1950 footnotes to her essay: 'The view that the earliest relation was negative and hostile was expressed by Freud. Later work leads to a correction of this hypothesis', referring to two

later papers by Klein included in the 1952 collection;
and in her Introduction to the book: 'it will be seen from
Chapters VI and VII that this is not Melanie Klein's
view.'[38] Likewise she will answer those who objected to
the weakness of the Kleinian ego by insisting on its
integrative powers. But in the overall context and feel of
the papers, these qualifications sit oddly – symptomatic
presence of something which it became too difficult to
sustain? Another way of putting this would be to ask how
an unconscious identification with death *could* – theoretically, institutionally – be sustained. This would be just
one way of reading the editing, the start of a theoretical
shift between the original discussions and the 1952 publication of the book.

In these earlier papers, it is stated over and over that
the subject first comes to experience itself negatively.
Self-alienation gives the colour of the subject's coming-
to-be: 'nothing good within *lasts* . . . the first conscious
idea of "me" is largely coloured by painful associations';
'It would seem with every infant that we have to give far
more experimental weight to the felt hostility of the
external world over a considerable period in early development than we had thought'; 'the relation of hate to objects
is older than that of love.'[39] The persecutory object-
relation rises up as the first defence against something
without 'definite name and shape' (like the patient Klein
describes in *Narrative of a Child Analysis* who dreamt of an
'indefinite object' stuck to a car, something which 'she
both wished to see and not to see'[40]). Object-relations
are 'improvements on' and 'protections against' primordial narcissistic anxiety; distrust of the object is better
than despair.[41]

More than primitive instinct, therefore, the Kleinian
concept of negativity appears as a psychic activation of
the *fort-da* game as famously described by Freud, an
answer of a sort to this question which, as Klein and
Heimann both point out, was left in suspense by Freud:

'When does separation from an object produce anxiety, when does it produce mourning and when does it produce pain? Let me say at once that there is no prospect in sight of answering these questions.'[42] Freud did not believe that absence of the mother could be connoted as loss of love or anger, whereas for Klein the mother rapidly comes to be experienced as bad. 'This fundamental fear of loss of the loved object', Klein states, 'seems to me psychologically well-founded' – 'predetermined, one may say, in the infant from the experience of birth'.[43]

It is at this point that the account offered here of psychic beginnings starts to sound uncannily like that of Jacques Lacan; so it is perhaps not surprising to discover Klein and Lacan converging on Freud's paper on 'Negation' (the link is not wholly coincidental, since this was the time when Lacan was working on his never to be completed translation of Klein).[44] 'Negation' was the key text for Rivière, Isaacs, and Heimann, who took it as the model for their theory of the subject's relation to its object-world.[45] Given the awkwardness as we have seen it of their relation to Freud's legacy, the terms with which Rivière declares this affiliation are at least worthy of note: 'one of the richest and most highly condensed productions that he ever composed . . . Melanie Klein's theories dovetail with exquisite precision into its tight and rigorous propositions.'[46] Easy or forced entry? What more fitting image for an intimacy uncertain of the legitimacy of its own claims. As if it were being acknowledged that the only passage for these doubtful inheritors was to come up on Freud from behind (sphincter theory, we might say).

The problem of beginnings, it would seem, is at least partly tributary to the problem of descent. What 'Negation' offers is a way of theorizing a subject who comes into being on the back of a repudiation, who exists in direct proportion to what it cannot *let be*. If there is no presupposed category of the subject in Kleinian theory, then the subject can emerge only in a moment of self-differentiation, as a difference from itself: 'when exactly does the ego, the differentiation from the amorphous id, begin?'[47] It is through the category of negation, the category in which Lacan locates the fundamental negativity of the symbolic function, that Klein and her followers find the reply. Let's consider first what Lacan reads in this famous – and famously cryptic – text by Freud.

Lacan's discussion of Freud's article takes up three chapters of the full version of his 1966 *Écrits* – an analysis by the Hegelian scholar Jean Hyppolite with an introduction and commentary by Lacan.[48] All three were originally part of Lacan's first seminar of 1954 on the technical writings of Freud[49] – the only works by Freud, interestingly, not included in the Pelican Freud, a comment in itself on the severance between psychoanalysis as clinical and as wider cultural discourse in Great Britain today. Hyppolite focuses on this sentence from the end of Freud's paper: 'Affirmation – as a substitute (*Ersatz*) for uniting – belongs to Eros; negation – the successor (*Nachfolge*) to expulsion – belongs to the instinct of destruction (*Destruktionstrieb*).'[50] He reads in Freud's distinction between 'substitute' (or 'equivalent') and 'successor' a crucial difference in the way affirmation and negation relate to the instincts from which they are said to derive. For Hyppolite that 'successor' (as opposed to 'equivalent') opens up a gap between negation and destruction; they are precisely not equivalents, not the same thing. Hence, he argues, we can read in Freud two concepts of negation: on the one hand, a pleasure of denying which results simply from the suppression of the libidinal components under the domination of the instincts – this already suggests, in a way that troubles some cherished boundaries, that the instinct of destruction is attached to the pleasure principle (Riviere: 'many psychic manifestations show that a threat from the death instinct produces a strong uprush of Eros'[51]) – and, on the other, negation as the basis of the symbolic function: 'a fundamental attitude of symbolicity (symbol-making capacity) made explicit'.[52] What Freud's article shows is that this capacity emerges in a 'space of suspension', from a 'margin of thinking' where thinking – and being – can only emerge through what they relegate to non-being, to the not-thought: 'what one is in the mode of *not* being it'.[53]

It is this second emphasis which is picked up by Lacan: 'negativity of discourse, insofar as it brings what is not into being, sends us back to the question of what non-being, manifested in the symbolic order, owes to the reality of death.'[54] Negation, for Lacan, is death in the structure, or what he also calls the 'real', which, for symbolization to be possible, has to subsist outside its domain. Negation shows the subject, and its world, arising in an act of demolition. For the subject to enter into the possibilities of language and judgement, something has to be discarded, something falls away. For Lacan, therefore, negativity resides on the edge of speech. In an account which is strikingly resonant of this vision, Ella Sharpe reinterprets Melanie Klein: '[the breasts] become the symbol of that undecomposed world which was once the baby's before knowledge entered to start him on the path of detachment.'[55] Knowledge, as much as – inseparably from? – aggression, breaks up the unity of the world. We could say that Lacan goes furthest in detaching negation from the destructive impulse – 'successor' precisely, but not 'equivalent' – because the moment of negation posits the end of equivalence, the end of unity, as such. As Hyppolite puts it: 'primordial affirmation is nothing other than to affirm, but to deny is more than to want to destroy.'[56] For those accustomed to reading Freud in terms of the concept of 'after-effect' (*Nachtraglichkeit*), it is easy to read in that *Nachfolge* or 'following after' the idea that what precedes has not necessarily come before.

In this commentary by Lacan, the reference to Melanie Klein, moreover, is explicit. A discussion of

Klein's 1930 paper on symbol formation ('The Importance of Symbol-Formation in the Development of the
Ego') follows immediately after Hyppolite's commentary
when it was originally presented to Lacan's seminar in
1954, and the discussion ends with a link between Hyppolite and Klein for what they each demonstrate regarding 'the function of destructionism in the constitution of
human reality'.[57] In his reply to Hyppolite, Lacan makes
a passing reference to a paper by Melitta Schmideberg,
identifying her as the first analyst of a patient of Ernest
Kris whose acting out of a prematurely cut short orality
might explain, he suggests, the relative failure of that
earlier analysis with Schmideberg.[58] Thus Lacan's commentary on Freud's 'Negation' leads, in a beautiful circularity, back to Melanie Klein.

In fact, the reference to Schmideberg could be seen
as the vanishing-point of Lacan's commentary, as well
as of the history and theory being discussed here – a part
of analytic literature which, as Lacan says, has 'unfortun-
ately become very difficult of access',[59] and an orality em-
bedded somewhere in a paper by an analyst, the daughter
of Melanie Klein, who, one could argue, as an effect of
its unbearable intensity, its acting out inside the analytic
institution, will finally reject all such concepts and sever
her links with the pychoanalytic world. Ella Sharpe: 'I
assume hopefully a possibility of discussing Mrs. Klein's
theory, of being critical in the constructive meaning of
that word, of accepting some things without its being
interpreted that one has swallowed Mrs. Klein and her
work whole.'[60]

It is through orality that Isaacs and Heimann read
Freud's paper on 'Negation'. For them, this is the key
passage:

> Expressed in the language of the oldest – the oral –
> instinctual impulses (*Triebregungen* – impulses of the
> drives), the judgement is: 'I should like to eat this', or

'I should like to spit it out'; and, put more generally: 'I should like to take this into myself and keep that out.'

That is to say: 'It shall be inside me' or 'it shall be outside me'. As I have shown elsewhere, the original pleasure-ego wants to introject into itself everything that is good and to eject from itself everything that is bad. What is bad, what is alien to the ego and what is external are, to begin with, identical.[61]

For Isaacs what this passage reveals is that the function of judgement is derived from the primary instinctual impulses. This is the famous 'instinctual reductionism' for which Klein is often criticized.[62] Indeed, Isaacs stresses the concept of derivation, and dismisses Freud's phrase 'expressed in the language of the oral impulses' as 'picturesque'.[63] But, as her commentary on this passage makes clear, it is the mechanisms of introjection and projection which are crucial, and the role of phantasy as the operational link between the two, 'the means by which the one is transmuted into the other': ' "I want to eat that and therefore I have eaten it" is the phantasy which represents the id impulse in the psychic life; it is at the same time the subjective *experience* of the mechanism or process of introjection,' an interpretation in turn, therefore, of the symbolic process of taking in.[64] Judgement devours and expels its objects: it derives from an orality which in turn becomes a metaphor for judgement itself. This, as I read it, is less derivation than circularity: 'one of the "results of the phantasy of introjection" is the process of introjection.'[65] No less than Lacan's commentary, which turns on the concept of foreclosure, the ability of the psyche under pressure of denial to wipe something out, this is a process which can have as its logical outcome the effacement, or scotomization, of the world:

the mechanism of denial is expressed in the mind of the subject in some such way as 'If I don't admit it [i.e. a painful fact] it isn't true.' Or: 'If I don't admit it, no one else will know that it is true.' And in the last resort this argument can be traced to bodily impulses and phantasies, such as: 'If it doesn't come out of my mouth, that shows it isn't inside me'; or 'I can prevent anyone else *knowing* it is inside me'. Or: 'It is all right if it comes out of my anus as flatus or faeces, but it mustn't come out of my mouth as words.' The mechanism of *scotomisation* is experienced in such terms as: 'What I don't see I need not believe'; or 'What I don't see, other people don't, and indeed doesn't exist.'[66]

What is striking about this passage is the way it seems to undermine the very causal sequence from which it claims to derive. For, if the body can become a mechanism of disavowal for language ('it is all right if it comes out of my body as flatus or faeces, but it mustn't come out of my mouth as words'), then the body is already being inscribed in a linguistic process, is being called up as metaphor even as it is metaphor – the passage of bodily process into language – that the subject resists. So the more Isaacs carries out her derivation of phantasy from impulse, the more the impulse becomes after the fact ('successor' we might say) the metaphoric correlate of the phantasy it supports. Thus the Kleinians flesh out the structure of negation. At one level it is without doubt a more literally – vulgarly – corporeal reading than that of Lacan; but no more than his can it guarantee the reality of the world which it constitutes but can equally efface. Orality appears here as the transcription or metaphor of itself. What primacy is being given here to the concept of the impulse – 'mythological beings superb in their indefiniteness' as Heimann and Isaacs put it, citing a famous remark of Freud's?[67]

It is, I think, worth stressing this question of transcription because, in relation to Klein, it is most often misread. Thus Nicolas Abraham and Maria Torok criticize what they call Klein's 'panfantastic instinctualism'; while

Jean Laplanche and J. B. Pontalis takes Isaacs's definition of phantasy as the 'mental expression' of the impulse as evidence of a potential reductionism in Klein,
one which Klein herself resisted but which has been
exacerbated by other interpreters and followers of her
work.[68] In her Introduction to the 1952 collection, Rivière cites Isaacs's definition together with the lines from
Freud on which it is based: 'Freud said: "We suppose
that it [the id] is somewhere in direct contact with somatic
processes and takes over from them instinctual needs
and gives them mental expression." Now in the view of
the present writers, this *mental expression is* unconscious
phantasy.' But, Rivière continues, the passage goes on:
'There is no impulse, no instinctual urge or response
which is not experienced as unconscious phantasy.'[69]
The two propositions are clearly not symmetrical: to say
that one thing is the *expression of* another is not the same
thing as to say that one thing *has to find another* in terms
of which it can be expressed. As Isaacs summarized in
her original paper, 'instinctual urges . . . cannot operate
in the mind without phantasy.'[70] The second implies
translation, mediation, or, as Isaacs puts it, 'operative
link'; that is, it implies interpretation, or rather mis-
interpretation, the word used explicitly by Rivière: 'on
Freud's own hypothesis, the psyche responds to the reality
of its experiences by interpreting them – or rather *mis*-
interpreting them – in a subjective manner.'[71] Subjective
experience involves the child in perpetual misreadings of
the world: '[the child's] misunderstanding of the situation is precisely that subjective interpretation of his
perception.'[72]

Phantasies, Isaacs writes, are the 'expression of wishes
and passions': 'It is primarily because he *wants* his urine
to be so very powerful that he comes to believe it is so.'[73]
The destructive impulse therefore turns on a tautology –
destructive because of the omnipotence with which the
child wields and translates it to or her or his own ends.

This is the impulse 'pressed into the service of need' of phantasy, to use Riviere's expression, far more than phantasy as the 'mental expression of' instinctual need;[74] not a reduction of phantasy to a biological instinct, but a massive inflation of the power of phantasy to make, and break, the world.

What emerges most strongly from these papers is the impossibility of assigning some simple origin to destruction. Hate may be older than love, but Melanie Klein's conclusions: 'do not stand or fall on the concept of the death instinct.'[75] What seems to be outrageous – paradoxically harder to manage than death as a pure force, as something which assaults the subject from outside – is this internalization of death into the structure. If death is a pure point of biological origin, then at least it can be scientifically known. But if it enters into the process of psychic meanings, inseparable from the mechanisms through which subjects create and recreate their vision of the world, then from where can we gain the detachment with which to get it under control?

It is clear that for the critics of Klein and her supporters, it was the priority accorded to subjective experience and the implications of this for knowledge which was at stake. (Recently Meltzer has suggested that this is *the* philosophical problem posed by Klein.[76]) Klein, Isaacs, and Heimann were confusing 'the mental corollary to instinct' with 'what we are used to call phantasy', subjective definition with mental mechanism – 'The mixing-up of conceptions impresses all of us as most undesirable'; 'What happens when the distinction is lost?'[77] Each time, Isaacs and Heimann respond by insisting on the impossibility, within the logic proper to psychoanalysis, of holding the elements apart: '*What I believe is that reality-thinking cannot operate without concurrent and supporting Ucs phantasies*' (emphasis original); 'A rigid separation between "mechanism" and "content" is a danger to psychological understanding . . . it springs from a basic fallacy: a rigid divorce between the id and the ego'; 'perception and image-formation cannot be sharply separated from unconscious phantasy'; 'the suggestion that we should discuss "the nature of the process itself" rather than its content seems to rest on a false assumption. The nature of mental process, as well as of the structure and mechanisms of the mind, is partly determined and characterised by phantasies, that is to say, by the subjective content of the mind.'[78] Compare Anna Freud from her 1945 paper 'Indications for Child Analysis': 'All through childhood a ripening process is at work which, in the service of an increasingly better knowledge of and adaptation to reality, aims at perfecting these functions, at rendering them *more and more independent of the emotions until they become as accurate and reliable as any non-human mechanical apparatus*' (my emphasis).[79]

What seems to be involved, therefore, is something in the nature of a boundary, or category, dispute. How much is subjective experience allowed to *take in* (can the category of cats be a member of itself)? Marjorie Brierly proposes that 'introjection' be kept as the term for the mental process, 'incorporation' for the experience of taking things in: 'When the baby is trying to put everything into its mouth, it comes across many things that won't go in. Image formation as a function of mind will not go in to incorporation.'[80] To which Heimann replies: 'Mentally, anything can go into anything.'[81] But if anything can go into anything – both mentally and theoretically – then what is there to distinguish psychoanalysis, as a form of mental activity, from the all-devouring, all-incorporating child?

Or, to put it another way, what is left of identity and its (self-)definition if these distinctions cannot be sustained? If incorporation cannot be distinguished from introjection, or introjection from identification (as Sharpe points out, Freud often blurred the distinction between the two), then the idea of identity as distinct from, even if created through, its objects becomes unclear. How can incorporation be the foundation of identity when it seems to imply as a concept a dissolution of the separateness on which identity relies?[82] The issue here is not whether these distinctions can, or cannot, be theoretically mounted, but the form of loss that seems to threaten when they fail. What do these uncertainties imply for an adult subject (an adult science)?

Brierly makes it explicit that the distinction between subjectivity and mechanism carries with it the distinction between first and third person, between identification and object-relationship, between knowledge and science.[83] If psychoanalysis cannot distinguish between knowledge and phantasy, it becomes an infant incapable of taking its measure of reality, incapable of stepping out into the world. So when Glover insults his adversaries – accusing, for example, Klein of projecting into children, Heimann of playing with Freud's theories like a 'kitten plays with a ball of wool' – I read this as more than personally symptomatic.[84] He has, like others of Klein's critics, spotted one of the most far-reaching and troubling implications of her theories: not just the point convincingly made by many recent commentators of Freud – that psychoanalysis can be only a speculative form of knowledge, that it must, if it is to remain loyal to its object, undo its claims to authority as it goes[85] – but that, in relation to the project of child analysis, that same undoing propels the analyst *and her theories* back into the realm of the child. Psychoanalysis cannot ignore, cannot separate itself from, the unconscious conditions of knowledge. Could it be the force of this recognition during the 'Controversial Discussions' that led, in reaction, to what today is often seen as the opposite – the rigidity of Kleinian interpretation, the fierceness with which Kleinian thinking now lays claim to its status as science? Walter Schmideberg: 'I listened to [the papers] in silence and some of them made me think that the accusations of our enemies that it is impossible to distinguish between the phantasies of the patients and those of the analyst contained more than a grain of truth'; Karin Stephen: 'Do we really know what we are doing?'[86] What happens if we read this as the insight and not the failure of the dispute?

Clearly, then, it is the status of psychoanalysis as scientific knowledge which is at stake – what might be called its coming of age. Is psychoanalysis an adult science? Do children develop from point A to point B, or do they evolve according to a different sequence, one which throws into crisis our idea of what a sequence should be? Thus the question of development arises logically out of the question of knowledge and science. It is, writes Brierly, 'to put the cart before the horse' if you make introjection, based on bodily behaviour, responsible for image formation.[87] If mental mechanisms are partly determined by phantasy, then 'expressed in theoretical terms this would mean that the end results of mental processes determine the processes themselves which is absurd'.[88] Complicated emotional attitudes are assumed to be in existence before instinctual urges; the infant interprets its experience in terms of a superego not yet in force: 'Coming events cast their shadow before.'[89] What has happened to sequence and causality? What priority – theoretically – is being given to unconscious time?

Once again the theoretical point takes its colour from the psychic processes being described. What Brierly and Glover have identified is that Klein's account of beginnings, of the infant's first being in the world, inaugurates circular rather than sequential time. This is how Rivière describes the 'vicious circle' which is the child's first apprehension of cause and effect: ' "You don't come and help, and you hate me, because I am angry and devour you; yet I *must* hate you and devour you in order to make you help." '[90] The child is caught in an impasse, 'the fear of destroying the mother in the very act of expressing love for her' and of 'losing her in the very process designed to secure her possession'.[91] Incorporation does not only take everything in; it also abolishes its object. If we go back to those moments of primordial absence and negation and put them together, we can watch this scenario emerge. What is lost is a persecutor; the only way of being of the object is as something devoured or expelled; the lost object is bad *because* the only way of being the object is as something devoured or expelled. If this is a vicious circle, it is also, in these early papers, a process without end; inherently contradictory, these mechanisms serve the very impulses against which they defend, and they founder on the 'problem of preservation' as emptiness, aggression, and sadistic impulses all return: 'The omnipotence of phantasy is a weapon which cuts both ways.'[92] Similarly, what is seen to resolve the cycle belongs no less in circular time: 'Here we have a benign circle.'[93]

One of the most interesting things about these papers, therefore, is that they lay out so clearly the problem of generating an account of positive development out of the processes they have described – positive as in psychic, positive as in linear time. Not that Klein does not add, as Rivière insists, a new emphasis on the mother as good object, on the early love relation, on the depressive phase in which the child takes everything back (as opposed to 'in') and subjects it to a meticulous and loving repair. 'Even during the earliest stage,' Klein writes, 'persecutory anxiety is to some extent counteracted by the experience of the good breast.'[94] And yet, even inside this account (and on the same page), the experience of gratification turns into idealization, which then sets up the object as 'perfect, inexhaustible, always available, always gratifying'.[95] As Klein puts it in the discussion following her paper in 1944: 'Even when the feeding situation is satisfactory, hunger and the craving for libidinal gratification stir and reinforce the destructive impulses';[96] and again in an earlier paper: 'some measure of frustration is inevitable . . . what the infant actually *desires* is unlimited gratification.'[97] Gratification therefore sets up the terms of its own demise. Or, where it repairs, it also repeats: 'The experience of gratification at the mother's breast after frustration' develops the infant's confidence that 'bad things go and good things come'[98]; it enters into the logic of explusion and projection that it is also intended to subdue.

Klein's contribution to the debate can be read at least partly as a reaffirmation of love against what has come before. But this love, she insists, is complex; it is not a value or thing in itself. If it is present from the earliest stages, it none the less comes at least partly in reply to the mother's demand ('an infant knows intuitively that his smile and other signs of affection and happiness produce happiness and pleasure in the mother'); turning on her pleasure, it seeks out her desires and her words. Klein provides a graphic image of this early relation in the five-month-old patient who put his fingers in Klein's mouth in 'an attempt to fetch the sounds out' (introjection, as Lacan would put it, as 'always introjection of the speech of the other').[99] These feelings, Klein states in reply to Brierly, are not a 'primary simple affect'.[100]

Likewise, reparation can reinforce omnipotence. (Although Klein herself had insisted on the distinction from 1935, one point of dispute was whether it simply derived from Freud's concept of reaction formation and obsessional undoing.[101]) In these discussions the concept of reparation appears less as a part of a naturally evolving development, more as a *requirement*, something enjoined – internally and externally – on the child. It is, in fact, striking the way it appears as a concept in the imperative mode: 'The objects within, feelings about people *must* be put right'; 'The external objects, real parents, brothers and sisters and so on, *must* be pleased and made happy'; 'the full internalisation of real persons as helpful loved figures *necessitates* abandoning this defence-method of splitting feelings and objects into good and bad'; 'good and bad feelings *have to be* tolerated at one and the same time.'[102] Manifestly replying to criticisms from the earlier debate, Rivière states: 'The significance of the phantasies of reparation is perhaps the most essential aspect of Melanie Klein's work; for that reason her contribution to psycho-analysis *should not be* regarded as limited to the exploration of the aggressive impulses and phantasies.'[103]

To what *necessity* we might ask – theoretical and institutional as well as psychic – does the concept of reparation correspond? Two recent Kleinian commentators have described the development of the concept as something of a mystery in Klein's work. For Meltzer, at the point where Klein starts to distinguish between manic reparation 'as defence against persecutory or depressive anxiety' and 'something more genuinely in the service of the objects', it begins to take on a 'more mysterious meaning'; in the discussion cited at the start of this chapter, Elizabeth Bott-Spillius described as 'mysterious' the shift of attention from sadism to love in Klein's later work: 'I don't know where it came from.'[104] It is as if reparation can theorize itself only as absolute necessity and/or absolute unknown. What these papers suggest is that reparation cannot be detached from the issue of knowledge. Indeed, one might say that, as psychic process, reparation requires a suspension of absolute knowledge if it is not to turn into pure omnipotent defence. It is not, therefore, to deny the validity of the experience of reparation to note that it has often come to serve in the Kleinian corpus as a solution to difficulties – of negativity, causality, and knowledge – which, in this earlier debate, seem to be without end. The point is made, although from very different perspectives, by both Glover and Lacan.

For it is central to Kleinian theory that the anxiety which leads to fixation and regression in both sexes also plays its part in precipitating the libido on its forward path: 'each of the fixations and pathological symptoms apt to appear at successive stages of development have both a retrogressive and progressive function, binding anxiety and thus making further development possible.'[105] Which is to say that development is in some sense pathological – Heimann calls this the 'negative aspect of progression'.[106] Klein herself states repeatedly, with reference to the depressive position, that each step in unification leads to a renewed splitting of the imagos – of necessity, since the depressive position genetically derives from the paranoid state that it is meant to surpass. What Heimann and Isaacs refer to as a 'benign circle' follows the same logic: 'These ego achievements . . . are prime factors in the fight against anxiety and guilt. A certain degree and quality of guilt and anxiety stimulate reparation and thus encourage sublimation.'[107]

Thus, when Isaacs writes, *'the established principle of genetic continuity is a concrete instrument of knowledge'* (emphasis original), 'the essence of Freud's theory lies in just this fact of detailed continuity', this is not a developmental paradigm in any straightforward sense.[108] The movement is constantly in two directions – progression being constantly threatened by the mechanisms which move it on. Hence the well-known paradox that, in Klein's account, homosexuality arises out of the anxieties of heterosexual phantasy; that if heterosexuality is somewhere pre-established for the subject, it is so only as part of an unmanageable set of phantasies which are in fact incapable, in the theory, of ensuring heterosexuality itself.[109] As much as the idea of a developmental sequence, this could be argued to be the logic proper to Kleinian thought: 'Anxiety and guilt at times check and at other times enhance the libidinal development'; 'while in some ways these defences impede the path of integration, they are essential for the whole development of the ego.'[110] Thus, as Lacan points out in his commentary on Klein's paper on symbol formation, the ego appears twice over and in the space of a single sentence as precocious or overdeveloped and as what, through its weakness, is preventing normal development from taking place: 'The early operation of the reactions originating on the genital level was the result of premature ego development, but further ego development was only inhibited by it' (Lacan: 'She says that the ego was over precociously developed . . . and then in the second part of the sentence that it is the ego which is preventing development from taking place').[111]

Too much and too little of an ego whose role it is to master the anxiety out of which it has itself been produced. Anna Freud objects: 'According to the theory of the English school of analysis, introjection and projection, which in our view should be assigned to the period after the ego has been differentiated from the outside world, are the very processes by which the structure of the ego is developed.'[112] Only if the ego comes first is development assured. Those who criticize Klein for developmental normativity (the idea that subjects progress naturally to their heterosexual goals) would do well to note that, at least as much as regards Freud's own normative moments, it is not in these terms that Klein's writings can theoretically sustain themselves.[113] The value of the stress on negativity would then reside in the trouble it poses to the concept of a sequence, the way that it acts as a bar, one could say, to what might elsewhere (and increasingly) appear as normative and prescriptive in the work and followers of Melanie Klein.

For Glover, in his long critique of Klein, a central problem – if not *the* central problem – was that 'the author cannot tell a developmental story straight'.[114] (For those in the humanities seeking after the trials of writing, this would be the ultimate accolade.) The 'subversive nature' of Heimann and Isaacs's paper on 'Regression' is precisely that 'if fixation can be regarded as a reaction to (result of) regression and if regression itself works backwards through a developmental aggression series, it follows that progression must be attributed to the same factors'.[115] For Glover, this is to undermine – or deviate from – the 'biological progression of an instinct-series' – that is, the whole conception of libidinal development as laid down by Freud: 'It subverts all our concepts of progressive mental development.'[116] Only 'if we stick to Freud's elaborated categories', writes Hoffer, are we 'able to conceive the primitive psychical make-up of an infant and the elaborate organisation of an adult personality as a *lawful continuity*'.[117] Thus Melanie Klein, in the eyes of her critics, theoretically disinherits herself.

The objections to these papers thus make it clear that the emphasis on negativity operates not as a primordial, biological pre-given from which an orderly sequence ('an orderly series and correlations') can be derived, but as the subversion of sequence and biology alike. And Glover is explicit that this subversion is the direct consequence of the emphasis on phantasy in the work of Klein. It is at that moment of primitive hallucination when, whe argues, the child misinterprets its experience 'against the whole weight of the biological evidence of survival' that the instinct loses the 'realistic aim' on which such a concept of orderly progression relies. And what, Glover asks, does this make of the infant if not 'fantast' and 'fool'?[118]

It seems to me that this is the problem which then works itself out inside the analytic institution and specifically in relation to the analysis of children. Let's note that the genesis of the persecutory object in Kleinian thinking casts a shadow over interpretation, since, according to the logic of negation, interpretation comes as a stranger from the outside. And let's note too that if Klein makes of the analyst a fool and a fantast, it is from this place that the analyst has to try to speak, bridging the gap, as Rivière puts it at the end of her Introduction, between the baby ignorant of the external world and the scientist aware of nothing else. For the baby derives and imputes meanings which, because they do not relate to external or material reality, the scientific worker cannot appreciate. And the analyst can bridge the gap only in so far as 'she can assume the baby's condition'.[119] What is this, other than to require psychoanalysis to enter into what Kleinians seem to theorize, to the consternation of their critics, as an infinite regress? a place which Rivière assigns to those 'gifted and intuitive mothers and women' who know that the child inhabits a world of psychic significance and who are 'almost as inarticulate as babies themselves'.[120] Leaving aside this extraordinary image of women's relationship to language in an introduction to a book in which only women in fact speak,[121] the question has to be asked: What problems must it pose for an analytic school to situate itself in the place of an infant to whom interpretation is by definition unwelcome and who is fantast and fool?

A point finally about the wider political resonance of this dispute. The discussions, as is well known, were staged at the height of the Second World War. The emphasis on negativity, the ambivalence about reparation (reparation as ambivalent), takes its reference from, even as it casts light on, the conflict going on all around. Ella Sharpe comments: 'For a belief in the actual good object the actual bad one results in world affairs with a Hitler-ridden Germany and pipe-smoking optimists elsewhere who say "God's in His Heaven, all's right with the world".' And again: 'The "status quo" is a frequent phrase heard today. The full phrase is "the status quo ante". How many people still hope that the end of the war may mean a restoration of the pre-war conditions for which they are most homesick, although progressive minds on every hand warn us that restoration of old conditions could only lead to renewed disaster.'[122] What clearer statement of the political provenance of theory? What clearer indication that, for this analyst at least, if psychoanalysis concentrates on the good and the restorative, it heads straight into a theoretical and political blind?

A POSTSCRIPT ON BLACK HOLES

During the course of working on this chapter, I read Stephen Hawking's *A Brief History of Time* (I am one of thousands, as it has been at the top of the best-seller list in Britain and the United States since it was first published in 1988).[123] I could not help but be struck by the remarkable analogies between what Hawking was describing in the realm of cosmology, the theoretical difficulties and points of tension of that description, and what Melanie Klein confronted in her attempt to theorize the negative components of psychic life. Hawking's investigation of black holes and the Big Bang theory of the universe can be read as an investigation of how to think negativity and outer boundaries, the points where what we take to be the recognizable and at least partly knowable universe comes into being, goes off its own edges, collapses into itself, ceases to be – all questions which are central to the psychoanalytic discussion of the boundaries, coming into being, and internally intractable limits of the psyche. As Paula Heimann put it: 'when exactly does the ego, the differentiation from the amorphous id begin?'[124] Compare Hawking: 'What really happens during the very early (. . .) stages of the universe? (. . .) Does the universe in fact have a beginning? (. . .) What were the "boundary conditions" at the beginning of time?' (pp. 115, 122)

In his book, Hawking discusses the famous concept of the black hole – points (or singularities) in the universe where all matter collapses in on itself: stars which have contracted to the point where light cannot escape, and if light cannot escape, since nothing can travel faster than light, 'neither can anything else; everything is dragged back by the gravitational field' (p. 87). All-incorporating, the black hole has, at the very least, extraordinarily metaphoric resonance for anyone thinking about Melanie Klein's work (irresistibly, current attempts at unified theory in physics are called 'grand unified theories' or GUTs).[125] However, it is in the relation between the black hole and its conceptual theorization that I think the most interesting points of connection appear. How can a black hole – how can negativity – be thought? This, as much as resistance to the idea of a destructive force in all of us, is what I consider to have been at the heart of the dispute with Melanie Klein.

It is central to Hawking's account of the black hole that what happens inside it cannot, by definition, be known. Since anyone entering a black hole is destroyed by it, she or he cannot observe it; inversely, those at the distance that allows observation are protected from the breakdown of the laws of science which occurs inside a black hole. If you are inside, you lose the capacity and conditions for knowledge; outside, you retain knowledge, but cannot grasp what it is you need to know. The black hole thus provokes two complementary anxieties: too close, it devours you; safely outside, you don't know what's going on. This is called the 'cosmic censorship hypothesis' (rephrased by Hawking as 'God abhors a naked singularity': p. 88). Like the unconscious, a black hole is censored, and can be known only by its effects. As a concept, the black hole wipes out the possibility of knowledge, of its own total or absolute theoretical grasp. It is therefore the place where not only all light and matter, but our laws of science in relationship to them, as well as the relationship we presume between observation and knowledge, equally disappear.

Lacan, in a passage cited by Shoshana Felman, draws on the Heisenberg uncertainty principle, also discussed by Hawking (pp. 53–61) – that it is impossible to locate exactly the speed and place of a particle at the same time (the process of locating one affects the other, and conversely): 'as soon as [the elements] are interrogated somewhere, it is impossible to grasp them in their totality.'[126] Hawking's discussion constantly returns to this question of the possibility of knowledge (although in relation to the uncertainty principle he in fact suggests that some forms of unpredictability might be removed). Thus, for example, the question arises as to why this universe, among the possibility of many different universes or regions of a single universe, developed in such a way that complicated organisms are possible, and why the universe is the way that we see it – to which the reply, according to what is called the strong 'anthropic principle' is: 'If it had been different, we would not have been here' (pp. 124–27). Not everyone accepts this principle of course – Hawking himself is committed to a unified theory of physics which would ultimately reveal the mind of God. But what is striking about the principle is that the state of the universe is explained as the consequence of the subjects who, according to a more obvious logic, should appear as its effect. Or to put it another way, in this account, it is only through a fantasy of our being-in-the-world that we can theorize the fact that the world comes to be.[127]

It is, therefore, not just that contemporary science points to the 'irreducibility of ignorance' (Felman's expression for the epistemological principle proposed by Lacan[128]), but that the question of knowledge and the question of origins – the question of the origins of knowledge – appear to be inextricably linked. At the very least, the terms of this discussion should act as a caution to any attempt to legitimate psychoanalysis through a naïve appeal to science (since today science itself will not support the idea of definitive knowledge to which such descriptions of psychoanalysis make their appeal). More, and in a way that echoes the insistence by Isaacs and Rivière on the inseparability of knowledge and subjective experience, fantasies are always in on the (scientific) act. 'It is greatly to be hoped', writes Hawking, 'that some version of the censorship hypothesis holds because close to naked singularities it may be possible to travel into the past. While this would be fine for writers of science fiction, it would mean that no one's life would ever be safe: someone might go into the past and kill your father and mother before you were conceived!' (p. 89). The point of quoting this is not to reduce scientific investigation to the status of oedipal fantasy or 'primal scene' (what exactly *did* parents get up to before one was born?), but, resisting any reduction of psychoanalysis to cosmology or the reverse, to suggest that if knowledge always borders on fantasy, fantasy is always in part fantasy about (the borders of) knowledge. Where does the possibility of knowledge come from? Can we conceive of a limit point where it ceases to be?[129]

It is the advantage of theories like that of the black hole or the Big Bang that they are so apocalyptic. The drama of their imagining compensates for what scares. The idea of something negative as explosion or pure inexplicable force seems oddly to be more manageable or acceptable than the idea of something negative which is at once less certain and which seems to wipe out the conditions through which it can, or should, be known. This, it seems to me, is what we saw in relation to Klein: leave the death drive in the sphere of biological science; don't mix it with meaning, with the psychic glosses and qualifiers of the inner world. It is not just that this brings the death drive in closer (Rivière's comment on psychoanalytic 'resistance' to the death drive); it is also paradoxically that this same proximity weakens its visionary force. In the Kleinian account, it was exactly in proportion as negativity entered the psychic structure that it slipped from the realm of logic and sequence – for the theory and for the psychic development being charted – and out of any totalizing grasp.

It seems significant, therefore, that Hawking has qualified the concept of the black hole – one chapter is entitled 'Black Holes Ain't So Black' – but this is much less often talked about (pp. 99–113). More difficult than the idea of the black hole as total destruct or all-incorporating negativity is the idea that the black hole emits something positive, radiation, which 'seems to imply that gravitational collapse is not as final and irreversible as we once thought' (p. 112). Hawking says that when he presented this result at a conference, he was greeted with incredulity. The images that Hawking offers here are in themselves graphic for psychoanalysis: negative virtual particles which fall into a black hole leaving their positive partner with nothing to 'annihilate with', at which point the partners either also fall into the black hole or, having positive energy, escape (p. 106). Perhaps we could substitute this strange image of partnership for the dualism of the life and death principles – 'pairing' as an alternative to the notions of 'balance' or 'triumph of one principle over the other' through which the link between them is most often described.

Again, more difficult than the idea of the Big Bang is the idea of a universe without beginning or end. This might be why Hawking's new proposal about the initial state of the universe – no boundary to space-time: 'The boundary condition of the universe is that it has no boundary' (p. 136) – is so unsettling. A universe without boundary disturbs, not just because it leaves so small a role for a creator (the Pope instructed the participants at one conference which Hawking attended not to enquire into the Big Bang itself because it was the work of God), but because, paradoxically, it is the idea of something *without* a limit that pushes us conceptually *off* the edge.

The issue then seems to be not how much we can take of negativity, but how much negativity itself can take. If it appears to be the potential black hole of psycho-analytic theory, it is perhaps even more disturbing to think that it might not be such an absolute, that there might be random particles which escape (not a collision between two absolute principles but particles left with no one 'to annihilate with'); that the black hole, like theory, cannot get everything under its sway. It is as if negativity can be taken on board only as Big Bang or black hole (without qualification), either pure origin or end.

It feels to me that, against the grain of this way of thinking, Hawking can be fruitfully read alongside Melanie Klein: negativity as the limit of theory or total knowledge; negativity as caught up in the positive partner as much as antagonist, and not something to which the positive can only be opposed. The concept of negativity will not provide us with a clear account of origins (even if it affects the way that the idea of origins can be thought); nor can we place it at the distance from which it could be conceptually controlled; if it is mixed up with the positive, it ceases to be a pure entity; at the same time the positive, implicated in its process, cannot be appealed to as the counter-principle which will placate and subdue it or get it back under control (the relationships are more shifting than this). In Hawking's universe, as I read it, negativity is unavoidable – on condition that we do not reify it, but recognize its place in the speculations which we cannot but choose to spin about the world and about ourselves.

NOTES

1 Leo Bersani gives a largely critical appraisal of Klein in 'Death and Literary Authority: Marcel Proust and

Melanie Klein', in *The Culture of Redemption* (Cambridge, Mass., and London: Harvard University Press, 1990) ch. 1; *Women – a Cultural Review* devoted a large section of its second issue, *Positioning Klein*, to Melanie Klein (November 1990). These appear, however, to be exceptions. There is no full discussion of Klein, e.g., in the influential collection *The Trial(s) of Psychoanalysis*, ed. Francoise Meltzer (Chicago: Chicago University Press, 1988). For discussion of feminism and Klein see n. 3 and 4 below.

2   Elizabeth Bott Spillius (ed.), *Melanie Klein Today – Developments in Theory and Practice*, vol. 1, *Mainly Theory*; vol. 2, *Mainly Practice*, New Library of Psychoanalysis, vols. 7 and 8 (London and New York: Routledge in association with the Institute of Psycho-Analysis, 1988).

3   The clearest statement of these criticisms, focusing more directly on Ernest Jones but also addressing Klein, is given in 'The Phallic Phase and the Subjective Import of the Castration Complex', in *Feminine Sexuality – Jacques Lacan and the école freudienne*, ed. Juliet Mitchell and Jacqueline Rose (London: Macmillan; New York: Norton, 1982), pp. 99–122; also Juliet Mitchell, Introduction to ibid., pp. 1–26; and Jacqueline Rose, 'The Cinematic Apparatus – Problems in Current Theory', in *Sexuality in the Field of Vision* (London: Verso, 1986), p. 211n. Bersani, 'Death and Literary Authority'; Noreen O'Connor, 'Is Melanie Klein the One Who Knows Who You Really Are?', *Women – A Cultural Review*, 1, no. 2, pp. 180–8. For a suggestive discussion of Lacan and Klein, see Malcolm Bowie, *Lacan* (London: Fontana Modern Master; Cambridge, Mass.: Harvard University Press, 1991), pp. 144–8.

4   See, e.g., Madeleine Sprengnether, '(M)other Eve: some revisions of the fall in fiction by contemporary women writers', in *Feminism and Psychoanalysis*, ed. Richard Feldstein and Judith Roof (Ithaca, NY: Cornell University Press, 1989), pp. 298–322. The absence of Klein, both in this article and in Sprengnether's more recent book, *The Spectral Mother – Freud, Feminism and Psychoanalysis* (Ithaca, NY: Cornell University Press, 1990), which describes the absence of/haunting by the mother

in Freud's work and the place of the pre-oedipal mother in subsequent analytic theory, seems striking. In discussion following the original presentation of '(M)other Eve' as a paper at 'Feminisms and Psychoanalysis', a conference held at the University of Illinois, Normal, in 1986, Sprengnether explained the absence of Klein in terms of the negative component of Klein's work. See also *The (M)other Tongue: essays in feminist psychoanalytic interpretation*, ed. Shirley Nelson Garner, Claire Kahane, and Madeleine Sprengnether (Ithaca, NY: Cornell University Press, 1985) and Jane Gallop's critique in terms of what she calls 'the dream of the mother without otherness' ('Reading the Mother Tongue: psychoanalytic feminist criticism', in Meltzer (ed.), *Trial(s) of Psychoanalysis*, p. 136).

5 *The Freud–Klein Controversies 1941–45*, ed. Pearl King and Riccardo Steiner, New Library of Psychoanalysis, vol. 11 (London and New York: Routledge in association with the Institute of Psycho-Analysis, 1991); and Melanie Klein, Paula Heimann, Susan Isaacs, and Joan Rivière, *Developments in Psycho-Analysis*, ed. Joan Rivière, preface by Ernest Jones, International Psycho-Analytic Library, vol. 43 (London: Hogarth, 1952, and Maresfield, 1989).

6 The fullest and most informative account is given by Riccardo Steiner, 'Some Thoughts about Tradition and Change Arising from an Examination of the British Psychoanalytical Society's Controversial Discussions (1943–44)', *International Review of Psycho-Analysis*, 12, 27 (1985), pp. 27–71; see also Pearl King, 'Early Divergences between the Psycho-Analytical Societies in London and Vienna', and Teresa Brennan, 'Controversial Discussions and Feminist Debate', both in *Freud in Exile*, ed. Edward Timms and Naomi Segal (New Haven Conn., and London: Yale University Press, 1988), pp. 124–33, 254–74; and Gregorio Kohon, 'Notes on the History of the Psychoanalytic Movement in Great Britain', Introduction to *The British School of Psychoanalysis – The Independent Tradition*, ed. Gregorio Kohon (London: Free Association Books, 1986), pp. 24–50. For a discussion

of the controversy, specifically in relation to the concept of phantasy, see Anne Hayman, 'What do we Mean by "Phantasy"?', *International Journal of Psycho-Analysis*, 70 (1989), pp. 105–14.

7 Janet Sayers, *Mothering Psychoanalysis – Helene Deutsch, Karen Horney, Anna Freud, Melanie Klein* (London: Hamish Hamilton, 1991); *Women – A Cultural Review*, 1, no. 2. The first reappraisal of Klein in this context, although not explicitly addressed to feminism, is Juliet Mitchell's introduction to *The Selected Melanie Klein* (Harmondsworth: Penguin, 1986). Nancy Chodorow discusses Klein in *The Reproduction of Mothering* (Berkeley, Calif., and London: University of California Press, 1978), criticizing her for instinctual determinism, but praising her recognition, *contra* Freud, of the girl's early heterosexuality.

8 Nicholas Wright, *Mrs Klein* (London: Nick Hern Books, 1988); and review by Elaine Showalter, 'Mrs Klein: the mother, the daughter, the thief and their critics', *Women – A Cultural Review*, 1, no. 2, pp. 144–8. Paul Roazen, *Freud and his Followers* (New York: Knopt, 1974; London: Allen Lane, 1975).

9 François Roustang, *Un Destin si funeste* (Paris: Minuit, 1976) trans. Ned Lukacher, *Dire Mastery* (Baltimore and London: Johns Hopkins University Press, 1982); Jacques Derrida, 'Du tout', in *La Carte postale – de Socrate à Freud et au-delà* (Paris: Flammarion, 1980), pp. 525–49, trans. Alan Bass, in *The Post Card: from Socrates to Freud and beyond* (Chicago: University of Chicago Press, 1987), pp. 497–521; Phyllis Grosskurth, *Freud's Secret Ring: Freud's inner circle and the politics of psychoanalysis* (London: Cape, 1991).

10 Derrida. 'Du tout', p. 548; trans. p. 520.

11 Julia Kristeva, 'The True-Real', in *The Kristeva Reader*, ed. Toril Moi (Oxford: Blackwell, 1986), pp. 214–37. Kristeva is undoubtedly the French psychoanalytic theorist who draws most consistently on the work of Melanie Klein.

12 None of the papers published in the 1952 *Developments in Psycho-Analysis* correspond exactly to the versions delivered to the scientific meetings of the British Society.

I therefore use the different versions where appropriate, always indicating the source in the notes.

13 Donald Meltzer comments: 'Any systematic attempt to teach Melanie Klein's work runs almost immediately into difficulties that are the exact opposite of the problems facing one in teaching Freud. Where the theoretical tail wags the clinical dog with him, hardly any theoretical tail exists to be wagged with her', *The Kleinian Development*, Part 2, *Richard Week by Week* (Perthshire: Clunie Press for the Roland Harris Educational Trust, 1978), p. 1.

14 *Complete Freud–Jones Correspondence*, ed. R. A. Paskauskas (Cambridge, Mass.: Harvard, 1993); cf. also Steiner 'Some Thoughts'.

15 Ernest Jones, Preface to *Developments in Psycho-Analysis*, p. v.

16 Joan Rivière, ibid., p. 1.

17 Ibid., p. 2.

18 Ibid.

19 Susan Isaacs, opening statement, 'Fifth Series of Scientific Discussions', 19 May 1943, in *Freud–Klein Controversies*, p. 444.

20 Marjorie Brierly, opening comments on Paula Heimann's paper 'Some Aspects of the Role of Introjection and Projection in Early Development', 'Sixth Discussion of Scientific Controversies', 20 October 1943, in *Freud–Klein Controversies*, pp. 538–9.

21 Paula Heimann. 'Seventh Discussion of Scientific Controversies', 17 November 1943, in *Freud–Klein Controversies*, pp. 569–70.

22 Rivière, Introduction to *Developments in Psycho-Analysis*, pp. 23–4.

23 Meltzer sees this as *the* central problem of Kleinian thought: 'It requires an immense shift in one's view of the world to think that the outside world is essentially meaningless and unknowable, that one perceives the form but must attribute the meaning. Philosophically, this is the great problem in coming to grips with Kleinian thought and its implications' (*Kleinian Development*, p. 86).

24 Rivière, Introduction to *Developments in Psycho-Analysis*, pp. 2–3.

25 Heimann, 'Some Aspects of Introjection and Projection', p. 511.

26 For a critique of Klein's 'instinctual reductionism', see 'Phallic Phase', and Chodorow, *Reproduction of Mothering*; Jean Laplanche and Jean-Bertrand Pontalis, 'Fantasme originaire, fantasme des origines, origine du fantasme', *Les Temps modernes*, 215, (1964); trans. 'Fantasy and the Origins of Sexuality', in *Formations of Fantasy*, ed. Victor Burgin, James Donald, and Cora Kaplan, (London and New York: Methuen, 1986), pp. 5–34; first published in English in *International Journal of Psycho-Analysis*, 49 no. 1, (1969) (their criticisms are directed more at Susan Isaacs than Klein); also Nicolas Abraham and Maria Torok, who refer to Kleinian 'panfantastic instinctualism', 'Deuil ou melancolie, introjecter-incorporer', in *L'Écorce et le noyau* (Paris: Flammarion, 1987), pp. 259–74; trans. 'Introjection-Incorporation: Mourning or Melancholia', *Psychoanalysis in France*, (New York: International Universities Press, 1980) ed. Serge Lebovici and D. Widlocher, pp. 3–16.

27 Isaacs, Balint, Lantos, in *Freud–Klein Controversies*, pp. 272, 347, 349; Edward Glover, 'Examination of the Klein System of Child Psychology', *Pscho-Analytic Study of the Child*, 1, (1945), p. 103.

28 Rivière, 'On the Genesis of Psychical Conflict in Earliest Infancy', in *Developments in Psycho-Analysis*, p. 43; paper originally published in *International Journal of Psycho-Analysis*, (1936), pp. 395–422.

29 Isaacs, replying to discussion of her paper 'The Nature and Function of Phantasy', 'Second Discussion of Scientific Controversies', 17 February 1943, in *Freud–Klein Controversies*, p. 373.

30 Anna Freud, *The Ego and the Mechanisms of Defence* (London: Hogarth Press and the Institute of Psycho-Analysis, 1937), p. 57; passage cited by Susan Isaacs, 'The Nature and Function of Phantasy', in *Freud–Klein Controversies*, p. 295. See also Anna Freud, 'Notes on Aggression', 1949 (1948): 'The presence of mental conflicts and of the guilt feelings consequent on them presupposes that a specific, comparatively advanced stage in ego development

has been reached' (*Indications for Child Analysis and other papers 1945–56*, in *The Writings of Anna Freud*, vol. 4 (New York: International Universities Press, 1968) p. 70.

31　Glover, 'Klein System', p. 88n. citing his own paper 'Grades of Ego-Differentiation', *International Journal of Psycho-Analysis*, (1930), pp. 1–11.

32　Barbara Lantos, 'Third Discussion of Scientific Controversies', continuation of discussion of Isaacs's 'Nature and Function of Phantasy', 17 March 1943, in *Freud–Klein Controversies*, p. 413.

33　Isaacs, 'Fifth Discussion' concluding discussion on 'Nature and Function of Phantasy', p. 460.

34　Rivière, 'Psychical Conflict in Earliest Infancy', p. 45.

35　Rivière, Introduction, p. 29.

36　Rivière, 'Psychical Conflict in Earliest Infancy', p. 45.

37　Melanie Klein, 'The Emotional Life and Ego-Development of the Infant with Special Reference to the Depressive Position', in *Freud–Klein Controversies*, p. 781.

38　Rivière, 'Psychical Conflict in Early Infancy', p. 45n.; Introduction, p. 15.

39　Rivière, 'Psychical Conflict in Earliest Infancy', pp. 54–5; Isaacs, 'Nature and Function of Phantasy', p. 302; Heimann, 'Some Aspects of Introjection and Projection', p. 518.

40　Klein, *Narrative of a Child Analysis: the conduct of the psycho-analysis of children as seen in the treatment of a ten-year-old boy*, in *Writings of Melanie Klein*, vol. 4 (London: Hogarth, 1961, 1975 and Virago, 1988) p. 339.

41　Riviere, 'Psychical Conflict in Earliest Infancy', pp. 47, 49.

42　Klein, 'On Observing the Behaviour of Young Infants', also cited by Rivière in Introduction, pp. 270n., 30; compare Heimann: 'Freud did not enter into the question of what happens in the infant's mind when he abandons the object' ('Certain Functions of Introjection and Projection', p. 145).

43　Klein, 'Emotional Life of the Infant', pp. 763–4.

44　See Phyllis Grosskurth, *Melanie Klein – Her World and Her Work* (New York: Knopf; London: Maresfield. 1986 pp. 376–7.

45   Isaacs, 'The Nature and Function of Phantasy', *Develop-ments*, pp. 103–7; Isaacs, 'Fifth Discussion', 'Sixth Discussion', pp. 466–7; p. 554; Heimann, 'Some Aspects of Introjection and Projection', pp. 505–6.
46   Riviere, Introduction, p. 10.
47   Heimann, 'Certain Functions of Introjection and Projection', p. 128.
48   Jacques Lacan, 'Introduction au commentaire de Jean Hyppolite sur la "Verneinung" de Freud'; 'Réponse au commentaire de Jean Hyppolite sur la "Verneinung" de Freud'; Appendice 1: Commentaire parlé sur la "Verneinung" de Freud, par Jean Hyppolite', in *Écrits* (Paris: Seuil, 1966), pp. 369–80, 381–400, 879–88. Throughout this section, where I cite these articles in English, I am making use of Anthony Wilden's unpublished translations of the texts kindly made available to me by Richard Macksey.
49   Lacan, *Le Seminaire I: les écrits techniques de Freud* (Paris: Seuil, 1975), pp. 63–73; trans. John Forrester, *Freud's Papers on Technique* (New York: Norton; Cambridge: Cambridge University Press, 1988), pp. 52–61.
50   Freud, 'Negation', 1925, in *The Standard Edition of the Complete Psychological Works of Sigmund Freud*, ed. and trans. James Strachey (London: Hogarth) vol. 19, p. 239; Pelican Freud, 11. p. 441.
51   Rivière. 'Psychical Conflict in Earliest Infancy', p. 52.
52   Hyppolite, 'Commentaire parlé sur la "Verneinung" de Freud', p. 886.
53   Ibid., p. 880. Hyppolite's reading, and Lacan's through Hyppolite, derives strongly from Hegel: 'The dissimilarity which obtains in consciousness between the ego and the substance constituting its object, is their inner distinction, the factor of negativity in general. We may regard it as the defect of both opposites, but it is their very soul, their moving spirit' (*The Phenomonology of Spirit*, trans. J. B. Baillie, rev. ed. (London: Allen and Unwin; New York: Humanities Press, 1949), pp. 96–7; cf. too Kojève's commentary: 'In contrast to the knowledge that keeps man in a passive quietude, Desire dis-quiets him and moves him to action. Born of Desire, action tends to

satisfy it, and can do so only by the "negation," the destruction, or at least the transformation of the desired object: to satisfy hunger, for example, the food must be destroyed or, in any case, transformed. Thus, all action is 'negating' (Alexandre Kojève, *Introduction à la lecture de Hegel* (Paris: Gallimard, 1947), p. 11; trans. James H. Nichols, Jr. *Introduction to the Reading of Hegel*, (Ithaca, NY, and London: Cornell University Press, 1969), pp. 3–4. For a discussion of negativity in relation to Hegel and psychoanalysis, see Kristeva, 'La negativité, le rejet', in *La Révolution du langage poétique* (Paris: Seuil, 1974), pp. 101–50, trans. Margaret Waller, *Revolution in Poetic Language* (New York: Columbia University Press, 1984), pp. 107–64.

54 Lacan, 'Introduction au commentaire de Jean Hyppolite', pp. 379–80.

55 Ella Sharpe, 'Ninth Discussion of Scientific Differences', discussion of Melanie Klein's paper 'Emotional Life of the Infant', 1 March 1944, in *Freud–Klein Controversies*, p. 811.

56 Hyppolite, 'Commentaire', p. 883.

57 Klein, 'The Importance of Symbol-Formation in the Development of the Ego', 1930, in *Love, Guilt and Reparation and Other Works, 1921–1945*, in *Writings of Melanie Klein*, vol. 1 (London: Hogarth, 1975, and Virago, 1988); Lacan, *Le Séminaire I*, pp. 81–3, p. 95–103, 83, trans. pp. 68–70, p. 78–8, 70. For a discussion of Lacan's reading of Klein's paper, see Shoshana Felman, 'Beyond Oedipus: the specimen story of psychoanalysis', in *Jacques Lacan and the Adventure of Insight – Psychoanalysis in Contemporary Culture* (Cambridge, Mass.: Harvard University Press, 1987), pp. 105–28. For a discussion in relation to Lacan and Kristeva, see Mary Jacobus, ' "Tea Daddy": poor Mrs Klein and the pencil shavings', *Women – A Cultural review*, 1, no. 2, pp. 160–79.

58 Melitta Schmideberg, 'Intellektuelle Hemmung und Ess-Störung' ('Intellectual Inhibition and Eating Disorders'), *Zeitschrift für psychoanalytische Pädagogie*, 8 (1934), p. 110–16; Lacan, 'Réponse au commentaire de Jean Hyppolite', pp. 396–8. A translation of Schmideberg's article, 'Intellectual Inhibition and Eating Disorders', is included as

an appendix to this book and is discussed in chapter 6, 'War in the Nursery'.

59 Lacan, 'Réponse an commentaire de Jean Hyppolite', p. 396.

60 Sharpe, 'Ninth Discussion', pp. 804–5.

61 Freud, 'Negation', pp. 236–7, Pelican Freud, p. 439; cited by Heimann, 'Some Aspects of Introjection and Projection', pp. 505–6; by Isaacs, 'Sixth Discussion', pp. 554–5; by Klein, 'Tenth Discussion of Scientific Differences', formal reply to discussion of 'Emotional Life of the Infant', 3 May 1944, in *Freud–Klein Controversies*, pp. 838 and 843n. (Klein offers a different translation from the version cited here; see Editor's note, p. 843).

62 See n. 26 above.

63 Isaacs, 'Nature and Function of Phantasy', *Developments*, p. 104.

64 Ibid.

65 Isaacs, 'Sixth Discussion', p. 555.

66 Isaacs, 'Nature and Function of Phantasy', *Developments*, p. 106.

67 P. Heimann and S. Isaacs, 'Regression', paper presented 17 December 1943, in *Freud–Klein Controversies*, p. 706. See also Ella Sharpe's 1940 paper on metaphor in which she describes all speech as metaphor – 'an avenue of outer-ance' (in itself a play on words) – through which the child, gradually controlling its bodily orifices, makes speech the outlet for tensions no longer relieved by physical discharge: 'So that we may say that speech in itself is metaphor, that metaphor is as ultimate as speech' ('Psycho-Physical Problems Revealed in Language: an examination of metaphor', in *Collected Papers on Psycho-Analysis*, International Psycho-Analytical Library, vol. 36 (London: Hogarth, 1950), pp. 155–69.

68 See n. 26 above.

69 Rivière, Introduction, p. 16, citing Isaacs, 'Nature and Function of Phantasy', *Developments*, p. 83. Note that in a footnote to this remark Rivière insists that, contrary to responses to Isaacs's paper at the time, this is central to Klein's conceptualization and not an innovation by Isaacs.

70　Isaacs, 'Nature and Function of Phantasy', in *Freud–Klein Controversies*, p. 313.

71　Rivière, 'Psychical Conflict in Earliest Infancy', p. 40.

72　Isaacs citing Freud, 'Nature and Function of Phantasy', in *Freud–Klein Controversies*, p. 280.

73　Ibid., pp. 96, 94.

74　Rivière, 'Psychical Conflict in Earliest Infancy', p. 50.

75　Heimann, 'Some Aspects of Introjection and Projection', p. 518; Klein, 'Eighth Discussion of Scientific Differences', discussion of Heimann and Isaacs's paper on 'Regression', 16 February 1944, in *Freud–Klein Controversies*, p. 747.

76　See n. 23 above. Cf. too Steiner: 'The term phantasy . . . after being bounced back and forth throughout these lengthy discussions, seems to have assumed an enigmatic, evocative power. For one side it came to be synonymous with new discoveries – the more the term was analysed, the more it was enriched with new meanings. For the others it seemed to mean something not unlike belief in a new and hazily-defined mysticism. Some of the latter even saw it as something to be exorcised by the expulsion of the entire group led by Klein'. (Steiner, 'Some Thoughts about Tradition and Change', pp. 49–50).

77　Kate Friedlander, Marjorie Brierly, Friedlander, Brierly, in *Freud–Klein Controversies*, pp. 409, 536, 539, 536.

78　Isaacs, *Freud–Klein Controversies*, p. 467, Heimann, ibid., pp. 580, 572, 570.

79　Anna Freud, 'Indications for Child Analysis', in *The Psycho-Analytic Treatment of Children* (London: Imago, 1946), p. 86. For a discussion of Anna Freud's dispute with Klein, see ch. 6 below.

80　Brierly, 'Sixth Discussion', p. 537. For a discussion of the possibility of distinguishing between incorporation and introjection in terms of metaphor, see Abraham and Torok, 'Introjection-Incorporation'.

81　Heimann, 'Seventh Discussion', p. 571.

82　Sharpe, 'Seventh Discussion', p. 582. For a discussion of these problems in relation to Freud's writing, see Mikkel Borch-Jacobsen, *Le sujet freudien* (Paris: Flammarion, 1982), trans. Catherine Porter, *The Freudian*

Subject (London: Macmillan; Stanford: Stanford University Press, 1982); also Abraham and Torok, 'Introjection-Incorporation'.

83 Brierly, 'Sixth Discussion', p. 536.
84 Glover, 'Sixth Discussion', pp. 559, 562.
85 See, e.g., Samuel Weber, *The Legend of Freud* (Minneapolis: University of Minnesota Press, 1982); Derrida, 'Speculer sur Freud', in *La carte postale*, pp. 257–409; Borch-Jacobsen *Le sujet freudien*.
86 Walter Schmideberg, 'The Second Extraordinary Business Meeting'; Karin Stephen, 'Resolutions and the First Extraordinary Business Meeting', in *Freud–Klein Controversies*, pp. 86, 50.
87 Brierly, 'Sixth Discussion', pp. 536–7.
88 Glover, 'Seventh Discussion', p. 586.
89 Friedlander, 'Discussion on "Regression" ' (discussion circulated only), December 1943, in *Freud–Klein Controversies*, p. 728; Glover, ibid., p. 715.
90 Rivière, 'Psychical Conflict in Earliest Infancy', p. 47.
91 Heimann, 'Certain Functions of Introjection and Projection', p. 161.
92 Rivière, 'Psychical Conflict in Earliest Infancy', p. 53.
93 Heimann and Isaacs, 'Regression', p. 703.
94 Klein, 'Emotional Life of the Infant', p. 201.
95 Ibid.
96 Klein, 'Tenth Discussion' p. 836.
97 Klein, 'The Oedipus Complex in the Light of Early Anxieties', 1945, in *Love, Guilt and Reparation*, p. 408.
98 Heimann, 'Some Aspects of Introjection and Projection', p. 523.
99 Klein, 'Emotional Life of the Infant', pp. 777–8; Lacan, *Le Séminaire I*, p. 97; trans., p. 83.
100 Klein, 'Tenth Discussion', p. 834.
101 Isaacs in reply to Glover, 'Fifth Discussion', pp. 456–7; Klein, 'A Contribution to the Psychogenesis of Manic-Depressive States', 1935, in *Love, Guilt and Reparation*, p. 265.
102 Rivière, 'Psychical Conflict in Earliest Infancy', pp. 60, 62.
103 Ibid.

104 Meltzer, *Kleinian Development*, pp. 46–7. Meltzer relates this issue to Klein's uncertainty about the conceptual status of the depressive position: 'She had never absolutely crystallised this in her mind, for sometimes she speaks of "penetrating" the depressive position, "overcoming", "surpassing", all of which have different implications regarding the meaning of the "depressive position" ' (p. 114).

105 Heimann and Isaacs, 'Regression', p. 183; cf. also: '[Klein] has shown too that specific anxieties not only contribute in both sexes to fixations and regressions, but also play an essential part in stimulating the libido to move forward from pre-genital positions to the genital one', (p. 175); and Meltzer: 'The badness must be sufficiently split off . . . [but] it must not be so widely split off as to diminish the anxiety below the level that is sufficient for development' (*Kleinian Development*, p. 64).

106 Heimann, 'Certain Functions of Introjection and Projection', p. 162.

107 Heimann and Isaacs, 'Regression', p. 703.

108 Isaacs, 'Nature and Function of Phantasy', *Developments*, p. 75.

109 See esp. Klein, 'Early Stages of the Oedipus Conflict', 1928, in *Love, Guilt and Reparation*, pp. 186–98.

110 Klein, 'Emotional Life of the Infant', pp. 223, 209.

111 Klein, 'Importance of Symbol-Formation', p. 227; Lacan, *Le Séminaire I*, p. 102; trans. p. 87.

112 A. Freud, *Ego and the Mechanism of Defence*, p. 57, cited by Isaacs, 'Nature and Function of Phantasy', in *Freud–Klein Controversies*, p. 295.

113 Despite the stress on development in Anna Freud's writing, one could equally argue that it is a simplification to read her work exclusively in such terms. Her famous paper 'Studies in Passivity' gives an extraordinary account of the possible vicissitudes of sexual identification and desire in relation to masculinity and of the resurgence in adulthood of the most primary forms of identification, at the same time as recognizing the limits of its own model of explanation: 'These interpretations are not satisfying . . . What is left unexplained', etc – i.e.

the text can be read aporetically as much as development-
ally (A. Freud, 'Studies in Passivity', 1952 (1949–51),
in *Writings of Anna Freud*, vol. 4, pp. 245–59.

114 Glover, 'Klein System of Child Psychology', p. 112.
115 Ibid., p. 110.
116 Ibid., p. 116.
117 Hedwig Hoffer, 'Fourth Discussion of Scientific Controversies', continuation of discussion of Isaacs's paper
'Nature and Function of Phantasy', 7 April 1943, in
Freud–Klein Controversies, p. 428 (my emphasis).
118 Glover, 'Klein System of Child Psychology', p. 99.
119 Rivière, Introduction, pp. 18–19.
120 Ibid., p. 36.
121 As Groskurth comments: 'The Discussions were dominated by women – and what women they were!' (*Melanie
Klein*, p. 316). This quote from the manuscript of Virginia
Woolf's *To the Lighthouse*, however, relates interestingly
to Rivière's remark: 'Don't we communicate better
silently? Aren't we (women at any rate) more expressive
silently gliding high together, side by side, in the curious
dumbness which is so much [more] to our taste than
speech'; cited by Lyndall Gordon, *Virginia Woolf – A
Writer's Life* (Oxford: Oxford University Press, 1984),
p. 195. A whole history of women's relationship to
language and of psychoanalysis's relation to modernism
is implicit in Rivière's extraordinary comment.
122 Sharpe, 'First Discussion of Scientific Controversies',
'Some Comments on Mrs. Klein's theory of a "depressive position",' in *Freud–Klein Controversies*, pp. 340, 805.
123 Stephen W. Hawking, *A Brief History of Time – From the
Big Bang to Black Holes* (London and New York: Ban-
tam, 1988). (subsequent references are cited in the
text).
124 Heimann, 'Certain Functions of Introjection and Projection', p. 128.
125 In his Brazilian lectures of 1974, Bion refers to black
holes: 'I am familiar with a psycho-analytic theory of the
mind which sounds like the astronomical theory of
the "black hole" ', (W. R. Bion, *Bion's Brazilian Lectures*,
vol. 2, (Rio/São Paulo, 1974; Rio de Janeiro: Imago,

1975), p. 61). Discussing this passage, David Armstrong suggests that the theory of the mind alluded to is Bion's own ('Bion's Later Writing', *Free Associations*, 3, 2, no. 26 (1992), p. 267).

126 Felman, 'Psychoanalysis and Education', in *Jacques Lacan and the Adventure of Insight*, p. 78.

127 In his Inaugural Lecture to the University of Cambridge, Hawking states that a quantum theory of gravity (as central to the not yet attained complete unified theory of physics) is essential if the early universe is to be described and its initial conditions explained without 'merely appealing to the anthropic principle' (Hawking, 'Is the End in Sight for Theoretical Physics?', Appendix to John Boslough, *Stephen Hawking's Universe* (Glasgow; Collins, 1984), p. 120). For a critique of Hawking in relation to the anthropic principle, see Feliz Pirani, 'The Crisis in Cosmology', *New Left Review*, 191 (January/February 1992), pp. 69–89.

128 Felman, 'Psychoanalysis and Education', p. 78.

129 Cf. Bion on the question of reduction: 'Why should a psycho-analyst invent a theory to explain a mental phenomenon and, independently, the astronomers elaborate a similar theory about what they think is a black hole in astronomical space? Which is causing which? Is this some particularity of the human mind which projects it up into space, or is this something real in space from which derives this idea of space in the mind itself? . . . I have used this idea of modern cosmology as a model for psycho-analysis, but I would also use psycho-analysis as the starting point of an investigation of the human mind' (Brazilian Lectures, pp. 61–2).

6 War in the Nursery[1]

When Anna Freud first published her 1926–27 technical lectures on child analysis in England in 1945, she prefaced them with this explanation for the delay:

> It is not the author's fault that the early material contained in this publication is presented to the English reader at such a late date. An English version of the *Introduction to the Technique of Child-Analysis* was published in America. Attempts at publication in England were not successful. For the general publisher the subject matter was still too remote and controversial. Professional psycho-analytic circles in England, on the other hand, were at that time concentrating their interest on Mrs. Melanie Klein's new theory and technique of the analysis of children. The British Psycho-Analytical Society devoted a *Symposium on Child-Analysis* to a severe criticism of the author's efforts, which ran counter to Mrs. Klein's outlook. The *Introduction to the Technique of the Analysis of Children* was rejected when offered to the International Psycho-Analytical Library for publication, and the matter lapsed, so far as England was concerned.[2]

The correspondence between Ernest Jones and Freud at the time suggests that this is, predictably, a one-sided account. When Freud accused Jones of arranging a campaign against his daughter, Jones replied that Melanie Klein's written response to Anna Freud's paper to the Berlin Society had been suppressed. It was because the *Zeitschrift* (*Die Internationale Zeitschrift für Psychoanalyse*) was barred to Klein that she had turned to the *International Journal of Psycho-Analysis* to publish her critique.[3] In this dispute across national boundaries and languages, Melanie Klein seems to occupy the same position for Jones as Anna Freud does in relation to Freud. It is a strange scenario in which two men already in a father–son relation battle it out over who in turn is the true daughter – as if the intensity of the dispute over *which* daughter is warding off the greater anxiety, their shared recognition that the legacy is passing to the female child.

It is perhaps not surprising, therefore, that the question of child analysis immediately finds itself caught up in a set of conflicts over the relationship of psychoanalysis to pedagogy, over the issue not only of whether one can, but equally if not more centrally, whether one should analyse a child. At one level, the move to child analysis can be seen as the logical next step after Freud (although as Juliet Mitchell has pointed out with reference to Klein, it can be seen as reversing the true order of analytic time).[4] But that idea of a logical next step conceals a more important factor, which is that this turn to child analysis was also coincident with – might even be seen as a form of acting out of – a crucial moment or difficulty in the transmission of psychoanalysis itself. It seems that, for the psychoanalytic community, child psychoanalysis has not fulfilled its promise. In 1945, Berta Bornstein was to comment that the expectation that every training analysis should include child analysis 'was disappointed'.[5] In 1962 Esther Bick wrote of the 'neglect' of child analysis, of the few adult analysts who go on to train in the field, of the 'specific difficulties interfering with the development of child analysis' (the developmental model is noteworthy in itself).[6] The question then arises as to what this 'symptomatic blockage' is expressive of – it is apparently still present, since Bick's essay was reprinted in a 1988 anthology *Melanie Klein Today*. How, from this historical distance, might its moment of emergence be read?

What does analysis *do* to children? What is the accountability, or otherwise, of psychoanalysis to social law? What is the social law, the binding and bonding, of the psychoanalytic world? If the psychoanalysis of children can be reconciled with pedagogy (adjunct, enabler, accomplice), then the risk is that it will drive the unconscious to the wall. But if it retains its separate identity, recalcitrant to what is most coercive and invidious about social norms, then it is not clear how psychoanalysis, or the children it analyses, can avoid the status of eternal outlaw, nor indeed how it can legitimate – how it can transmit – itself. There will be no transmission if the second generation refuses the legacy of the ancestors; a rebellious daughter will not obey or perpetuate her father's law. But if that law is the law of the unconscious, then a subservient one paradoxically disobeys and undoes his heritage no less at the very point of her surrender. Nor is it only the order of fathers and daughters which is at play. For Melanie Klein also found herself involved in an impossible drama of legacy when her daughter became, before the most absolute of repudiations, a Kleinian analyst in turn. So what happens when the problem of transmission plays itself out between mother and daughter – that relationship in which Klein herself was the first to locate a violence no less than that which Freud had identified between fathers and sons? In this dispute over child analysis between Melanie Klein and Anna Freud – the quarrel over pedagogy, transference, and the superego – we can uncover some of the most intractable knots of our psychoanalytic inheritance. Rather than reading it as a war of invective, proof of the self-infantilizing – in the bad sense – of the analytic scene, we might use it instead to identify something about the limits or boundaries of psychoanalysis, as procedure, as discipline, as history; we might ask what the difficulty of analysing children tells us about the transmissibility of psychoanalytic (of any) law.

When, in the course of their correspondence, Jones suggested that Anna Freud had been insufficiently analysed, Freud replied: 'I must point out to you that such a criticism is as dangerous as it is impermissible. Who, then, has been sufficiently well analysed? I can assure you that Anna has been more deeply and thoroughly analysed than yourself.'[7] Not untypically, Freud's mutually exclusive propositions (true logic of the unconscious as he defines it elsewhere) capture the central dilemma in which the two men are caught: are some analyses more sufficient than others, or is psychoanalysis interminable (to use Freud's later expression), something – like the subjectivity it addresses – necessarily insufficient and incomplete? Since Freud analysed his own daughter, we might see both these propositions as the most blatant self-defence (she was adequately analysed; if she wasn't, then nor is anyone else). But Anna Freud will inherit the knot of these intertwining and self-cancelling propositions when she turns to the question of how, or whether, to analyse a child. Let's start by stating the obvious, that in so far as Anna Freud will argue that there can be no child analysis in the full sense of the term, she is issuing the most thinly veiled of reproaches against Sigmund Freud (she was twenty-three when he analysed her, but she was also, and would always remain, his child). It has become customary to criticize her, especially in the early stages of her work, for forcing psychoanalysis into an educational mould. But when she argues for a psychoanalysis in tandem with pedagogic ideals, her apparent social compliance, her plea for a measure of normality, may also be her way of warding off a more ferocious legislator, the too intrusive and pressing reality of the paternal word. Maybe, as we will see, the issue is not whether you are for or against the law, but *where* you want to situate it, how – the question may be unanswerable – to negotiate between the law inside and the law outside the mind. Maybe – but this is to anticipate – there is not, finally, such a total opposition between Anna Freud and Melanie Klein.

It is generally accepted that Anna Freud's 1922 paper 'Beating Fantasies and Daydreams' is an account of her own analysis with her father. In it she expands on Freud's paper 'A Child is being Beaten', picking up his reference to two female patients who overlaid their beating fantasies with an 'elaborate superstructure of daydreams', offering as her own illustration the fantasy life of a fifteen-year-old girl (it is because Anna Freud was not qualified in 1922 that it is assumed that the patient is herself).[8] The paper starts with the contrast between the fantasy of beating, with its barely concealed sexual encounter with the father, and the 'nice stories' produced in compensation, inspired by a boy's story-book of medieval heroism: a medieval knight is engaged in a long feud with nobles leagued against him; a youth imprisoned by the knight's henchman is first tortured but finally released. Although the daydreams end with reconciliation, the beating fantasies with an act of violence, it is clear that they are thinly disguised versions of the same theme. The identity between them, which transcends the apparent distinction between pleasurable and painful outcome, is made clear when Anna Freud recounts the version of the story which, several years later, the patient wrote down: 'It began with the prisoner's torture and ended with his refusal to escape' (p. 154). In this compacted summary, there is no mention of the reconciliation which might be expected to explain the youth's desire to stay (elaborating, Anna Freud comments: 'Its aim – harmonious union between the former antagonists – is only anticipated but not really de-scribed': p. 154.) Strikingly, then, it appears that it is not reconciliation – the alleviation of torture – which produces the bond between the youth and his captor, but the process of torture itself.

That Anna Freud should become the theorist of 'al-truistic surrender' or 'overgoodness' has often been seen as the logical theoretical accompaniment of, and way of protesting, her life time's devotion to her father.[9] Some-where between '*gutseins*' ('being good') and '*etwashaben-wollen*' ('wanting something of her own'), it is almost too easy to track the partially sublimated expression of her own interminably repeated surrender and escape.[10] In her biography, Elizabeth Young-Bruehl presents this more in terms of a narrative of self-discovery and eman-cipation; from her father to Lou Andreas-Salomé, to Max Eitingen, Anna Freud painfully constructs a path to analytic and personal autonomy. That narrative of progress looks less assured, however, when we remember that Anna Freud sent Dorothy Burlingham, centre of the family which she finally made her own, into analysis with Sigmund Freud.

At the end of 'Beating Fantasies and Daydreams' Anna Freud charts the emergence of the writer: 'the private fantasy is turned into a communication ad-dressed to others . . . regard for the personal needs of the daydreamer is replaced by regard for the prospective reader' (p. 156). But if this is an account of the emer-gence of sublimation (a self-created representational space), it is none the less worth noting that it is the version of the story in which the prisoner's father ap-pears for the first time: 'the story being presented in the frame of a conversation between the knight and the prisoner's father' (p. 154). In the very activity of writing, the father 'frames' the scene. The youth may be the hero of the story, but it is not to him that we look for the symbolic capacity to narrate. Anna Freud thus transposes herself in fantasy into a boy only to come straight up against paternal law. It is therefore a symbolic as well as a sexual trajectory which the different stages of the story describe. If this paper draws on fantasy material from Anna Freud's analysis, could we not read it as referring, as much as to the sexual contents of her unconscious (beating as the expression of forbidden desire) to the process – tortuous, pleasurable – of the analysis itself?

At the end of this paper, Anna Freud describes the developmental gain of writing: 'renouncing her private pleasure in favour of making an impression on others, the author has accomplished an important developmental step: the transformation of an autistic activity into a social activity' (p. 155). Narcissism, as Freud himself theorized, is the key social affect ('the satisfaction which the ideal offers to the participants in the culture is of a narcissistic nature'[11]). By 1926, when Anna Freud delivered the first of her lectures on the technique of child analysis ('An Introductory Phase in the Analysis of Children'), an author's ability to hold on to her audience has become the model of the analytic scene: 'My way was rather like that of a film or a novel which has no other intention than to attract the audience or reader to itself' (p. 10). Manipulating her audience – in 1926 her patient – Anna Freud passes from the pleasures of torture into her analytic role: 'My first aim was in fact nothing else but to make myself interesting to the boy' (p. 10). With the unerring clarity of symptomatic logic, what then surfaces in the lecture, as the rite of passage into analysis, is a drama of mastery whose ultimate objective is the child's total surrender to her will: 'he got the habit of relying on analysis as a protection from punishment and claiming my help for repairing the consequences of his rash acts; he let me restore stolen money in his place and got me to make all necessary and disagreeable confessions to his parents . . . I had however only waited for this moment to require of him in turn . . . the surrender, so necessary for analysis, of all his previously guarded secrets' (pp. 10–11).

Thus Anna Freud seems to carry over into her procedure something which looks like a parody of an earlier parental-cum-analytic scene. We can criticize her, as the Kleinians did at the time, for the crudest manipulation of her patient; or we can note what this bizarre process of transmission reveals about the perverse components – punishment as torture and pleasure – of analytic and social norms. What seems clear is that the question of the child's criminality and the question of subjection and mastery are intimately related to each other. Acknowledge my criminality for me, take me under your wing. In a move which strangely anticipates Melanie Klein's famous papers on crime,[12] Anna Freud seems inadvertently to be suggesting here that crime is not, at the deepest level, antisocial behaviour, but the means through which the subject tortuously affirms her or his social being, surrenders her or himself.

In terms of the most immediate opposition between Anna Freud and Melanie Klein, Anna Freud is on the side of convention. Although this dispute has been well documented, it might be worth laying out the basic argument again here.[13] Anna Freud believed, at this stage in her work, that there could be no full analysis of children.[14] For her, the still vivid presence of the parental figures meant that the transposition from person into imago from which transference proceeds could not take place. Unlike the adult, the child is not ready to produce 'a new edition of its love-relationships' because the 'old edition is not yet exhausted' (p. 34). Reluctant to make the transition (to leave, psychically, the family home), the child must be won. It is because the child is still in a state of total psychic dependence on the parents that the analyst has to woo and manipulate her or his way into the child's mind. The more positive the attachment of the child to the parents, the harder this will be, the more essential it becomes for the analyst to take up a positive role. Idealization of the parent–child relation thus leads straight into the production of a parallel idealization of the analyst on the part of the child.

It follows from this first point – the still present reality of the parents – that the analyst becomes no less real. In the analysis of adults 'we remain impersonal and shadowy, a blank page on which the patient can transcribe his transference-fantasies, somewhat after the way in which at the cinema a picture is thrown upon an empty screen' (the image of the cinema again) (p. 35). But the child's analyst must be 'anything but a shadow' because of the way she must seek the collaboration of the child and because of the 'educational influences' involved in the analysis of children, which mean that the child knows full well what it is that the analyst desires, what he sanctions, of what he disapproves (p. 35). The argument thus seems to move in two directions at once: there must be pedagogy because there is no transference; there can be no transference because pedagogy is the final aim. At the end of this lecture, Anna Freud argues that, even were it possible to generate a full transference by removing the child from the parents, the outcome on the child's return would be either renewal of the neurosis or open rebellion, something which may therapeutically appear as an advantage, but which in terms of social adjustment, which 'in the child's case most matters in the end, is certainly none' (p. 37). For Anna Freud, the child's superego, undetached from the parents, is weak; there is always the risk, therefore, that this childish superego will not withstand the lifting of repression in analysis and that the outcome will be direct, and unmanageable, gratification of libidinous and aggressive impulses on the part of the child. The analyst must, therefore, *'succeed in putting himself in the place of the child's Ego-ideal'* (p. 45); (emphasis original).

Once again, it is hard not read this as a veiled account of the dangers, the seduction, that Anna Freud felt herself courting in analysis with Freud, hard not to see it as her way of commenting on the extraordinary tension, if not tease, behind the analytic injunction to speak but not act. And from where – if not from an analysis with one's own father – would the conviction that parent and analyst are indistinguishable, the belief in their joint and indissoluble reality, be more likely to arise?

It is customary to read the emphasis by Anna Freud on the pedagogic function of analysis as betraying true analytic goals (in a 1931 paper entitled 'Some Contrasted Aspects of Psycho-Analysis and Education', Nina Searl insists on their 'irreconcilable' nature[15]). Freud himself, on more than one occasion, has been described as an 'anti-pedagogue'.[16] It may be, however, that Anna Freud is revealing something about the analytic contract which a mere insistence on the incommensurability between analysis and education cannot quite resolve. In her essay on psychoanalysis and pedagogy, Shoshana Felman discusses the links between transference and the function of authority.[17] Since transference bestows authority, there is a sense in which the analyst is always already a pedagogue. Conversely, since education always contains a transference component, it could be argued that the analytic scenario is present, *in potentia*, wherever a relationship to knowledge is at play. (Lacan wrote: 'As soon as there is somewhere a subject presumed to know, there is transference.'[18]) In a famous comment, Freud described analysis, teaching, and government as the three impossible professions, but he did not elaborate on the transferability, so to speak, of their authority and/or pedagogic aims.[19] Felman cites this passage from Freud's essay on schoolboy psychology to illustrate the link between teaching and transference in the analytic sense of the term: 'These men [the teachers] became our substitute fathers. That was why, even though they were still quite young, they struck us as so mature and so unattainably adult. We transferred to them the respect and expectations attaching to the omniscient father of our childhood.'[20]

From fathers to teachers to analysts, Anna Freud seems to be doing no more than uncovering something about authority, something startlingly focused by her own experience, but unavoidable in the analytic scene (something which her own insistence on the absence of full transference in child analysis cannot finally remove). If the debate over child analysis is so fierce, it might be because it forces on to the agenda, over and above the differences between the protagonists, an insoluble problem of analytic authorization and how it transmits itself. How can you pass on knowledge from generation to generation – how can you secure the child's passage into the adult world – without precisely generating, indeed relying on, the transference and its latent pedagogic imperative which psychoanalysis is meant ultimately to dissolve? The question of psychoanalytic inheritance and the question of pedagogy are in fact one and the same thing.

In a passage from the paper on schoolboy psychology not cited by Felman, Freud says some more about those earlier teachers: 'We courted them or turned our backs on them, we imagined sympathies and antipathies in them which probably had no existence, we studied their characters and on theirs we formed and misformed our own. They called up our fiercest opposition and forced us to complete submission.'[21] The passage graphically fills out what is psychically at play – courting and rejection, projection, identifications which form and malform what the child comes to be (compare from the other passage: 'we transferred to them the respect and expectations attaching to the omniscient fathers of our childhood'). From deference to projection, the difference almost anticipates one conceptual shift from Freud to

Melanie Klein. Even more striking in this context is that acknowledged relation between rebellion and the utmost defeat, as if it were not only the authority professionally accruing to the teacher which engineers the final submission, but also the pleasures and dangers internal to the relation, not to say the process of resistance itself. In a way which anticipates the daydreams of his daughter – youths tortured by henchman in service to their beleaguered knight – Freud offers us an account here not just of the pedagogic relation, but of what we might call fealty, its perversions and its discontents.

Melanie Klein's main disagreement with Anna Freud turned on the question of the superego. For Klein, far from the childish superego being weak, it was fierce and inexorable, the product of the internal rage attendant on the extravagance of the child's impulses and its thwarted being in the world. The task of analysis, child analysis included, was not to align with or reinforce the superego, but to reduce and assuage the inexorability of its law: 'what is needed is not to reinforce this superego, but to tone it down.'[22] No less than for Anna Freud, the child was, for Klein, a potential criminal; but in her account this is because the child is warding off, through socially unacceptable behaviour, the edicts of an internal persecutor compared with which the chastisement of an external authority is a positive relief. Crime does not engender guilt; it is the consequence of a guilt that is already there. As Klein puts it in her paper 'On Criminality' of 1934: 'it is not lack of conscience, but the overpowering strictness of the superego, which is responsible for the characteristics of asocial and criminal persons'.[23] (The row between her and Melitta Schmideberg over this paper is put at the centre of the play *Mrs Klein*.) For Anna Freud, on the other hand, it is the collapse of the superego precipitated by mental illness or criminality in the parent that is responsible for asocial tendencies in the child. If the child is guilty, it is because the parent was guilty before it, guilty of a failure at the site of the superego – whereas for Klein the problem is precisely that the superego *never* fails.

It follows for Klein that the aim of the analysis must be to attract on to the analyst everything that is most negative in the child's inner world so as to dissipate, finally, its unbearable force: 'My method presupposes that I have from the beginning been willing to attract to myself the negative as well as the positive transference' (p. 145). That negativity will be necessarily, if relatively, autonomous from the reality of the parental figures in the outside world. For Klein, the child is a phantasy-spinner from the start – hence the possibility, and painful nature, of the psychoanalysis of children. What we see here are the repercussions of Klein's emphasis on the destructive impulses for the activity of analysis. Precisely because of that irreducible negativity, we could say, transference – phantasy driven by its own inner process – is something assumed in the analysis of children by Melanie Klein.

Is it surprising that the one who holds on to the image of the analyst as essentially benevolent is none other than the daughter of Freud? At the same time it is important to acknowledge that Klein's stress on negativity could also be seen – was seen by her critics – as playing a defensive role.[24] The attraction of hostile impulses on to the person of the analyst, far from endangering the child's relation to the parents, protected them from the worse ravages of their effects. At the same time, an emphasis on the negative inner imago of the parents – the insistence that this was *only* an imago – could paradoxically serve their idealization, an acceptance at face value of the way they see themselves (for Melitta Schmideberg this will be the fundamental reproach).

It is usually assumed that on the issue of the superego Anna Freud was in agreement with her father. Indeed, he intervened on her behalf over this specific issue in the course of the debate. In his correspondence with Jones, Freud argued that Klein's belief in a superego belonging in the early years, prior to Oedipus and autonomous from the parents, was simply wrong: 'I would like to challenge Frau Klein's statement that the superego of the child is as independent as that of the adult. It seems rather to me that Anna is right in emphasizing the point that the superego of the child is still the direct parental influence.'[25] So much, so clear. But is it? Anna Freud may talk of the 'prestige' of the superego, whose authority rises and falls with the benevolence with which the parents are viewed, while Melanie Klein charts its fierce and manic oppression; yet each of their accounts of psychic and social regulation appears to contain something which, in the very name of the control it promises, is completely beyond their (anyone's) sway. Internal persecutor or henchman, the images are remarkably close; in fact, they can both be seen as sketching out, for children and for the psychoanalytic institution, the 'unpsychological proceedings of the cultural superego', to cite a famous definition of Freud's.[26] In doing so, they confront us with an impasse at the heart of social identity, one which, one could argue, was dislodged or displaced on to the dispute about how or whether to analyse a child. Before lining up Anna Freud and Melanie Klein on either side of the law – indeed, before asking whether psychoanalysis supports or undermines social regulation – we should perhaps first ask what exactly, for psychoanalysis, the law *is*. For if the law is a henchman, the question is not whether to obey it, but what exactly obedience, no less than disobedience, might involve.

More than one commentator has read *Civilisation and its Discontents* as an account of the perverse nature – tortuous and self-defeating – of social law.[27] Indeed, it is hard not to see this text as the Urtext for many of the fantasies and narratives which we have been tracking so far. For it is central to the Freudian account of the

superego that it draws its force from the violence it
controls and, in the form of its terrifying injunctions,
repeats it. (This is why if we turn our attention to the
question of the superego, we at once make psychoanalysis more directly socially accountable and remove the
possibility of using it for a simply liberationist goal.) The
superego inherits the aggression of the drives it curtails;
in fact, it appears as nothing other than their deflection.
Subjects introject their own aggressiveness, sending it
back, so to speak, to where it originally belonged: 'There
it is taken over by a portion of the ego, which sets itself
over against the rest of the ego as super-ego, and which
now, in the form of "conscience", is ready to put into
action against the ego the same harsh aggressiveness that
the ego would have liked to satisfy upon other, extraneous individuals.'[28] The superego even incorporates the
subject's resistance to the superego itself, entering into
possession of 'all the aggressiveness which a child would
have liked to exercise against it'.[29] Inside the child is a
degraded relic of the father's authority: 'Here as so often
the [real] situation is reversed: "If I were the father and
you were the child, I should treat you badly".'[30] The
model for the superego is therefore a drama of torture
which takes place between father and child. If we refer
back to Freud's essay on schoolboy psychology, what he
seems to be providing here is the ferocious underside of
transference to the pedagogue.

This superego sounds uncannily like the master who
tortures at whim: 'the new authority, the superego has
no motive that we know of for ill-treating the ego', which
it none the less 'torments'.[31] Strictly without reason, this
instructor offers to the subject its first model of social
control. Relentless, it pronounces an ethical imperative
which is self-defeating and impossible to obey. Conscience torments the saint far more than the sinner:
'virtue forfeits some part of its promised reward; the
docile and continent ego does not enjoy the trust of its

mentor and strives in vain, it would seem, to achieve it.'[32] The less we offend, or rather the more we obey this law, the crueller it becomes. As Lacan points out in his seminar on ethics, this logic does not work the other way round. If the saint is troubled by his conscience in proportion to his virtue, it is not the case that the sinner, in proportion to his pleasure, finds himself liberated from his debt to the law.[33] It is, we could say, the superego which is the prime culprit – the purveyor, not the assuager, of guilt.

When the Kleinians insist, *contra* Anna Freud, that a rebellious child is in fact testing or appealing to the law which she appears, wildly, to be free of, I would suggest that they are repeating in the frame of child psychology this impasse or impossible dictate which psychoanalysis exposes at the heart of socialization. In fact, Lacan is nowhere closer to Klein than on this very issue: 'It is a capricious, arbitrary, oracular law, a law of signs where the subject is guaranteed by nothing, in regard to which he has no security or safeguard [*Sicherung*], to use another Kantian term. Which is why, this *Gute* [the Good], at the level of the unconscious, is also, and fundamentally, the bad object, which Kleinian articulation still speaks of.'[34] As Rivière put it during the symposium of 1927, the child's sense of goodness, its superego, is derived from the bitterness of its experience in frustration.[35] In this context, reparation, as theorized by Klein, can be seen as an attempt to keep the ethical instance (the good) separate from the bad object – despite the fact (or because) it is from the bad object that it so clearly and unavoidably derives.

If we turn back to the dispute between Anna Freud and Melanie Klein, we can now see how the ethical question and the question of negativity, as discussed in the last chapter, might be linked. What Klein allows us to do is to delve one step deeper into what it is that this punishing ethical imperative is trying to control, what it is that, every time it voices its injunction, it draws on and repeats. One of Anna Freud's own examples can be used to suggest what might be involved – the case of a six-year-old girl which runs through the lectures, who, as soon as the analysis relaxed her inhibitions, turned from obsessional to pervert, cheerful, and overbold, whose pleasure in recounting her anal fantasies at the dinner table destroyed the appetites of all the grown-ups. Faced with which, Anna Freud decided that she had made a serious blunder, and admonished the child, thereby making her once again inhibited and apathetic. Compare Isaacs: 'It is all right if it comes out of my anus, but it mustn't come out of my mouth as words.'[36] If this little foulmouth transgresses, it is because she is more than happy – indeed, finds her happiness – in the effluence which pours out of her mouth – one kind of oral production (the child's verbage) which makes it impossible for everyone else to eat.

The issue would thus seem to be not just the child's social manageability, but what that same manageability is designed to ward off: an unspeakable orality and anality where the drive, as theorized by Klein and her supporters, transmutes itself in an uncomfortable and dangerous proximity into the fact of speech. Which is not to say, as we have already seen, that language is the untranslated or direct expression of the drives, but something about the inextricability of the two. The aggression of the drive does not seem here to precede language, but rather to be its effect, as it is speech which makes of it a projectile, seizing it in that logic of expulsion which is the basis of judgement as such. After all, instinctual gratification in this instance (the feared outcome of child analysis for many critics who objected to it as early as the case of 'Little Hans') means talking about it.

What does it mean to ask that this process be managed? What – equally if not more to the point – would it mean to ask that it not be? What is Anna Freud being asked, or trying, to put back in place? As we watch her describe her attempt to calm the child's guardian who presumably, along with the whole household, was on the verge of starvation (they had lost 'all appetite'), it seems as if something is being expressed not just about the child, but about the whole family scene. In a comment remarkably resonant for this case, Rivière commented on the way that a real, objectifiable situation can take on the weight of what is unmanageable within: 'the destructive condition (starvation) becomes equated with the destructive impulses', giving the impulses an object and turning them into less of an internal threat.[37] Like Dora, this little girl seems to be refusing to be the 'prop for the common infirmity' of those around her (the expression is Lacan's), by speaking in her symptoms what the family cannot bear.[38] In Dora's case, we know that Freud was only partially able to recognize the reality she was refusing (her exchange for her father's lover), that he first acknowledged Dora's protest but then demanded that she once again comply.[39] I see Anna Freud as caught in an equivalent dilemma, only this time it is not a question of an oedipal triangle, but precisely of what that narrative – as Freud later recognized – repressed: a primitive orality which it is impossible to extricate from the very fact of judgement and speech. Is this the horror which underlies the injunctions which issue from the voice of the law? The scandal of the Kleinians would then be that they force us to look inside the mouth of God.

For Freud, as we know, the law was always the law of the father. He never – a point made by Julia Kristeva[40] – retheorized his account of social bonding subsequent to his later writings on femininity; he never asked whether his narrative of inter-male rivalry and truce-making might need to be altered in view of the 'discovery' of pre-oedipality and of the crucially important early relation between the mother and the girl-child (the fact that he assumed that women were never quite 'in' culture is a related but separate point). The dispute between Melanie Klein and Anna Freud can be seen as enacting for the participants this unwritten version of social lineage: in the content of the dispute – in the negativity, orality, and incorporation which appear as the underside of that finally more civilized, or socially familiar and acceptable, war of identification between men; in its frame – what this group of women succeed and fail in transmitting among themselves. A logical, or perhaps even inevitable, outcome once you add to the image of knights and henchmen as arbiters of the law what Melanie Klein uncovered in the unconscious of the child.

In the course of her lectures, Anna Freud acknowledged that hostility towards the mother was something she was unable analytically and, one can speculate, personally to approach. In the case of the six-year-old girl it appears as the 'climax' of the analysis, as well as a type of vanishing-point of the whole dispute: 'At the climax of her analysis it was a matter of elucidating for her her hatred of her mother, against the knowledge of which she had previously defended herself by the creation of her "devil" as the impersonal deputy for all her hate impulses. Although up to now she had co-operated readily, she began at this stage to shrink from further progress' (p. 25). Alongside, or behind, the struggle with the (paternal) master, hostility towards the mother, and even more the struggle over its resistance to knowledge and articulation, appears to propel and set the limits to the analytic scene: 'Finally she surrendered outwardly before these constantly recurring proofs, but demanded to know from me also the reason for such a hostile feeling towards her apparently well-loved mother' (ibid.). But at the very point where she gets the child to surrender, it is her own knowledge which comes abruptly to an end: 'Here I declined to give further information, for I too was at the end of my knowledge' (ibid.).

For Melanie Klein this moment is crucial. In her intervention during the 'Symposium on Child Analysis', she seizes on it as the moment when the 'substitution' of analysis by pedagogy takes place (pp. 161-2). It signals for her that Anna Freud's refusal to negotiate the negative transference has resistance – resistance to knowledge of hostility towards the mother – as its base. Today, what is equally striking is the way in which Anna Freud's language reiterates in the field of child analysis that tension between forcing ('finally she surrendered') and the failure of knowledge ('I too was at the end of my knowledge') which readers of the Dora case have commented on in relation to Freud: his oppressive assertiveness in tandem with his inability to recognize the presence of transference and the homosexual factor in the case.[41] This is a strange irony for a feminism which has wanted to read behind Freud's own resistance to knowledge a positive orality for women, the founder – potentially – of another femininity to be located in the earliest relation between the mother and the girl-child. As Anna Freud puts it, hostility to the mother is the hardest thing to incorporate (it was the little girl's only 'serious resistance' in the 'progressive reincorporation' of all her impulses (p. 61); just as death, in Paula Heimann's formulation, is the one thing which cannot be expelled.[42]

How then do Melanie Klein and her supporters get round this seeming 'impasse' (how do they incorporate it, we might say)? One way is clearly through the figure of Melanie Klein herself. In the symposium, Nina Searl describes how her hesitance to use direct interpretation with a pre-latency boy was traced, after conversations with Klein, to fears about the stability of her early superego, fears which her analysis subsequently resolved.[43] Her remarks give a sense of that always present overlap between theory and institution in what is unmistakably here the founding of a school (the creation of the Kleinian group will follow the 'Controversial Discussions' of 1941–5); or rather, between theory, institution, and founder, since Klein so clearly occupies the place of knowing subject, site of interminable transference, as François Roustang put it in relation to Freud. If Freud held off the more negative or psychotic instance by binding filiation to his person, Melanie Klein effects no less of a binding when she chases up that instance and forces it in turn to speak. We should hardly be surprised that if it works, as it seems to – at least at this moment – for Nina Searl, it was unlikely to work for her own daughter.[44]

It is the case reported by Ella Sharpe during the symposium, however, which gives the most dramatic illustration of the way this difficulty inscribes itself in the framework of analytic space – a case which reads like a cross between that of Dora and Henry James's *The Turn of the Screw*.[45] Not quite child analysis, it involves a fifteen-year-old girl brought to analysis by her horrified parents when she is sent home from school after she is discovered writing what was described as an obscene letter to a boy (in fact, she was brought by her mother because the father promptly retired to his bed). In her preliminary meeting with the analyst, the mother immediately made clear that, for her, the aim of the analysis was to ensure that the daughter does not begin to think that mothers do not understand their daughters, that she remain dutiful and obedient, and that she get these things, which she had learnt from the boy and were not her own thoughts, 'out of her mind in a month so that she could go back to school' (p. 381). Until a year ago, the mother insisted, she had known all her daughter's thoughts, and she could not see what good it could do to talk to the analyst (true self-cancelling logic, this, where the analysis is deemed pointless at the same time as it is ordered to have instant effects). What is perhaps most chilling is that the girl's head is clearly to be emptied so that the mother can get back in.

Ella Sharpe immediately lays out the ramifications of this situation for the analytic process, whose aim must be, she states, to make the girl 'mistress of her own sexual thoughts':

> not only is the mother negative to the suspect analyst, but the analyst is in immediate opposition to the wishes of the mother. The analyst is aware that not only does the parent here represent in reality the deepest layers of the infantile superego in the analyst, but that the conscious purposes of the analyst are in accord with the deepest levels of that hostile negative attitude to the parent who forbade sexual activity and knowledge. (p. 381)

What is this other than analysis as a declaration of war, against a mother who concretely attempts to repress the sexual thoughts of her daughter, but – and this is more difficult – against the dictates of the infantile superego, a superego by definition in excess of the mother, but which the mother cannot fail, for both patient and analyst, to represent? Repeating a primitive childhood conflict, the analyst's conscious (her *analytic*) purpose re-enacts the battle once raged against the unreasonable dictates of the superego by the child: 'I detected here reverberations never stirred by an adult analysis' (p. 382). Thus Ella Sharpe anticipates Esther Bick's observation of 1962 that unconscious conflict in relation to the child's parents is a key factor in explaining why counter-transference stresses are so much greater in the analysis of a child.[46] When the patient sides with the mother against the analyst, recognizing, not unreasonably, that in so far as the analysis requires her to talk about sexuality, it is asking her to repeat the original offence, Sharpe catches herself thinking: ' "It isn't *my* fault you have had to come, you should not have written that letter, then you wouldn't be coming to me!!!" ' (p. 382); that is, she catches herself in an identification with the parent, 'at the mercy of the infantile superego condemnation of myself' (ibid.). The only way out of this impasse is, as she sees it, to dissolve the severity of the superego, by recognizing its autonomy and detaching it from the mother who seems to embody it with such force: 'The freedom to speak plainly to the mother corresponded to a release in myself from the deeper levels of the unconscious negative to the condemning parent in my own mind' (p. 383). Only when this detachment has been effected can the analyst proceed to analytic interpretation, hampered up to then by unconscious guilt. It is therefore the severity of the infantile superego which stops interpretation, stops the analytic engagement with the word. For Sharpe, only this concept of interpretation can bring about a transference in the full analytic meaning of the term: 'I proved in the last analysis that transference occurred through interpretation alone' (p. 384). Another way of putting this would be to say that negativity must, finally, be seen to be its own master if the analytic process is to proceed.

Not that this ensures a successful outcome of the analysis. By making herself the ally of the girl's unconscious wishes, Sharpe provokes her conscious hostility; she sides with the mother, and the analysis is brought to an abrupt end (this in itself should serve as a caution against seeing women patients who walk out of analysis – a point often made in relation to Dora – as casting a type of proto-feminist vote). In this context, however, what matters is the effects of this scenario for child analysis itself: 'The problem of child analysis seems more subtly implicated with the analyst's own deepest unexplored repressions than adult analysis' (p. 384). Sharpe's final comments are clearly directed against Anna Freud: 'Rationalisations that the child is too young, that the weakness of the superego makes an admixture of pedagogy with analysis indispensable, and so on, are built upon the alarms of that very same infantile superego in the analyst that he has to deal with in the child before him. That infantile "supergo" in the last resort becomes the dictator between analyst, child and parent' (ibid.).

All of which leaves a further question: how can analysis proceed, how can it institutionalize itself, when it has so clearly identified as persecutory (as dictator) nothing other than the bearer or instance of the social institution as such? Thus, not for the first time will women have the privilege of identifying the violence – not to say perversity – of the social tie (the point is made by Julia Kristeva in her essay 'Women's Time'[47]). But what Ella Sharpe's example shows is that it is not easy for this insight to pass from one woman to another, even less from mother to daughter, since their interaction is bound to be a site – if not *the* site – where that problem or conflict is played out. Since Freud could not, any more than his daughter, talk about the mother, it was his blindness that he passed as legacy to his (psychoanalytic) child. In different ways it was a legacy which could not help but be enacted by both Anna Freud and Melanie Klein. Note that this has nothing to do with 'mothering' psychoanalysis,[48] but everything to do with the difficulty for psychoanalysis, as practice and institution, of what the mother represents.

So what, then, of Melanie Klein's daughter? It is tempting, although also too easy, to see her as the element which, for the Kleinians to constitute themselves *as* Kleinians, had to be expelled. (When I asked Hanna Segal, the best-known commentator on Klein's work, about Melitta Schmideberg during the course of an interview in 1990, it was the one topic on which she was unwilling to reply.[49]) Melitta Schmideberg was analysed by Melanie Klein; it is generally assumed that she is the girl referred to in the 1921 paper 'The Development of a Child' and named as Lisa in the 1923 paper 'The Role of School in the Libidinal Development of the Child'. (In the play *Mrs Klein*, Melitta reproaches her mother for having analysed her, as well as for describing her in

the first paper as of 'only average intellect'.[50]) Commentary on the dispute that developed between Klein and
her daughter has tended to pathologize Melitta (in one
letter Klein herself referred to her 'illness'[51]), although
not consistently. Paula Heimann, for example, suggests
that she was driven from England; Phyllis Grosskurth,
Klein's recent biographer, discusses the ethical and
psychic issues raised by Klein's analysis of her own children, as one among a number of grounds for potential
reproach, including Melanie Klein's mourning of her
brother during her pregnancy with Melitta and her frequent absences when Melitta was a child.[52]

What seems to me important in this context, however,
is not the question of legitimate or illegitimate recrim-
ination by either party (how, from this distance, or even
at the time, could one decide?), but the way that Melitta
Schmideberg's writings resonate with the problems of
psychoanalytic transmission as I have tried to outline
them here. Seen in these terms, the importance of
Melitta Schmideberg resides not in the question of her
participation – interestingly rebellious or virulently ob-
structive – in the controversy surrounding Melanie
Klein, but in what she reveals about the institutional and
theoretical difficulties of the collective project in which
all the participants were caught.

'A neurotic woman patient said: "In fact everything –
reading, going to the theatre, visiting – is like eating.
First you expect a lot, and then you're disappointed.
When I come to analysis, I eat your furniture, your
clothes, your words. You eat my words, my clothes, my
money." '[53] In her 1934 paper 'Intellectual Inhibition
and Eating Disorders', Melitta Schmideberg provides
one of the clearest accounts of the relationship between
orality and intellectual production, between eating and
mouthing, between taking in and giving out words.
Since it can be read as an extended gloss on the concerns
of the last chapter, I have included a translation as an

Appendix here (it is this paper to which Lacan refers as part of psychoanalytic material which has become difficult of access today). It was written in her mother tongue, but remained untranslated into the language which both mother and daughter finally made their own – the clearest statement of the allegiance between them, it never passed into the language of their falling out.

Already Schmideberg lays out in it something of a psychic double bind: the woman who rejects her mother's nourishment or experiences it as bad will be bound to that same mother, in the apathy of failed autonomy, for life; the woman who achieves intellectual and personal independence acknowledges, in that very gesture, the indissoluble nature of her – oral – debt (it is exactly the oedipal drama that Freud describes for fathers and sons rewritten for girls). Ironically, then, according to her own account, Melitta Schmideberg's final repudiation of her mother – the daughter strikes out on her own – is a form of perverse tribute, the point of her greatest allegiance, to the body of Klein's work. This trajectory would then have to be placed alongside – it does not neutralize it, but gives it a different refrain – the journey from the endless citation of her mother in her early papers ('M. Klein has shown . . .'; 'M. Klein points out . . .'; 'M. Klein believes . . .'; 'Mrs Klein has emphasized . . .'; 'Cf. the writings of Melanie Klein'; 'these conclusions agree with those which Melanie Klein has embodied [sic] in her book'[54]) to the utter repudiation of her work and the entire psychoanalytic project for which she is most renowned.

Even in those early papers, however, we can see Melitta Schmideberg making some kind of bid for herself – in her frequent allusions to a primordial narcissism, a concept she saw as discarded by current theory, in which reality is equated not with the mother's body, but with the child's own.[55] Anna Freud, in a related but distinct movement, will argue in her paper on passivity that there is a point, prior to object love, of primordial identification with the object which in later life threatens the subject with the complete dissolution of self.[56] Parodies of total autonomy and total surrender – how far back, in order to bypass the object which most immediately confronts them, do these daughters of psychoanalysis feel they have to go?

This searching back would then be the other face of the opposite and more obvious move in her writing – away from psychoanalysis and outwards into a larger world, from the impulses and phantasy life of the infant to the factors of environment and external reality which, she argued, Melanie Klein ignored.[57] Certainly she saw her trajectory very much in these terms – from 'external factors can probably contribute' ('The analysis of these patients showed that their anxiety derived from instinctual sources and not from the ill-treatment they suffered') to 'the fateful effect of unfavourable reality', to 'I was criticized because I paid more attention to the patient's actual environment and reality situation', to the reproach that analysis had become the hallmark of a liberalism untested by 'the stress and possible dangers inherent in being involved in social and racial issues'.[58]

Thus Melitta Schmideberg seems to cross from one side to the other of the inner/outer boundary which, as I discussed in chapter 3, has so often been at the heart of the psychoanalysis and politics debate. In fact, even when she became involved in social work, she never relinquished her commitment to the complexities of the inner life; her 1948 book *Children in Need* can be seen as exemplary of a psychoanalytically informed project of social reform.[59] And in the 1971 paper in which she attacks the institution of psychoanalysis most strongly, she herself acknowledges, in the face of alternative therapies, the importance of the 'scrupulousness and rigid adherence' to psychoanalytic rules.[60]

But there is, I would suggest, another way of reading her writing that can avoid this inner/outer dichotomy which, in her dramatic shift of allegiance and identity, she none the less seems so starkly to embody or repeat. And that is to read her repudiation in terms of a problem theorized by psychoanalysis which has recurred throughout these texts: the problem of how subjects take on, in the fiercest and most punishing core of their identities, a social legislator both unavoidable and impossible in any simple way to obey. If this cannot be reduced to an inner/outer dichotomy, it is because it is precisely the point where inner and outer worlds clash and coalesce. (As Lacan puts it, it is the psychoanalytic account of social exigency which makes it incompatible with any theory based on the distinction between the individual and her or his social world.[61])

Like Anna Freud, Melitta Schmideberg provides her own commentary on the way in which this problem rebounds on the process and dynamic of analysis itself. When she talks of the patient's reality, it is the reality of the *analytic scene* that she is most often talking about. When she introduces the element of reassurance into her technique, it is not – as with Ferenczi (she insists on the difference[62]) – 'active' or 'relaxation' therapy attached to the principle of pleasure, but a way of trying to alleviate what she sees as the punishing elements of analysis, the extent to which the analysis itself, as much as the analyst, can take on the role of the superego who puts, or rather takes, its subject to task. The superego, she writes after Klein in her paper on 'asocial' children, 'is never lacking', unlike the more beneficent figures of the ego-ideal (another reproach against her mother?) which can fail.[63] If the superego is a persecutor – site of 'psychotic anxiety [*Gewissensangst*]'[64] – then how can analysis proceed; how can interpretation reach its object, since once it is uncovered in the course of analysis, the obvious place for the superego to take up residence is in the speech of the analyst herself?

What Melitta Schmideberg seems to be asking is whether, finally, Kleinian analysis (whether analysis) can dissolve the ferocity of this superego or whether, despite its best intentions, it can only drive it further in. It is this question of the superego as *generic* to the analytic scenario which underlines the more obvious questions about ethics and procedures which she raises. Thus, when analysis aims for the relinquishment of pre-genital defences, how can it be certain that it has not simply ensured that they are more successfully repressed? When the child gives up its asocial habits, is reduced anxiety or an increase in inhibition the cause? What does it mean to require of the patient that he or she be depressed? What, finally, is normality in a Kleinian world? 'The objection that a patient cannot be well because he still has manic defences, unconscious paranoid anxieties or an anal fixation would be justified only if it could be proved that there are people without them.'[65]

To put it at its crudest, the risk is that the Kleinian analyst, no less than the Anna Freudian, will identify with the police:

> Thus a patient may remain homosexual or polygamous, continue to bite his nails, or to masturbate, though usually not to excess, without feeling guilty about it. In evaluating symptoms, I should be disposed to attach greater importance to those representing inhibitions of instinct than to manifestations of primitive instinctual life. This policy might usefully be adopted if only to counteract the analyst's unavoidable moral bias . . . especially when he fears the disapproval of parent-substitutes: other analysts, the patient's parents, the police, probation officers., etc.[66]

(There is an interesting slide here from authorities inside to those outside the analytic community – is it really the police who disapprove of masturbation?)

Health, Melitta Schmideberg seems to be arguing, can be the ultimate form of consent. What is the fantasy of a 'fully analysed person'?, she asks, rejoining the question which Freud put to Jones at the very beginning of the dispute.[67] The point here is not to evaluate her contribution to analytic technique, but at least to hand back to her the validity of her dilemma and of the questions which she raised. How could the analytic theory which most graphically described the fierceness of the superego be expected to avoid, clinically or institutionally, the worst of its effects? (The history of the analytic institution – of most institutions – suggests that the Kleinian aim of dissolving its severity is not in itself enough.) How, as Fornari puts it, can you analyse the unconscious components of political violence without provoking a transference war?[68] How, finally, can you pass on the legacy of the unconscious, so stunningly elucidated by Melanie Klein, without founding an institution, without – for all the differences with Anna Freud – setting up school?

We come back, therefore, to the beginning of these essays, or at least to the general principle that has informed them. That psychoanalysis is political in two senses: in what it has to say about the fantasies which inform our political identities and, in what it reveals in its own history about the vicissitudes and blind spots of political allegiance, the two senses linked by the question of what it means to try and constitute oneself as any kind of social or political group. For those of us still committed to some form of socialist vision, the fourth Conservative election victory in Britain has forced us to recognize this as one of the most difficult and challenging issues today. One of the things that the Conservatives seem to have mobilized so effectively in the last election is, not so much the opposition between collective and individual priorities, as a fear of the group; the only group that can be trusted, they constantly reiterated, is the one that tells you to trust only yourself. ('[The Labour Party] is still too closely identified with groups. It is thought to be the party that, as one interviewee said, "would rather group you together".[69]) As Rivière puts it, if individual security depends on autonomy in phantasy, then sharing and co-operation, the condition of collective security, threatens at the very moment it protects.[70] While the concept of rights starts from that recognition, we could say that what distinguishes Conservatism is that it exploits the fear on which it rests.

In his 1955 paper 'The Freudian Thing' (in some senses the basis for the seminar on ethics of 1959–60), Lacan suggests that there has been a move in psychoanalytic theory from guilt to frustration.[71] The issue of guilt, he writes, its meanings, its discovery in the action of the subject, dominated the first phase of psychoanalysis, to be superseded by the concepts of emotional frustration and dependence. Something which Freud recognized as a fundamental aporia at the heart of social identity was, as Lacan saw it, taken over by an emphasis on what was needed for the subject to be socially, no less than sexually, completed or fulfilled. In one of his first public interventions, Lacan argued that what distinguished human subjects was the existence of the superego, the internal arbiter of the mind (he was repeating something of a pattern, since he was speaking against, indeed addressing, his analyst, Loewenstein).[72] Although he is closer than anywhere else to Klein on this subject, he none the less felt that she detached the superego from the moment of social recognition, running it back to the mythic body of the mother towards which the subject must then make restitution, thereby repairing the mother and securing a harmonious social participation at one and the same time.[73] The subject and social redeem themselves together (everybody makes up).

It is, I have suggested, arguable whether Klein ever in fact theorized this moment with the singular completion that this reading suggests. Meltzer, for example, distinguishing between manic and true reparation, where objects repair each other or are repaired not defensively but for their own sake, describes the way in which reparation takes on a more 'mysterious meaning' at this point in Klein's account.[74] Certainly the institutional history and the writings on war, conducted at the same time as the disputes described in these two chapters, offer a type of caution to the more redemptive movement in Klein's own work.[75] In this context and reversing the normal order of things, the political component might be seen as the 'repressed' of the clinical debate.

There is, however, a more general point to be made. It has become commonplace, especially for feminism, to argue, that psychoanalysis reveals a failure of sexual norms, that the meaning of the unconscious is that it always knows more than what our socially circumscribed sexual identities appear to declare to the world. But for the most part that recognition has not been accompanied by an equivalent acknowledgement of the social aporia, or impasse of social identity, which psychoanalysis simultaneously describes. It is as if there has been a type of lag in the theory – sexuality as trouble against a social reality theorized as monolithic in its origins and effects (the idea of patriarchy, for example, as efficient or functioning exchange). But if social being is slashed with the same bar that distances the subject from her or his sexual roles, then it becomes impossible to pit 'another' sexuality as simply antagonistic to social law. There is no simple 'outside' of the law any more than there is a simple 'outside' of sexual norms – it is the participation in *and* refusal of those norms which psychoanalysis so graphically describes (take the first without the second and you get normalization; take the second without the first and you get a euphoric but ineffective liberationist version of Freud).

At a time when we seem to be confronted with the blandest and most terrifying versions of a seemingly interminable Conservatism in Britain, when claims for national identity at the heart of Europe seem barely to articulate their legitimate aspirations before tipping over into their most disturbing separatist and absolute forms, the idea that we are by definition at odds with a social reality in which we cannot at the same time help but participate might be worth restating once again. Against those accounts that turn to Klein for a redemptive account of social and political being, I would suggest that the value of Klein's insights resides precisely in their negativity, in their own points of internal resistance to narratives of resolution, even if it is those narratives which her own writings and those of her followers have increasingly come to propose. The history of her (but not only her) institution suggests that we are never more vulnerable to the caprices of the superego and to the potential violence of identities than when we take it at its word.

NOTES

1   I take my title from Denise Riley's brilliant account of the relationship between psychoanalysis, social policy, and politics, with special reference to Melanie Klein and John Bowlby, at the end of the Second World War; *War in the Nursery – Theories of the Child and Mother* (London: Virago, 1983).
2   Anna Freud, *The Psycho-Analytical Treatment of Children*, 1945, Preface, p. ix (subsequent references are cited in the text).
3   Riccardo Steiner, 'Some Thoughts about Tradition and Change Arising from an Examination of the British Psychoanalytical Society's Controversial Discussions (1943–44)', *International Review of Psycho-Analysis*, 12, no. 27 (1985), pp. 33–4; cf. also *Complete Freud–Jones Correspondence* (Cambridge, Mass.: Harvard, 1993).
4   Juliet Mitchell, Introduction to *The Selected Melanie Klein*, ed. Juliet Mitchell (Harmondsworth: Penguin, 1986), pp. 25–30.

5 Berta Bornstein, 'Clinical Notes on Child Analysis', *Psycho-Analytical Study of the Child*, 1 (1945), p. 151.

6 Esther Bick, 'Child Analysis Today', in *Melanie Klein Today – Developments in Theory and Practice*, ed. Elizabeth Bott Spillius, vol. 2, *Mainly Practice*, pp. 168–9. Bick draws attention to the fact that the symposium she was addressing was the first symposium on child analysis at an International Congress of Psycho-Analysis, the previous symposium of 1927 being held before the British Psycho-Analytical Society.

7 Cited by Steiner, 'Some Thoughts about Tradition and Change', p. 32.

8 A. Freud, 'Beating Fantasies and Daydreams', 1922, in *The Writings of Anna Freud*, vol. 1, 1922–35 (London: Hogarth, 1974), p. 138 (subsequent references are cited in the text); Sigmund Freud, 'A Child is being Beaten: a contribution to the study of the sexual perversions', 1919, in *The Standard Edition of the Complete Psychological Works of Sigmund Freud*, ed. and trans. James Strachey (London: Hogarth), vol. 17, pp. 177–204; Pelican Freud vol. 10, pp. 159–93; and commentary, Elizabeth Young-Bruehl, *Anna Freud – A Biography* (New York and London: Simon and Schuster, 1988), pp. 104–9.

9 Young-Bruehl, 'Being Analysed', in *Anna Freud*, ch. 3, p. 186; Adam Phillips, 'A Seamstress in Tel Aviv', review of *Anna Freud*, by Young-Bruehl, *London Review of Books*, 14 September 1989, p. 6. Anna Freud introduces the concept of 'emotional surrender' in 'A Form of Altruism', in *The Ego and the Mechanisms of Defence*, 1936, in *Writings of Anna Freud*, vol. 2, pp. 122–34.

10 Young-Bruehl, *Anna Freud*, pp. 127, 131–3, 135–8.

11 S. Freud, *The Future of an Illusion*, 1927, in *Standard Edition*, vol. 21, p. 13; Pelican Freud, vol. 12, p. 192.

12 Klein, 'Criminal Tendencies in Normal Children', 1927; 'On Criminality', 1934, in *Love, Guilt and Reparation and other works, 1921–1945*, in *The Writings of Melanie Klein*, vol. 1 (London: Hogarth, 1975, and Virago, 1988), pp. 170–85, 258–61.

13 See, e.g., Young-Bruehl, 'Psychoanalysis and Politics', in *Anna Freud*, pp. 140–84; Phyllis Grosskurth, 'London

1926–39' and 'The Controversial Discussions 1942–4', in *Melanie Klein – Her World and Her Work* (New York: Knopf; London: Hodder and Stoughton, 1986), pp. 151–246, 279–362.

14 See Anna Freud, *Psycho-Analytical Treatment of Children*, Preface, pp. xi–xii, for subsequent modification of her views.

15 Nina Searl, 'Some Contrasted Aspects of Psycho-Analysis and Education', *British Journal of Educational Psychology*, 2 (1932), p. 288.

16 Catherine Millot, *Freud – anti-pedagogue* (Paris: Bibliothèque d'Ornicar, 1979).

17 Shoshana Felman, 'Psychoanalysis and Education', in *Jacques Lacan and the Adventure of Insight – Psychoanalysis in Contemporary Culture* (Cambridge, Mass.: Harvard University Press, 1987), pp. 68–97.

18 Jacques Lacan, *Le Séminaire XI: les quatres concepts fondamentaux de la psychanalyse* (Paris: Seuil, 1973), p. 210; trans. Alan Sheridan, *The Four Fundamental Concepts of Psychoanalysis* (London: Hogarth, 1977), p. 232; cited by Felman, 'Psychoanalysis and Education', p. 85.

19 S. Freud, Preface to Aichorn's *Wayward Youth*, 1925, in *Standard Edition*, vol. 19, p. 273; cited by Felman, 'Psychoanalysis and Education', p. 70.

20 S. Freud, 'Some Reflections on Schoolboy Psychology', 1914, in *Standard Edition*, vol. 13, p. 242; cited by Felman, 'Psychoanalysis and Education', p. 85.

21 S. Freud, 'Some Reflections on Schoolboy Psychology', p. 242.

22 Melanie Klein, 'Symposium on Child Analysis', held before the British Psycho-Analytical Society, 4 and 18 May 1927, first published in *International Journal of Psycho-Analysis*, 8 (1927), pp. 339–91; Melanie Klein's contribution with a qualifying note on Anna Freud's subsequent modification of her views is included in *Love, Guilt and Reparation*, pp. 139–69: see esp. p. 164. Because of its greater availability I cite this edition for Klein's intervention (subsequent references are cited in the text).

23 Klein, 'On Criminality', p. 258.

24 Edward Glover, 'Examination of the 'Klein System of Child-Psychology', *Psycho-Analytic Study of the Child*, 1 (1945), p. 114.

25 Cited by Steiner, 'Some Thoughts about Tradition and Change', p. 31; cf. also *Complete Freud–Jones Correspondence*.

26 S. Freud, *Civilisation and its Discontents*, 1930 (1929), in *Standard Edition*, vol. 19, p. 143; Pelican Freud, vol. 12, p. 337.

27 Leo Bersani, *The Freudian Body – Psychoanalysis and Art* (New York: Columbia University Press, 1986), ch. 1, 'Theory and Violence', pp. 7–27; Mikkel Borch-Jacobsen, 'The Freudian Subject: from politics to ethics', *October*, 39 (Winter 1986), pp. 109–27: Lacan, *Le Séminaire VII: l'éthique de la psychanalyse* (Paris: Seuil, 1986), trans. Dennis Porter, *The Ethics of Psychoanalysis* (London: Routledge, 1992).

28 S. Freud, *Civilisation and its Discontents*, p. 123; Pelican Freud, p. 315.

29 S. Freud, *Civilisation and its Discontents*, p. 129; Pelican Freud, p. 322.

30 Ibid. At one point, Anna Freud gives a definition of the superego which is uncannily close to this one by Freud: 'What else is the superego than identification with the aggressor': discussion at Hampstead Centre on 'The Ego and the Mechanisms of Defence' (*Hampstead Bulletin* and Sandler et al., *The Analysis of Defence* (New York: International Universities Press, 1985)), cited by Young-Bruehl, *Anna Freud*, p. 212.

31 S. Freud, *Civilisation and its Discontents*, p. 125; Pelican Freud, pp. 317–18.

32 S. Freud, *Civilisation and its Discontents*, Pelican Freud, p. 126; p. 318.

33 Lacan, *Le Séminaire VII*, p. 208; trans., pp. 176–7. In her discussion of Klein, Anne Alvarez makes the distinction, after Money-Kyrle, between 'persecuting conscience or god, who demands penance and propitiation' and a 'more depressive god who . . . is felt to grieve at his children's moral failure rather than to threaten punishment' (*Live Company – Psychoanalytic Psychotherapy with Autistic,*

Borderline, Deprived and Abused Children (London and New York: Tavistock/Routledge, 1992), p. 142).

34 Lacan, *Le Séminaire VII*, p. 89: trans., p. 73 (translation modified).

35 Joan Rivière, 'Symposium on Child Analysis', pp. 374–5.

36 Susan Isaacs, 'The Nature and Function of Phantasy', in *Developments in Psycho-Analysis*, ed. Joan Rivière, International Psycho-Analytic Library, vol. 43 (London: Hogarth, 1952, and Manesfield, 1989), p. 106.

37 Joan Rivière, 'On the Genesis of Psychical Conflict in Earliest Infancy', in *Developments in Psycho-Analysis*, p. 47.

38 Lacan, 'Intervention sur le transfert', in *Écrits* (Paris: Seuil, 1966), pp. 215–26; trans. Jacqueline Rose, 'Intervention on Transference', in *Feminine Sexuality – Jacques Lacan and the école freudienne*, ed. Juliet Mitchell and Jacqueline Rose, (London: Macmillan, 1982), p. 70.

39 For various readings of the 'Dora' case, see *In Dora's Case – Freud, Hysteria, Feminism*, ed. Charles Bernheimer and Claire Kahane (New York: Columbia University Press; London: Virago, 1985), esp. essays by Suzanne Gearhart, Toril Moi, Neil Hertz.

40 Julia Kristeva, *Pouvoirs de l'horreur* (Paris: Seuil, 1980), 'De la saleté à la souillure', pp. 69–105, trans. Leon S. Roudiez, *Powers of Horror* (New York: Columbia University Press, 1982), 'From filth to defilement', pp. 56–89.

41 See essays by Gearhart, Moi, and Hertz in *In Dora's Case*.

42 Paula Heimann, 'Some Aspects of the Role of Introjection and Projection in Early Development', in *Freud–Klein Controversies*, p. 511.

43 Nina Searl, 'Symposium on Child Analysis', p. 379.

44 See Grosskurth, *Melanie Klein*, pp. 230–1 for an account of Searl's eventual resignation from the British Society.

45 Ella Sharpe, 'Symposium on Child Analysis', pp. 380–4 (subsequent references are cited in the text).

46 Bick, 'Child Analysis Today', p. 170.

47 Kristeva, 'Le temps de femmes', *33/44: Cahiers de recherche de science et de documents*, 5 (Winter 1979), pp. 5–19: trans. Alice Jardine and Harry Blake, 'Women's Time', in *The Kristeva Reader*, ed. Toril Moi (Oxford: Blackwell, 1986), pp. 187–213.

48 Janet Sayers, *Mothering Psychoanalysis – Helene Deutsch, Karen Horney, Anna Freud, Melanie Klein* (London: Hamish Hamilton, 1991).

49 'Interview with Hanna Segal', *Women – A Cultural Review*, 1, no. 2 (1990), pp. 198–214.

50 Klein, *Love, Guilt and Reparation*, pp. 1–53, pp. 59–76, p. 46.

51 Klein, cited in Grosskurth, *Melanie Klein*, p. 197; Grosskurth comments in a note on the same page: 'There is no indication that Melitta was suffering from any physical ailment. Is she suggesting that Melitta was schizoid?'

52 Ibid., pp. 381, 53, 90, 99–100, 218.

53 Melitta Schmideberg, 'Intellektuelle Hemmung and Esstorung', p. 109, trans. Robert Gillet and Jacqueline Rose, 'Intellectual Inhibition and Eating Disorders', p. 262.

54 Schmideberg, 'A Contribution to the Psychology of Persecutory Ideas and Delusions', *International Journal of Psycho-Analysis*, 12 (1931), pp. 343, 344, 349; 'Some Unconscious Mechanisms in Pathological Sexuality and their Relation to Normal Sexual Activity', *International Journal of Psycho-Analysis*, 14 (1933), pp. 228, 252, 256.

55 Schmideberg, 'Persecutory Ideas and Delusions', p. 344; 'Some Unconscious Mechanisms', p. 248.

56 A. Freud, 'Studies in Passivity', 1952, in *Writings of Anna Freud*, vol. 4, p. 259.

57 This is, at the very least, a difficult issue, and is a reproach often made against Melanie Klein. The 'Controversial Discussions' and the papers subsequently published in *Developments in Psycho-Analysis* make it clear, I think, that it involves a simplification of the complex significance which Klein and her supporters attach to the external world. While it is undoubtedly the case that their unique emphasis was on internal psychic factors, the intensity of the latter in fact *increased* the importance of the environment. In 'Psychical Conflict in Earliest Infancy', Rivière describes the way that 'inexorable internal need' is *'referred* as a demand upon the external mother' (p. 46; my emphasis); the fact that the child experiences the behaviour of real objects as a 'mirror

reflection' of its feelings towards them is what 'determines the importance of the child's real experience and of the environmental factors in development' (p. 56). Note too that Anna Freud's position is also a nuanced one; while she stresses external and environmental factors, she comments, for example, that conclusions drawn from home life can be 'as misleading in some cases as they are accurate in others' ('Certain Types and Stages of Social Maladjustment', 1949, in *The Writings of Anna Freud*, vol. 4, p. 85). In relation to Melanie Klein, it is in fact very hard to establish a clear causality between inner and outer. Cf. for example this passage from her late paper 'On the Theory of Anxiety and Guilt' (1948): 'The frustrating (bad) external breast becomes, owing to projection, the external representative of the death instinct; through introjection it reinforces the primary internal danger-situation; this leads to an increased urge on the part of the ego to deflect (project) internal dangers (primarily the activity of the death instinct) into the external world' (in *Envy and Gratitude and Other Works 1946–63*, in *Writings of Melanie Klein*, vol. 4, p. 31). In an unpublished paper, 'The Fissure of Authority: violence and phantasy in the work of Melanie Klein', John Phillips gives a very convincing description of how ambiguity between external and internal determination is integral to Klein's work.

58 Schmideberg, 'Persecutory Ideas and Delusions', pp. 349–50; 'The Psycho-Analysis of Asocial Children and Adolescents', *International Journal of Psycho-Analysis*, 16 (1935), p. 45; 'A Contribution to the History of the Psycho-Analytical Movement in Britain', *British Journal of Psychiatry*, 118 (January 1971), pp. 63, 67.

59 Schmideberg, *Children in Need*, with an introduction by Edward Glover (London: Allen and Unwin, 1948).

60 Schmideberg, 'History of the Psycho-Analytical Movement in Britain', p. 67.

61 Lacan, *Le Séminaire VII*, p. 126; trans., p. 105.

62 Schmideberg, 'Reassurance as a Means of Analytic Technique', *International Journal of Psycho-Analysis*, 16 (1935), p. 317.

63 Schmideberg, 'Asocial Children and Adolescents', p. 37n.

64   Schmideberg, 'The Play-Analysis of a Three-Year-Old Girl', *International Journal of Psycho-Analysis*, 15 (1934), p. 261.

65   Schmideberg, 'After the Analysis . . .', *Psycho-Analytic Quarterly*, 7 (1938), pp. 135–7.

66   Ibid., p. 140.

67   Ibid., p. 128; Freud to Jones, cited by Steiner, 'Some Thoughts about Tradition and Change', p. 32.

68   Franco Fornari, *The Psychoanalysis of War* (Bloomington, Ind., and London: Indiana University Press, 1975), p. 247.

69   Giles Radice, Labour MP for Durham North, reporting on research conducted in five South-East marginal seats that Labour failed to capture in April 1992: 'This is How Labour can win', *Independent*, 29 September 1992.

70   Rivière, 'Hate, Greed and Aggression', in Melanie Klein and Joan Rivière, *Love, Hate and Reparation, Psycho-Analytical Epitomes*, vol. 2 (London: Hogarth and the Institute of Psycho-Analysis, 1937), p. 8.

71   Lacan, 'La chose freudienne', in *Écrits*, p. 433; trans. 'The Freudian Thing', in *Écrits: a selection*, p. 142.

72   Cited by Elizabeth Roudinesco, *La Bataille de cent ans: l'histoire de la psychanalyse en France*, vol. 2, *1925–85* (Paris: Seuil, 1986), p. 136; trans. Jeffrey Mehlman, *Jacques Lacan & Co. – A History of Psychoanalysis in France 1925–85* (Chicago: University of Chicago Press; London: Free Association Books, 1990), p. 122.

73   Lacan, *Le Séminaire VII*, p. 127; trans., p. 106.

74   Donald Meltzer, *The Kleinian Development*, Part II (Perthshire: Clunie Press, 1978), p. 47.

75   Leo Bersani, *The Culture of Redemption* (Cambridge, Mass., and London: Harvard University Press, 1990) criticizes Klein in terms of the concept of redemption. Bersani's writing on violence and culture in relation to Freud anticipates some of the themes addressed here (cf. *The Freudian Body*: Columbia University Press, 1986, esp. Ch. 1, 'Theory and Violence'); see also Jessica Benjamin, *The Bonds of Love* (New York: Pantheon, 1986, London: Virago, 1988).

An Interview with Jacqueline Rose

Conducted by Michael Payne and Maire Jaanus

JAANUS I thought that the first question I would ask you is about questions, because it is so noticeable to me when I read you that both the beginnings and the ends of your essays are always questions. You take other people's – often feminists' – answers, and you undo them as questions, or you re-pose questions as new questions. As I was reading your essays, I thought that they are just propelled by questions. There's a motor movement, an unrest in the essays, and it makes them very difficult. I was reminded of Derrida saying that the question is the real discipline in philosophy. And Kristeva saying that a question is a suffering. And then I thought, I will ask her, what is a question for her?

ROSE I don't have my definition of a question; but a way of understanding what you are saying would be in terms of the difficult forms of compatibilities which I would like to put into play. On the one hand, there are political questions in the very substantial sense of the word, as in the feminist struggle to transform forms of oppressive social organization for women, questions which can be transmuted fairly directly into political demand. On the other hand, I would want to place alongside these the project, which I have always seen myself as part of, which is involved in trying to articulate problems of psychosexuality, the way subjects, and especially women, find themselves positioned within language, within sexuality, and within culture at the most fundamental level of their subjective and unconscious organization. And in that domain, everything is a question. That is to say, if you take the Freudian idea of the unconscious, it is the site of an interminable self-questioning which undermines any possible conclusion to self-definition. It has been said many times, and I agree, that it is not immediately evident what the terms of the dialogue could be between the notion of political demand in the first sense and this other project of a continuous and radical psychic self-questioning. But the kind of feminism that I want and see myself involved in would be one that saw the second – that is, radical self-questioning – not as a block or a bar to political process, but as a necessary part of its procedures and – this is not exactly utopian but more a bid for the future – would take this as feminism's specific contribution to other forms of political life. The argument would be that feminism, in so far as it is in touch with the sexual not just as assertion, important though that is, but as a self-questioning, can undo a certain rhetoric of certainty – one which has often dominated left-wing political discourse and whose bankruptcy seems more and more obvious today.

JAANUS Let me just ask you this question again, maybe because of what you said. When Lacan spoke of Socrates as a hysteric and as a questioner, and when he spoke of the witty butcher's wife, if I understand it correctly, he said that a question is a demand for knowledge, and that the hysteric makes this demand for knowledge. But he also said that a demand is not desire. Desire is for being. For Socrates, finally, there was a desire for knowledge; it was not a demand for knowledge, as for the hysteric. And being cannot be found in knowledge any more. There is too much uncertainty. And I just wondered, in the context of what you were just saying about your desire for a feminist politics – you used the word 'demand' just a little while ago – if there is a need for being, if desire is for being, in what will women find their being, or is being obsolete?

ROSE Another way of putting it would be to reinsert the question of being into the agenda of politics. Or, more simply, it would be to reformulate a politics that could – and you are right that I used the word 'demand' – make its demands for forms of social transformation in the most concrete and material sense without relinquishing the question of being; that is to say, without relinquishing the question of a subjectivity that will always be in excess of or in default of any concrete and particular demand. I think that feminism can do both those things at the same time. Let's take a couple of concrete examples. The one that comes to mind, which I discuss in 'Where Does the Misery Come From?', is the dispute about fantasy in relationship to the real event in psychoanalysis, and the charge that the psychoanalytic attention to fantasy deprives women of legitimate accusations against the real world, quite specifically against fathers or paternal sexual abuse, that Freud had to clean up on this, and that his 'repression' of the issue of abuse says a lot about Freud, obviously, but also about the bankruptcy of the psychoanalytic project – as in the famous Jeffrey Masson dispute. There is a situation in which you are presented quite dramatically with a choice: you either pay attention to the reality, the social reality of the event, and the plaint against it, or you talk about fantasy and the circulation and interminability of meaning.

If you ask psychoanalysts about this now, they will say that of course they acknowledge the reality of childhood abuse; the difference is that, for psychoanalysis, that is not the end, but the beginning, of the story – that is to say, that nothing can be done psychically for a patient who has been abused if you stop at the level of the first demand or if you stop at the level of the first recognition; and that the next and necessary psychoanalytic move would be to explore the range of meanings and fantasies generated by that experience for any individual woman subject up to and beyond the point at which they may or may not chime in with the appropriate political response or demand in the concrete sense. But if you turn to the concrete instances in which this has been played out, as for example the Cleveland case in England, where Marietta Higgs, the paediatrician working at Middlesborough Hospital in the North of England, brought in over a hundred children thought to have been sexually abused, leading to a huge controversy and a government-commissioned report on the matter, she will say that she cannot work in psychiatric time; she has to work in social work time. And in social work time, you simply take the children out of the home. Or if you read the special issue of *Feminist Review* (the feminist journal that is published in England) on child sexual abuse, Mary MacLeod and Esther Saraga argue that, faced with a child or even an adult remembering abuse, the therapist has a choice – either to ask in what way the child could feel responsible or to ask whether a small child can consent. That seems to me to be a psychically false alternative, although I can see how it might follow from the fact that in the field of law and social policy you do have to make a choice. Recognition of the immediate urgency appears literally to wipe out the possibility for these other forms of exploration. I think that this is improverishing for everybody involved in the concrete situation and impoverishing for the wider terms of political debate. It's as if you can have only one language or the other.

Asked about this, the Kleinian analyst Hanna Segal talked about a child who could both have been abused and have had a desire for the father. She made the point that this would not mean that the child had therefore wanted it to happen, rather that in such a situation the child would trust the parent even more not to act. I asked her whether one might not make a distinction between desiring something and wanting it, since the fact that you desire something doesn't mean that you want it to happen. But we don't have a language in the courts, we don't have a language in social work, and we don't have a language in demands for equal rights or freedom of choice in the realm of abortion or surrogacy, or in any area where the issue is that of equality or rights, for allowing that kind of complexity. Therefore I feel we deprive ourselves of whole components of the personal at the very moment when feminism is saying that the personal is its prerogative. I want to see if we can find a vocabulary for ending their mutual exclusiveness. So it's a question of incompatible forms of being, or a clash between demand and being, if you want to call it that, though I don't think I mean it quite in the Socratic sense.

PAYNE Just one further thing about the Socratic mode of your writing. Lacan also refers to Socrates as a midwife, and to psychoanalysis as a maieutic science or enterprise. Now I am curious as to what is getting born in this maieutic process of your text. Is it new knowledge? Is it a structure of value that you're after to make a transition between knowledge and politics? Or is there some more direct connection between knowledge and political action that you see as possible?

ROSE I think the issue is the possible relationships between those areas. In an article published in the anthology *Between Feminism and Psychoanalysis* edited by Teresa Brennan, Gayatri Spivak suggests that I run the epistemological/ontological question of woman too directly into the feminist axiological project of social transformation, whereas in fact it is because I see the former as caught in the throes of the unconscious that the link to feminism in the other, axiological sense precisely becomes an issue. So I would put your question in a slightly different way, which is; what are the possible connections between an interrogation of problems of self-identification and sexuality in the unconscious and a field that can be called one of (conscious) knowledge and politics in its most obvious sense?

For me, what remains crucial is that feminism brings sexuality on to the political stage. It has been responsible for an absolute whirlwind at the heart of what constitutes our political life. But that has often been conditional on the personal being assimilable to structures of identity that don't trouble politics or identities as they are usually understood. So it's as if we – and I say 'we' deliberately, because I'm caught in this problem as much as anybody else – we constantly, for good historical and political reasons, get cold feet. They are 'good' historical and political reasons because it is true that dominant social and legal institutions and discourses will abuse the employment of more nuanced forms of language. In rape cases, lawyers pleading for the defendant will argue that the accuser said no, but psychoanalysis tells us that a 'no' might cover an unconscious 'yes' (this would be an instance of the law using the category of the unconscious, but against women). The fact is that they haven't understood the distinction between the conscious and the unconscious, since what goes into the unconscious is precisely what you don't desire to happen in your concrete existence. But you're not going to last two minutes in a courtroom trying to make those kinds of distinctions. So when I argue that feminism brings the sexual into the personal arena and then stalls on what it allows as legitimate to be said about it, I think that has to be understood not as a failure of will or as an intel-

lectual inadequacy or theoretical mistake, but as a part
of the historical moment in which these things are both
happening and failing to happen. There has been in the
last five years an increasing exploration of the complexity of sexual life and identity on the part of many feminists, specifically in the realm of popular culture and
film and readings of literary texts, feminists who are
working to open up the field of sexual identifications, so
it isn't just me who is saying this.

JAANUS Your chapter on 'Daddy' at the end of *The
Haunting of Sylvia Plath* brings us back to some of these
questions on fantasy. In that chapter you made harrow-
ingly real the way that unconscious psychic space is so
vast and so infinite that within it one can stand in any
position, and the different identities one can assume, as
victim and executioner and as innocent and guilty and
so on; and the kinds of crises which can be caused for
the individual who has participated in this way in the
possibilities of his unconscious or who has been forced
to, because of an external situation, who has been driven
around in his own unconscious into these different positions. But then at the end of the essay you said something that struck me very much. First you asked whether
women may not have a special relationship to fantasy,
and then, even more radically, and I'm quoting you now,
whether 'women may not be most likely to articulate the
power of fantasy as such'. Do you see a real asymmetry
here in the fundamental power of fantasy?

ROSE Julia Kristeva says in her article 'Women's
Time' that, faced with the problem of psychic differentiation and separateness, it seems that women will try to
deny it and men will try to over-assert it. This proposition or insight could be seen as the basis of such very
different uses of psychoanalysis and feminism as Chris-
tiane Olivier's *Children of Jocasta* on the one hand and

Nancy Chodorow's work on the other. What I think Kristeva is saying there – it is one of those moments in her work where there is a clear recognition of the over-determination between psychic bodily self-recognition and socially sanctioned forms of identity and behaviour – is that men and women emerge out of a similar trajectory in slightly different positions, psychically. So, while at the same time I would want to insist on the bisexuality of the unconscious, because that was always and is being increasingly stressed as one of Freud's most radical insights, I don't think that this idea works unless it goes hand in hand with the simultaneous account in psychoanalysis of the production of a difference. One of the things that most interests me about psychoanalysis is the symmetry and the asymmetry in the field of sexual and unconscious life.

However, in suggesting that women may have a privileged relation to fantasy, I was also, as one only can at the end of a book, throwing out a statement to see what would happen to it. The excitement of working on Sylvia Plath was that she seemed to articulate together in the space of her writing – in a single text, a poem, a line of a poem – on the one hand a strong, articulate protest against social institutions such as medicine and psychiatry and marriage, while on the other and at the same time acknowledging women's complex and sometimes self-defeatingly pleasurable engagement in the very structures against which they protest. The ability of Plath to hold these two things together in such a way that they didn't cancel each other out, but if anything strengthened both, was, I'm sure, one of the reasons for my continuing fascination in and commitment to her. Plath allows us to think about a political language in which recognition of the 'perverseness' of the fantasmatic and the assertion of political protest and identity could be articulated simultaneously.

I realize that this raises the question of in what languages such a joint articulation is possible. There is a problem in pointing to a literary discourse or poetic writing as the place of such a possibility, because before you know where you are, you've slid into that privileging of the literary which I think is the weakest aspect of Kristeva's work and of the whole *Tel Quel* project. But I was also making another point about forms of feminist argument. For one feminism there is felt to be a tension between the discourse and language of the social sciences in their concrete specificity and the language of literary or psychoanalytic theory – the feeling, which we have already touched on, that if you are making concrete political demands or acknowledging the real oppression – not to say, in some contexts, victimization – of women, then you cannot also talk about women's fantasies or their 'complicity' at the level of the unconscious (in fact, it's not complicity, because it says nothing about what women actually want to happen). But it is true that to discuss this dimension of fantasy is a way of allowing that women might be mentally playing out, or with, the positions that they are simultaneously condemning and trying to exclude. But there is no place for this in the language of Andrea Dworkin or Catharine McKinnon, no discussion of psychoanalysis, because it would be seen to be undermining of the political project.

It is this position which I am deliberately trying to shift – not invert; I don't want to replace one vocabulary with the other. But it none the less involves a twist: which is to argue that precisely *because* it is so clear that in certain situations women are victims – and not just in the context of rape and child abuse, but let's come a little bit closer to home in the USA and the Clarence Thomas hearings and the testimony of Anita Hill, in which you did indeed see a woman being victimized as a huge legal and governmental apparatus tried to discredit her utterance on the issue of sexual harassment – precisely *because* it is so clear in certain contexts that women are the victims, this, then, should be seen as releasing a permission internal to the discourse of feminism to talk about fantasy. This would be to alter the received position on the relationship between fantasy and politics, by saying that because we can be so sure that women are oppressed and victimized, so we can also give ourselves permission to talk about the difficult, self-undermining, playful, contradictory aspects of our fantasy lives. Or, we must repeat again and again that to talk about the second is in no way incompatible with or undermines the first. As I've already said, I think we need a language in which both these things can be said at once. I want feminism to be able to talk about the psychic in a way that doesn't have to subordinate itself to the one-track, singular, surface-level rhetoric of the received available forms of political language and discourse.

JAANUS   When you were speaking, I was thinking that actually the one urgent political demand then is, if I understand you correctly – or would be, certainly – a reform in the law, because that's where you see most concretely women being punished or victimized. There are endless cases: divorce cases, adoption cases, rape cases. And the reform in the law that you are asking for is really that the law become more psychoanalytical in the true sense, rather than misusing psychoanalysis, as you said before. It seems to me it would involve a total transformation of the present language of the law to incorporate into itself a vocabulary of fantasy which is present in literature. It would be like a making literal, or literalizing, of legal language, the whole legal structure. It's an enormous task.

ROSE   That's a difficult question and relates to current debates about the law, but I don't think that's what I'm asking for. In fact, in certain areas of critical legal theory, the argument would be that legal discourse is already infused with the literary, already troped, and hence – in ways that contradict what is often its dominant project – inherently unstable and available to be read. One feminist project would be this form of unmasking or interrogating – linguistic/literary – of the law. But at another level, it's clear what, in the field of law, feminist demands are, like freedom of choice or equal pay, for example. What feminism so often encounters there are straightforward forms of reaction, prejudice, obfuscation, and obstruction of feminist demands. The point I have been making is that there are moments in the law where the personal is abused on the wrong side, where concepts from psychoanalysis are misused in order to foster reactionary legal decisions against women, which then increases the suspicion, reasonably enough, of feminists with regard to psychoanalytic discourse. Freud himself argued that psychoanalysis should never be appealed to in a court of law, because the realm it deals with cannot be used to decide things either way. In these instances, the aim would not be to introduce psychoanalysis into law, but to effect a clearer separation and demarcation of the separate realms.

But at the same time I agree that I am asking another question, to do with a wider field of political vocabularies – which is whether the nature of feminist legal and political demand, and its required forms of articulation, has to rule out the simultaneous exploration of the subjective or psychic experiences for women – in all their ambivalence, complexity, and ambiguity – of those demands themselves (the issue of abortion or surrogacy, for example). Can we find a way of expressing that dimension without sacrificing the force of the political demand or feeling that the argument has thereby been handed over to the opponents of legal advance for women? The point would therefore be to separate the legal issue from such areas where it is strategic to do so, but without ruling them out of what defines our forms of political self-understanding and definition. The writer who has come closest to this for me, or helped me to think how it might be possible, is Patricia Williams. Although her framework is not psychoanalytic, in *The Alchemy of Race and Rights* – which is, I know, famous in the States, just published by Virago in Britain – she seems to move across incompatible domains, bringing something of these forms of language together: the most intensely personal account of the psychic tracks and backtracks of her life, an epistemological critique and internal dismantling of the language and apparatus of the law, and a restated commitment (against some critical criminology) to the project of human rights, all this, crucially, in the name of a politics of race. This – the fact that Williams is writing about racial politics and about feminism – is also one instance which shows how feminism today has to define itself as something which exceeds its own earlier boundaries, as something which, in order to continue, has therefore to be more than itself.

PAYNE   As I read you, and you have to tell me if this is wrong, I see your theoretical projects as having three dimensions to them. First, and the basic one, is your reading in psychoanalysis. Out of that you are deriving a language of fantasy and desire and sexuality that complicates in interesting and politically important ways the second dimension of your project, which is feminism. But there is a third dimension: war, capital punishment, the political and social consequences of Thatcherism in Britain and Reaganism in America – which you see as related to problems of feminism and as potentially informed by psychoanalysis. My question is, is it the case that you are getting from the texts of psychoanalysis a theoretical ground for your feminist politics and your other politics?

ROSE   I don't want to hierarchize them as much as that – although it is up to readers to decide where they think the hierarchy lies – because I don't want to give psychoanalysis the status of a meta-discourse. The point is to use psychoanalysis selectively and not as a fixed body of 'truth'. The context in which one is deploying it also has crucial effects on how it can be used. So, for example, making available Lacan's texts on feminine sexuality was possible for me only in a context where there was already a feminist intellectual and political movement with which they could engage, even if controversially, and also outside the institutional parameters which made it impossible for many – although not all – women psychoanalysts in Paris finally to work with, or affiliate to, Lacan himself. Lacan's ideas cannot of course be completely detached from that world, but the difference of my history, being an outsider to the world of Lacan, was not just the actual but also the necessary condition for that project; it was what made it theoretically and politically feasible to translate his work. Had I been a feminist in France, I would not have been able to bring out a book entitled *Feminine Sexuality – Jacques Lacan and the école freudienne*, even if I still find many of Lacan's ideas immensely productive today.

What interests me in psychoanalysis now is, on the one hand, an effect of my feminist politics and, on the other, a desire to understand other aspects of politics and history: State legitimacy, the fantasy component of Thatcherism, the Holocaust in relation to the problem of historical memory. It's a two-way process between the field of psychoanalysis and politics. The question then becomes – again – what form of dialogue and compatibility there could be between them. All this in a context where it seemed to me that the feminist debate about psychoanalysis, certainly in terms of the opposition between a Lacanian account of feminine sexuality and the woman-centred accounts of French feminists such as Luce Irigaray, had got stuck. The phallocentric account gives you an account of femininity which is there or precisely not there to be constructed, and that's what is progressive about it; but it's phallocentric. The other account isn't phallocentric; but it gives a woman who is always already there. I don't think this issue is capable of theoretical resolution; all you can do is follow the effects of what is released and/or blocked by the two different versions.

It also seemed to me that so successful had feminism been in insisting on the political nature of the sexual and the psychic, that the sexual and psychic nature of the political in the other sense had become correspondingly neglected. And this sense coincided with a moment where there were certain things I felt the need to understand as a feminist, the first of which was the phenomenon of Thatcherism, since it was so shocking for feminists to see a woman achieve the summit of political power and then embody that power in a form which one would like to call parodic self-fashioning, but which somewhere was so clearly quite the opposite – an absolute literalizing, of a kind one suspects no man could carry off today in Britain, of the patriarchal and authoritarian structures of statehood to the point where she laid bare, and I think this was inadvertent, the extent to which all State authority rests on violence – as if a woman was, paradoxically, bringing the latent violence of State power to the surface of our social life. In that case, psychoanalysis wasn't the discourse from which I went to other questions. It was that there were things that were troubling me that I wanted to understand. And it seemed to me that bits of psychoanalysis could help me to do that.

JAANUS Did you see Thatcher as someone completely detached from the symbolic, empty and detached, really – let's go back to Lacanian terms – is that how you were also describing her?

ROSE I think she embodies the symbolic law at its most self-inflated and rigid, the symbolic law that is absolutely incapable of knowing its own points of failure. In relationship to the discussion of Lacan, I think it's crucial to bring back, as Slavoj Zizek has in his writing, especially in *The Sublime Object of Ideology*, the concept of the real, if only to make it absolutely clear that the symbolic is not a fixed structure. Most of the critiques made of psychoanalysis or Lacanian psychoanalysis accuse it of being over-deterministic, and argue that Lacan's concept of the symbolic order means that you are inscribed in language and therefore fixed for all time. If you reintroduce the category of the real, or even if you read what he says about the symbolic, the symbolic is always also the site of its own failing, hence the importance of his seminar on ethics and what he has to say about the aporia of the law. Thatcher can be seen, I think, as somebody for whom the law must not know its own sense of aporia, and must always entrench itself in a vision of its own self-fulfilment (which is why I make the link to Hofstadter's concept of politics in the paranoid style). But there is another point I want to make here, which is that if psychoanalysis is radical for women, it is not, as I see it, through a notion of writing-in-the-body which relegates psychoanalysis to its age-old allegiance with the literary institution in a celebration essentially of high modernist writing. The risk is that you render anodyne and safe and poeticize the unconscious.

I also think that there has been a problem in the relationship between psychoanalysis and social theory for feminism which can perhaps be traced back to Juliet Mitchell's book *Psychoanalysis and Feminism*, which, while opening up the question of sexuality and the unconscious for women, locked social organization – via Lévi-Strauss's account of kinship – into the structure of patriarchal exchange. So, following that lead, Gail Rubin wrote her famous essay 'The Traffic in Women', in which women are exchanged because the phallus is what is being circulated, and the phallus is what is being circulated because women are exchanged – a perfect functionalist 'fit' between psyche and social. The trouble was that it was so rigid that, in a later essay in the anthology *Pleasure and Danger* edited by Carole Vance, Rubin argues for a complete severing of questions of sexuality and sexual pleasure from the relations of gender. It seemed to be the logical consequence of the first move. If you've tied them so tightly together and you want a politics of sexuality of a more libertarian kind, you have to then resunder them as if the alternatives are too much of a tie or no link at all. I think this problem was a consequence of the fact that, whereas the emphasis in psychoanalysis and feminism on sexuality has been about the necessity and failure of female identity (with the stress for me on the latter), the concept of the social has not caught up with that. There has been literally a lag in the theory, where the concept of the social has remained at the level of a notion of efficient exchange. It's been a sort of baggage which has been carried along with the feminist account of sexual identities, so that the social, as a concept in psychoanalysis, has been relatively unexplored. So the other move behind the Thatcher–Ellis piece, the 'Daddy' chapter, and the 'Why War?' piece is an attempt to return to psychoanalysis to see what it can say about – as much as the failing of sexual identity – the failing of social identity and social self-positioning. It was the feeling that something had gone out of 'sync' in what we'd been taking from psychoanalysis and what we needed it or could perhaps continue to use it for.

PAYNE May I ask you where the aesthetic dimension stands in your cultural theoretical project, on the one hand, and your psychoanalytic work, on the other. Perhaps I should ask it this way: in the last chapter of your book on Sylvia Plath, the chapter on 'Daddy', you seem to be reclaiming the aesthetic dimension of the poem against those who have claimed the misuse and the inappropriateness of Plath's Holocaust metaphor. And so you offer really a meticulous New Critical reading of the poem, very carefully working through its poetic structure and its form. But then there's an undercurrent in your text that sort of disrupts that formalist reading of the text, in which there is a great deal of Lacanian theory at work. No?

ROSE Psychoanalytic theory. The main references are taken from the International Association of Psycho-Analysis 1985 conference in Hamburg, which was the first time that the Association had returned to Germany since their visit to Wiesbaden in 1932. Melanie Klein is also very present too.

PAYNE All right. Psychoanalytic theory. Now one other possible point of contact here with the question about the place of the aesthetic concerns the play *Mrs Klein*, which figures in your chapter on Melanie Klein and Anna Freud. Assuming that you don't want to claim an exalted place for the aesthetic *per se*, has the aesthetic become a means of getting access to certain cultural processes that are both politically and psychoanalytically charged?

ROSE Well, it's an interesting question because, of course, psychoanalysis is the practice of language, the talking cure. It is the realm of what Lacan defines as the 'function and field of speech and language' in his famous Rome discourse; but way before then, there is a historically accredited set of links between psychoanalysis and literature, in so far as they are both hermeneutic activities. So there is a kind of parallelism, often leading, problematically, to applied psychoanalysis, the kinds of

readings of literary texts by psychoanalysis that Shoshana Felman undoes so brilliantly in her essay on Henry
James's *The Turn of the Screw*. That was the essay which
initiated a shift from content analysis to a use of psychoanalysis which says more about the 'enunciative modality'
as one might call it, of textual utterances or speech acts,
but speech acts as informed by the psychoanalytic concept of the unconscious. Now to that extent, the reading
of 'Daddy' in the Plath book can be seen as a continuation of the ways in which a psychoanalytic attention to
language and a literary attention to the movements of
poetic discourses have certain objectives or strategies
or movements in common.

But the term 'New Criticism' of course makes me a
bit uncomfortable, because my understanding of New
Criticism is that, in the end, the reading of the poem
is in the service of underscoring the aesthetic integrity
of the object – that is to say, it reinscribes the literary
object back within the parameter of the literary, whereas
my attempt to read the 'Daddy' poem in the Plath text
tries to open it up, not to history in the sense of its
historical context or referent, but to historical processes
as in themselves determined by structures of linguistic
slippage, identification, and fantasy of the same kind as
are being explored in the poetic text. So there is a reference out to something which I'd want to call history and
also a reference out to a feminist sexual politics, or a
feminist sexual political concern with the question of
fantasy – on condition that you don't make those the
concrete base referents of the text, but see both of them
as caught up in problems of unconscious self-fashioning
or self-representation of the kind that is going on in the
language of the poem.

But I also see a more general point about literary
theory today in your questions. One of the oppositions
which often appears in literary theory is between a con-
centration on the literary or aesthetic movement of the

writing and a reading of literary texts in the name of something called history or materiality, with the corresponding insistence that the latter grounds the text in a more concrete, referential domain. But that distinction is one which I was trying, in the reading of 'Daddy', to unsettle, by suggesting that both halves of the opposition need to be troubled by what they encounter on either side of the binary. So there is an appeal to the category of the aesthetic, but through history and psyche on the one hand, and to that of history, but through linguistic and unconscious processes on the other.

I also think that the opposition between the aesthetic and the historical is further displaced by the issue of memory. In his introductory chapter to *The Drowned and the Saved*, Primo Levi really goes for Liliana Caviani's *Night Porter* for the way it suggests that there are sadists in all of us. For Levi, real, historically attributable injustice is merely obfuscated by any confusion of the boundary between victim and executioner, so he is issuing a very strong challenge to anybody trying to work with the mutability of fantasy. But one of the powerful things about the book is that he insists on this at the same time as discussing in the most extraordinary way the problem and difficulty of memory in relationship to the Holocaust and his own experience of it, while in his chapter on the grey zone, he also describes the forms of uncertain divison between, and inside, identities involved at the time.

Now this is not something which I can talk about in terms of my own historical experience, but there does seem to be an issue here about memory and history. And it goes beyond, although it is related to, the debate about the relativizing (or not) of history in relation to the Holocaust – Hayden White acknowledges in his article in Saul Friedlander's collection *Probing the Limits of Representation* that no event puts greater strain on the relativizing of history, provoked by recent developments in linguistic and literary theory, than the Holocaust. But it is rather a question of what the concept of memory – and the relation of memory to fantasy – does to the category of history. At one stage oral historians thought that oral evidence, evidence culled from the field of memory, was going to be an innovative, authentic form of evidence. A historian like Sally Alexander, one of the editors of and contributors to *History Workshop Journal* and author of the forthcoming collection *Essays in Feminist History*, will now say that the oral record has to be treated like a text, read for its gaps and silences and points of fantasy, because it is a self-selection and self-representation – even if she would also say that there is a difference between the oral and the written historical record.

JAANUS   Would you like to say anything about the question of ethics, because you raised the issue of the ethics of failure at the end of the piece on war, in which you also talked about the origin of the ethical commandment in Freud's second essay on war, where the death of the beloved hated other produces the commandment 'Thou shalt not kill'. What I was going to ask you is, if human relationships cannot be love–hate relationships, then do they not have to be relationships in the sense of indifference, or a kind of indifference? I wonder whether you had hopes for a feminine ethics, or whether it was possible, because again and again in your essays the crisis of morality and the crisis of ethics reappears.

ROSE   I think the notion of a specifically feminine ethics is always surrounded by real flashpoints of danger because it can so easily become a notion of women's priority over the domain of the ethical, which seems often to involve an idealization of the feminine unconscious. On the other hand, the argument that a different form of ethics would arise if mothering were seen as a more central component of how political dimensions define themselves seems to be a different and important point. Mothering not just as a set of different political priorities like child-care facilities, which are of course crucial, but mothering in the sense that Kristeva talks about, as an area of hybridity where the relationship between self and other is obfuscated, confused, and re-worked. I think there is something to be said for that, on condition that it's not literalized and that ethics doesn't get transposed into maternal duty, which I don't think Kristeva argues.

There is an obvious link from there to her book on racism, in which she uses Freud's concept of the un-canny. Ethics then appears as an extension of the ques-tion of self-othering. How – and with what force or violence – are the boundaries of difference between self and other produced, and what is it possible to reinteg-rate from what it is that you have got rid of in the very production and formation of identity? In the passages I quote from Freud's essay on war, it seems to me that he is saying something about that: that the ethical dimen-sion has to reside not just in the form of empathetic humanism that you get, for example, at the end of Olive Schreiner's novel *Story of an African Farm* or at points in Bessie Head's *A Question of Power*, where empathy is an invocation to cross-cultural identification and a general, human form of recognition, but an ethics that would include in that project a recognition of the alien-ness of self-identification, which makes it more difficult, but even more urgent. In fact, Bessie Head's novel does also move on something of that terrain.

To make a leap to today, this does seem to me to be one of the most acute political problems as the question of national self-identities erupts all over Eastern Europe and in the former Soviet Union. How to detach legitimate claims to national self-determination from the most de-structive forms of nationalist assertion. This is the domain in which the question of ethics and the question of politics are deeply implicated in each other. A certain reading of mothering as self–other differentiation and non-differentiation might be a metaphoric way of thinking about some of these questions, provided you don't literalize this as the task and/or inherent property of all mothers, and provided you don't end up idealizing women.

JAANUS   Can I just ask one more question? Obviously there are two aspects to the epistemological dimension of psychoanalysis – the kind of knowledge that we get from it and the rationalization of this knowledge in a sense, and the cure. They can't be separated. But in a sense, they can be separated if you are not in a clinical situation. I wondered how you related those two different dimensions of psychoanalysis and whether you do draw a hope in a sense from the aspect of the cure, that there is such a thing as a cure. I thought of this because I know you yourself have undergone psychoanalysis and feel that you've benefited from it, and because you raised this at the end of your article 'Why War?' where you say that the ultimate challenge for the psychoanalytic cure is really the problem of war. And so I wondered how you relate to those two dimensions and whether perhaps psycho-analysis was so important to you originally, also intel-lectually, because it has this other dimension of the cure.

ROSE   You asked me yesterday which one – psycho-analysis inside or outside the profession, in the clinic or in the 'academy' and wider intellectual culture – needs the other most, which is another version of the question you just put to me. I think they both need each other, not because I think that it is illegitimate to read psycho-analytic texts without reference to the therapeutic activ-ity, because I think psychoanalysis is a body of writing that can be read like any other, and there is a danger of fetishizing the clinical situation as the sole site of psychoanalytic truth in a way that denies the obvious fact that psychoanalysis has points of dialogue with education, law, social work, literary writing, the analysis of culture, politics, and history; that is to say, psychoanalysis has always also been involved in those forms of investigation and scrutiny, so I don't believe that it is somewhere in default of itself in the academy if it isn't constantly referring to the clinical setting. On the other hand, the complete severance between the two domains and the reading of psychoanalysis without the possibility of also discussing it in the context of clinical practice, which is after all where many of the psychoanalytic ideas being used in the humanities arise, is, I think, a problem. You do get a different set of questions and a different set of insights if you think about psychoanalysis in relationship to the therapeutic activity.

On the concept of the cure – we would have to have a much fuller discussion about what we think a cure is, what a cure is for different people, and the points at which the notion of the cure vary dramatically between different analysts themselves. For example, I have just read Michael Eigen's paper on catastrophe and faith in the work of Bion in *The Electrified Tightrope*, in which he argues – against Klein, who sees a transition from the paranoid-schizoid phase to the depressive position as the condition for creativity seen as an essentially reparative activity – that creativity arises out of a more dialectical interplay between the two stages, neither of which ever replaces the other. So, after Bion, Eigen reads creativity in terms not of reparation, but catastrophe. So even inside the clinical literature, the notion of the cure has to be read as much as anything else, and discussed.

JAANUS I was also asking something broader, whether just the fact that, no matter how it comes about, there has been a cure for individuals, whether this gives something additional, something beyond the intellect, beyond knowledge, that psychoanalysis offers, which certainly the university has never been able to offer.

ROSE I agree that you have to recognize that it is the objective of most psychoanalytic practice to effect some notion of transformation, if not cure, and that is not the objective of the university in the same way. In fact, I would argue that it is crucial not to see teaching as a therapeutic activity. However, there are points of overlap in so far as transference does occur in a teaching situation, and how you deal with it will depend on the institution's or teacher's relationship to knowledge. Shoshana Felman, in her book on Lacan, discusses the relationship between analysis and pedagogy and the way that, for Lacan, the objective of psychoanalysis is the dissolution of a fantasy of knowledge lodged in the person of the analyst. One could argue that the dissolution of such a fantasy will be the effect of a true learning experience, which brings us back to Socrates and being, which is where we began.

More obviously, to say that the cure is outside knowledge and outside the intellect is, I think, problematic, because the framework within which a cure is effected will be determined and over-determined by the intellectual parameters that any individual analyst brings to the concept of the cure. That is very clear in the row between Lacan and the ego psychologists; there is a big difference between saying, as Strachey translated Freud, 'where id was, there ego shall be', and retranslating it, as Lacan did, 'where it was, so must I come to be'. The ramifications of that for a concept of the cure, which is roughly a split between the American dream and the surrealist magazine *Minotaur*, are quite dramatic and monumental.

JAANUS Well, we know where you stand on this . . . [*laughter*]

ROSE Maybe you don't! Maybe one can't exactly 'know' that. But having said that about the cure as a concept, of course I also agree with you that there will be a dimension in the analytic process which defies its own theorization. Much of the work that goes on in the humanities in recent literary theory is about the limits of theory, the way theory constantly undermines its own speculative endeavour. So that point, the point at which psychoanalysis as a practice comes up against the limits of its own interpretive process, might be the point at which there could be the strongest dialogue between psychoanalytic practice and the readings of psychoanalysis in the humanities which stress the ultimate failure of controlling interpretive procedures.

Jacqueline Rose: *A Bibliography, 1974–1992*

compiled by Nancy Weyant

1974

1 (Trans.), 'Freud in Paris', by J. B. Pontalis, *International Journal of Psychoanalysis*, 55, pp. 455–8.

1975

2 'Writing as Auto-Visualisation: notes on a scenario and film of *Peter Pan,*' *Screen*, 16, no. 3 (Autumn), pp. 29–53.
3 Comment on *The Freudian Slip* by Sebastiano Timpanaro, *New Left Review*, 94 (November/December), pp. 74–9.

1976

4 'Paranoia and the Film System', *Screen*, 17, no. 4 (Winter 1976–7) pp. 85–104. Translated in *Ça Cinéma*; special issue, *Psychoanalyse et cinéma*, 16 (1978), pp. 44–60. Reprinted in *Feminism and Film Theory*, ed. Constance Penley (London and New York: Routledge, 1988), pp. 141–58.

1977

5 (Trans.), 'Suture – Elements of the Logic of the Signifier', by Jacques-Alain Miller, *Screen*, 18, no. 4 (Winter 1977–8), pp. 24–34.

1978

6 'Dora-Fragment of an Analysis', *m/f* 2, pp. 5–21. Reprinted in *In Dora's Case: Freud, hysteria, feminism*, ed. Charles Bernheimer and Claire Kahane (New York: Columbia University Press; London: Virago, 1985), pp. 128–48.

1980

7 'Woman as Symptom', in *Cinema in the Eighties* (Venice: Edizione Biennale), pp. 23–5.

1981

8 (With Elizabeth Cowie *et al.*), 'Representation versus Communication', in *No Turning Back – Papers from the Women's Movement 1975–1980*, ed. (London: The Women's Press), pp. 238–45.

9 'Jacques Lacan – An Intellectual portrait', *Times Higher Educational Supplement* (feature article), 2 October.

1982

10 'The Imaginary', in *The Talking Cure – Essays in Psychoanalysis and Language*, ed. Colin MacCabe (London: Macmillan), pp. 132–61.

11 'The Cinematic Apparatus – Problems in Current Theory', in *The Cinematic Apparatus*, ed. Teresa de Lauretis and Stephen Heath (London: Macmillan), pp. 172–86.

12 *Feminine Sexuality – Jacques Lacan and the école freudienne*, ed. Juliet Mitchell and Jacqueline Rose, trans. Jacqueline Rose (London: Macmillan; New York: Norton), Introduction II by Jacqueline Rose. Translated into Slovenian in *Zenska Seksualnost – Freud & Lacan*, Ljubljana, *Analecta* (1991), pp. 121–47.

1983

13   'Femininity and its Discontents', *Feminist Review*, 14, pp.
      5–21. Reprinted in *Sexuality: a Reader* (London: Virago,
      1987), pp. 187–98. Reprinted in *British Feminist Thought*,
      ed. Terry Lovell (Oxford: Blackwell, 1990), pp. 227–43.
      Reprinted in *Ethics: A Feminist Reader*, ed. Elizabeth
      Frazer, Jennifer Hornsby and Sabina, Lovibond, (Oxford
      and Cambridge, Mass.: Blackwell, 1992), pp. 236–58.
      Translated into Italian in *Cultura del Femminismo, Memoria,
      Rivista di storia delle Donne*, 15, no. 2 (1985) pp. 52–6.
      Translated into Slovenian in *Zenska Seksualnost – Freud
      & Lacan*, Ljubljana, *Analecta* (1991), pp. 201–18.
14   'Feminine Sexuality – Interview with Juliet Mitchell and
      Jacqueline Rose', *m/f*, 8 (Summer), pp. 3–16.
15   'Complete Diversity or Disarray?', Symposium on English
      Studies, *Times Higher Educational Supplement*, 11 February.

1984

16   *The Case of Peter Pan or The Impossibility of Children's
      Fiction* (London: Macmillan).

1985

17   'Sexuality in the Field of Vision', in *Difference: On Rep-
      resentation and Sexuality* ed. Kate Linker (New York: New
      Museum; London: Institute of Contemporary Arts),
      pp. 31–3.
18   'Sexuality in the Reading of Shakespeare: *Hamlet* and
      Measure for Measure', in *Alternative Shakespeares*, ed. John
      Drakakis (London and New York: New Accents),
      pp. 95–118.
19   'State and Language: *Peter Pan* as written for the child',
      from *The Case of Peter Pan*, ch. 5, in *Language Gender and
      Childhood*, ed. Caroline Steedman, Cathy Urwin, and
      Valerie Walkerdine, (London: Routledge and Kegan Paul),
      pp. 88–112. Another version of this text published in

Subjectivity and Social Relations, ed. Veronica Beechey, and James Donald, (Milton Keynes and Philadelphia: Open University Press), pp. 250–61.

1986

20   'Hamlet: the "Mona Lisa" of literature', *Critical Quarterly* 28, nos 1–2 (Spring/Summer) pp. 35–49. Reprinted in *Futures for English*, ed. Colin MacCabe (Manchester: Manchester University Press, 1987), pp. 35–49.
21   'Jeffrey Masson and Alice James,' *Oxford Literary Review*, 8, nos 1–2, pp. 185–92.
22   *Sexuality in the Field of Vision* (London: Verso).

1987

23   'The State of the Subject II: the institution of feminism', *Critical Quarterly* (Winter), pp. 9–15.
24   ' "The Man who Mistook his Wife for a Hat" or "A Wife is Like an Umbrella": Fantasies of the Modern and Postmodern', in *Identity: The Real Me*, ed. Lisa Appignanesi (London: Institute of Contemporary Art Publications); and in Andrew Ross, *Universal Abandon? The Politics of Postmodernism*, ed. (New York: University of Columbia Press, 1988), pp. 237–50.

1988

25   'Margaret Thatcher and Ruth Ellis', *New Formations*, 6 (Autumn), pp. 3–29. A short version of this article was published in the *New Statesman* (July) under the title 'Getting Away with Murder', pp. 34–7. Translated into French in Gilles Deleuze, and Felix Guattari, (eds), *Chimères*, 10 (Winter 1990–1), pp. 49–74.
26   'Sexuality and Vision', in *Vision and Visuality. Discussions in Contemporary Culture*, ed. Hal Foster, Dia Art Foundation (Seattle: Bay Press), pp. 115–27.

1989

27 'Shakespeare and the Death Drive – on *Measure for Measure*', in *L'Eros in Shakespeare*, ed. Keir Elam and Alessandro Serpieri, (Parma: Pratiche Editrice), pp. 29–46.
28 'Julia Kristeva – Take Two', in *Coming to Terms – Feminism, Theory, Politics*, ed. Elizabeth Weed, (New York and London: Routledge), pp. 17–33.
29 'Where Does the Misery Come From? – Psychoanalysis, Feminism and the Event', in *Feminism and Psychoanalysis*, ed. Richard Feldstein, and Judith Roof, (Ithaca, NY: Cornell University Press) pp. 25–39. Translated into Slovenian, *Problemi Eseji* 3 (1991), pp. 175–86.
30 'Psychoanalysis and History – A Comment', *History Workshop: a journal of Socialist and Feminist historians*, 28 (Autumn), pp. 148–54.

1990

31 'The Female Spectator', *The Spectatrix, Camera Obscura* (special issue), 20–1 (Autumn), pp. 274–9.
32 'Interview with Hanna Segal', in *Women – A Cultural Review*, ed. Isobel Armstrong, and Helen Carr, 2 (Autumn), pp. 198–214.
33 Review of *Sylvia Plath: The Critical Heritage*, by Linda W. Wagner; *Sexton – Selected Criticism*, by Diana Hume George; and *The Unbeliever – The Poetry of Elizabeth Bishop*, by Robert Dale Parker, *Journal of American Studies*, 24, no. 3, pp. 446–8.
34 Review of *Am I That Name? – Feminism and the Category of Women in History*, by D. Riley, *History Workshop: A Journal of Socialist and Feminist History*, 29 (Winter), pp. 159–62.

1991

35 *The Haunting of Sylvia Plath* (London: Virago). Reissued 1992 (Cambridge, Mass.: Harvard University Press).

36 'Why War?', *Winnicott Studies*, 6, pp. 66–83. Printed in *Bulletin of the Applied Section of the British Society of Psychoanalysis* (June), pp. 1–10. Trans. into Italian, *Psychologos*, 2 (January), pp. 36–47 (included in original, pp. 49–60).

37 'Strange Dissociation of Ideas', review of Elizabeth Roudinesco, *Lacan & Co.*, *Times Higher Educational Supplement*, 4 January.

38 Review, 'Faking it up with the truth – Anne Sexton: A Biography by Diane Wood Middlebrook', *Times Literary Supplement*, 1 November.

1992

39 *The Case of Peter Pan or The Impossibility of Children's Fiction*, rev. edn (Philadelphia: University of Pennsylvania Press).

Appendix: Intellectual Inhibition and Eating Disorders

Melitta Schmideberg,

Psychoanalysis has shown that the infant's first relation is to the mother's breast and that this, together with its relation to eating (*das Essen*), is significant for its whole relationship to the surrounding world. A neurotic woman patient said: 'In fact everything – reading, going to the theatre, visiting – is like eating. First you expect a lot and then you're disappointed. When I come to analysis, I eat your furniture, your clothes, your words. You eat my words, my clothes, my money. If you work, you're eaten up by your employer. But you are also eating yourself. One moment I am very hungry and the next I cannot eat a thing.'

Eating disorders provide a pathological indicator for disorders of object- and reality-relating. Little Beryl, who suffered from a severe eating inhibition, was also completely lacking in desire and affect, spoke to no one outside her closest family, and lived entirely in a fantasy world. As she started to show some appetite, so in proportion she began to express interests and wishes normally. In the case of Edna, three and a half years old and

Translated by Robert Gillett and Jacqueline Rose. First published as 'Intellektuelle Hemmung and Esstörong' *Zeitschrift für psychoanalytische Pädagogik*, 8, (1934), pp. 109–16.

feeble-minded, there was a complete inhibition in her capacity for identification and intellectual grasp. She suffered from a severe eating disorder, and as an infant had already shown an abnormal tendency to avoid putting things in her mouth and biting. As she gradually got over this in the course of the analysis and began to eat with pleasure and greed, so she also began to develop intellectually in a normal way.

Sense-organ functioning is put in the service of the self-preservative and libidinal aims (modified or unmodified) of the drives. Furthermore, taking things in (*das Aufnehmen*) by means of the sense-organs, like grasping things intellectually, is equated with oral incorporation, while affects such as greed, pleasure, anxiety, inhibition, etc., get transferred from eating on to the senses (cf. the expressions 'drunk on beauty', 'a feast for the eyes', 'a feast for the ears', and so on). Compulsive conflict can either inhibit or stimulate sense-organ functioning and the reality sense based on it in two ways: (1) through conflicts relating to the libidinal aims of the drives in whose service sensory perceptions are then placed (e.g. in the inhibition of, or urge to make, sexual observations); (2) through libidinal disorders which secondarily become fused with sense-organ functioning or with thought processes (e.g. in cases where looking, smelling, or thinking are experienced as oral acts, inhibitions in looking, smelling, and thinking can be substituted for eating inhibitions).

A woman patient who had suffered from severe eating difficulties as a child, only partially diminished in later life, had had unusual difficulty in learning to read. Even now she will constantly complain that she can't take things in (*aufnehmen*). She often can't hear or understand what is said to her. She has immense difficulty in taking cognizance of reality. She is frightened that I shall 'force reality' on her in analysis, just as eating and learning had been forced on her when she was a child.

Although at first she showed no obvious disorder in her object-relations, after many months of analysis she discovered that up to that point I had been completely unreal to her and that I was gradually becoming more real just as a wood carving emerges from the wood. After a stretch of analysis, it transpired that a reduction in her eating difficulties was accompanied by a sudden new ability to draw realistically, something which she had been unable to do before. At first when she did wood carvings, which were 'more real' for her than drawings, she would vomit. The first one she attempted represented a child. As the things and people around her became 'more real' for her, so her own feelings and conflicts felt clearer and more real. It was only after about a year of analysis that she really acknowledged the difficulties which had brought her to analysis. Prior to that, her shifts of mood, her depression, and thoughts of suicide had seemed unreal or mere play-acting to her, or else she completely forgot them as soon as they receded.

Our attitude to external reality generally corresponds to our attitude towards internal reality or the affects, since it is only by means of the latter that a relationship to the external world can be achieved. Usually one's own affects are equated with the contents of one's own body, as incorporated objects.

Abraham's statement that the incorporative function (*die aufnehmende Funktion*) of eating is a model for later intellectual comprehension has been confirmed by different analysts. All the cases of intellectual inhibition which I have analysed could be traced back to a previous eating inhibition. In those cases, where an intellectual inhibition is not substituted for the eating inhibition, however, this seems to be because intellectual acquisition is felt to be less real and less aggressive, thus calling for less anxiety, than the actual consumption of food.

The schizophrenic patient mentioned earlier had suffered from severe eating disorders in her childhood. Her eating inhibition stemmed from a reaction to her intense oral greed. At the age of about ten, she largely overcame this inhibition when anxiety forced her to overcompensate for the feelings of nausea and of aggression against the mother which had been expressed in her refusal to eat: better eat of her own accord than have her mother force her to do it, perhaps forcing the food into another orifice such as the eye or the anus. Her fear of people was conditioned by the same factors as her eating inhibition; but now a still greater anxiety forced her to overcome this first anxiety and be 'polite', to do everything like other people and to eat everything. The only things possessing real value for her were those which she obtained in secret – food which she stole outside mealtimes. But her excessive anxiety forbade her the satisfaction of these impulses. If anyone knew what she owned, ate, or studied, etc., then by that very token, it immediately became worthless; since they could take it from her or prevent her from enjoying it, she might as well relinquish it of her own accord.

This attitude towards food also determined her relationship to money and to knowledge. As a reaction to her wanting to obtain lots of money from her parents (oral greed), she had developed an extraordinarily strong sense of guilt. Because of this, she wanted to avoid accepting anything from her parents. But since this attitude was also bound up with the aggressive wish to be independent of them and grown up (oral defiance), she again had to overcompensate for it and to play the part of a small child dependent on its parents. The latter was also determined by her excessive fear of destitution (starvation).

She had a very strong urge to study, but was so extensively inhibited in this, as in her whole intellectual development, that the first impression she gave was one of complete feeble-mindedness. Her wanting to know everything and to use her knowledge to become omnipotent and independent of her parents, to be admired and feared, was an expression of her impulse to incorporate orally an omnipotent penis. Different subjects of study represented male, female, or sexless persons for her. She was incapable of studying because she had not to prefer one subject to another, one person to another, one form of food to another. She had to study all subjects at once so as to incorporate all human beings at once. Subjects she neglected she felt guilty about; subjects she started to study (half but not completely eaten food) made her feel anxious. If unable to deal with all subjects at once, she gave them all up. She thereby expressed her defiance: all or nothing. This was strengthened by her fear of the knowledge to be acquired (*das aufzunehmendes Wissen*).

The incorporation anxieties which had inhibited her eating now found expression in a host of different fears that study was bad for her health. She felt especially unable to study sociology because the different theories existing in the field would have the same effect in her mind as incompatible types of food in her stomach (it was dangerous to incorporate sadistic parents who fight each other). These incorporation anxieties were somewhat alleviated when she worked together with others and convinced herself that they were able to acquire knowledge, just as her anxiety had been alleviated when she ate together with her mother. On the other hand, she was inhibited by the anxiety and rivalry which she felt towards her female colleagues. Obviously she didn't want to have what others possessed but something quite new and hitherto non-existent. Once she had taken this into herself (by eating or learning it), she was like God. In order to be so, she had to be alone without human relationships or sexual impulses. She also had to be alone in order to escape her envy of others. Her anxiety was that her mother was giving her bad, noxious, or worthless food and that her female teacher was giving her the same type of knowledge. Hence, she had to make any valuable knowledge her own in secret. But in order not to arouse in others the suspicion that she was secretly searching for something better, she also had to incorporate the food and knowledge put before her. Since she did not know where the 'good' (breast, penis, fertilizing seed) was hidden, she thought she would have to devour everything in the world, and the impossibility of this completely paralysed her. Since she suspected that what was put before her as worthless was really valuable, she believed she had to pay special attention to all trivial and secondary things without, however, seeming to do so. She had a compulsion to buy old books, partly in the hope that they might turn out to be especially valuable, partly because these books with which she identified would otherwise, being unwanted by anybody else, decay. The feeling of guilt she experienced towards old books that she did not buy she similarly felt towards everything discarded that she did not pick up, towards all food she left, towards abandoned children, and also towards subjects of study she had not learnt. This was why she must not prefer one thing at the cost of another. However, this in turn produced the anxiety that she would be incapable of providing for so many children and that the starving children would then eat her up herself. Similarly, she wanted to keep lots of pets, but was afraid that she was incapable of being a good mother to them, of giving them enough food, time, etc., or that she would become sadistic towards them. She felt that she would only be able to study when she had kept mice and rabbits, had studied them, and proved herself in relation to them. But she was then afraid that if she did this well (was a good mother – i.e. feminine), she would not be allowed to give it up, to study (be a man). Her ideal was androgyny – which was why she had to have everything at once, incorporate everything into herself at once (father and mother simultaneously), be man and woman at the same time, so as to become as God. She thought that it was through sexlessness or androgyny that one came to resemble God.

I have been able to adduce here only some of the elements which caused the severe intellectual inhibition of this patient. What is striking about them is that they are diametrically opposed to each other, so that no compromise between them is possible. In this, as in other cases, I found the most important factors inhibiting oral-intellectual receptivity to be the following: anxiety about the envy of others, corresponding to the intensity of the subject's own envy of others' possessions; anxiety about the subject's own sadism (of destroying food, of damaging or depriving others of knowledge through one's own inability); numerous further incorporation anxieties. The element of oral defiance stressed by various authors is also important – an unwillingness to receive knowledge because it had not been given in the way desired or with the desired completeness in childhood.

Oral factors do not only have an inhibiting effect; in many cases they stimulate intellectual development. Hunger for knowledge, curiosity, greed for money, are often substituted for greed for food, so that knowledge is felt as substantial and is equated with the penis, contents of the body, etc. One male patient, not intellectually inhibited, only valued knowledge unavailable to others which he had acquired in secret or 'stolen'. His main anxiety was that a woman would eat up his brain or that his academic works would turn out to be plagiarism (stolen). He equated knowledge – thoughts – with the content of the head and the latter with the contents of the body. His primitive wishes to incorporate his mother orally made him afraid that the woman would eat up the content of his head in retaliation, or that his child (his academic work) would turn out to have been stolen from his mother. Academic or scientific work seems to be largely based on the oral theory of sexuality – that it is only possible to bear a child (the work) by first incorporating orally stolen parts of the parents' body (thoughts of other authors). That is why for psychology plagiarism appears to be a central problem of scientific work. Normally, the fear of retaliation is avoided by legalizing plagiarism through quotation (restitution to the author). This oral theory of sex also finds expression in the work ritual of a number of people who, for example, can only work well if they have first eaten a raw steak or if they eat sweets or smoke while working.

A male patient who had occasionally stolen things (mainly sweets and books) during puberty later had a certain inclination to plagiarism. Since activity for him was bound up with stealing and academic work with plagiarism, he could escape these disreputable impulses only by means of a very marked inhibition of his activity and intellectual efforts.

Intellectual disorders can extend to disorders of both input and output. For output, the symbolism of excretion and birth is of primary importance. The disorders arising from this are numerous: a number of people are able to write a piece of work only if they already have the next one prepared in their heads, due to a fear of being left infertile or empty (robbed of the contents of their body). One male patient felt guilty towards his completed work once he sent it to the editor; he had abandoned his child, sent it away to strangers. As long as it lay with him in the drawer, it was safe, like the child in bed. Anxiety can also often be felt towards the work itself: the different thoughts it contains (children, excrement) are like an army which has, with difficulty, to be controlled so that the soldiers do not fight (contradict) each other or rebel against their leader. A male patient with an insect phobia compared his work to a centipede, the footnotes representing the many feet. It is also very common for hypochondriacal fears and broodings to be transferred from the body to thoughts and from thoughts to work. However, I don't want to go into these factors more deeply now, but rather to emphasize the role of oral factors in inhibitions of output.

One male patient had given some lectures with great difficulty, and after a further lecture reported to me with real contentment that it had again – as expected – turned out badly. The bad lecture, like boring free association, proved to be revenge for all the bad lectures which he had had to listen to, for all the knowledge that had disappointed him, and in the last analysis for unsatisfying food. On another occasion, he cancelled a lecture at the last moment. By lecturing, he had power over the audience. In this way, he identified with the breast-feeding mother who is in a position to provide or to deny completely good or bad nourishment (knowledge).

The same elements which I have illustrated here with the examples from journalistic and scientific works and lectures can also be found in letter writing, doing homework, answering in class, reciting poems, and so on – indeed, in simple speaking in adults and children. Once again, these elements have an inhibiting effect only in certain cases, and can often constitute a vital stimulus to intellectual development.

In general, it can be said that oral factors have a positive influence on intellectual development in those cases where oral greed which has been sublimated in the hunger for knowledge is intense but does not call forth strong anxiety or feelings of guilt due to its sadism (or alternatively if anxiety and feelings of guilt are attached to other objects without inhibiting intellectual development). The most advantageous circumstance for intellectual production is identification with the good mother who provides nourishment and knowledge. This attitude can only be preserved without disorders if anxiety is not too intense.

Index